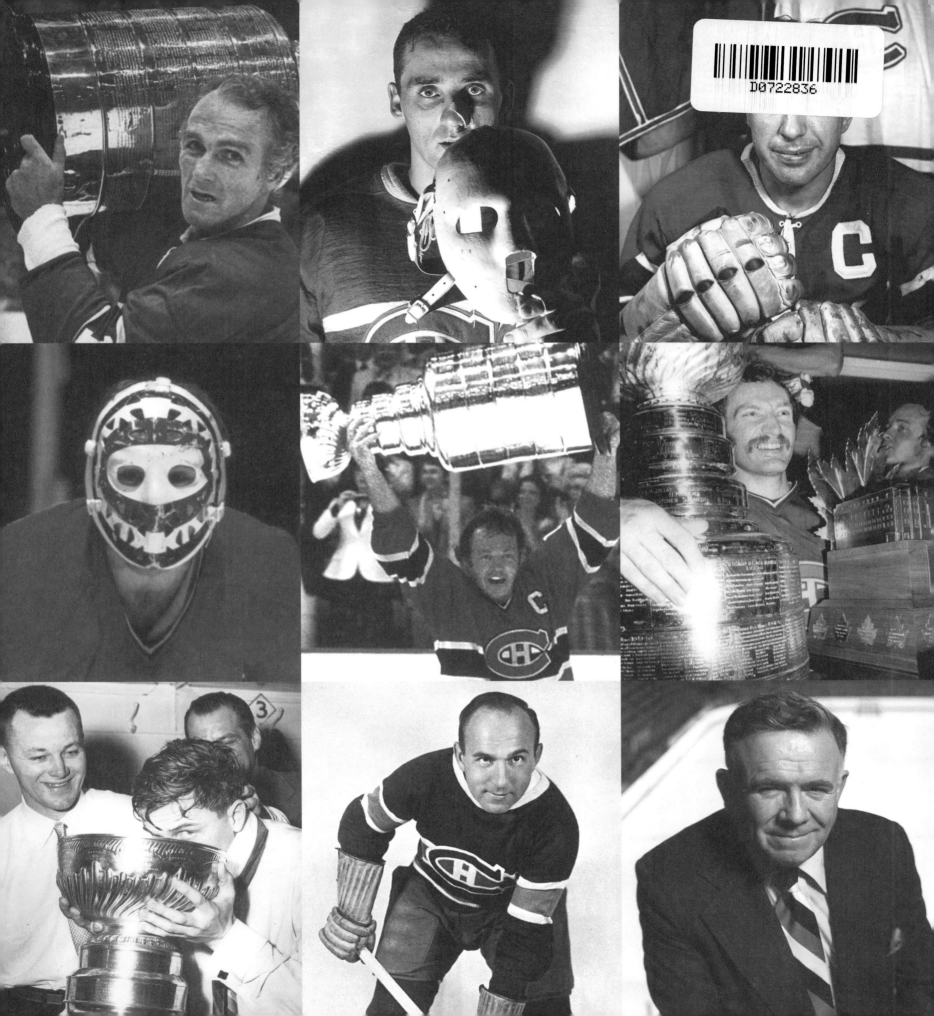

Honoured Canadiens

HOCKEY HALL *of* FAME

Fenn Publishing Company Ltd.

HONOURED CANADIENS
A Fenn Publishing Book / First Published in 2008

Fenn Publishing Company Ltd.
Bolton, Ontario, Canada
www.hbfenn.com

The publisher gratefully acknowledges the support of the Canada Council for the Arts and the Ontario Arts Council for its publishing program. We acknowledge the support of the Government of Ontario through the Ontario Media Development Corporation's Ontario Book Initiative.

We acknowledge the financial support of the Government of Canada through the Book Publishing Industry Development Program (BPIDP) for our publishing activities. Care has been taken to trace ownership of copyright material in this book and to secure permissions. The publishers will gladly receive any information that will enable them to rectify errors or omissions.

Text design: Laura Brunton

Printed and bound in Canada

Library and Archives Canada Cataloguing in Publication

Podnieks, Andrew

    Honoured Canadiens : Hockey Hall of Fame / Andrew Podnieks.

ISBN 978-1-55168-340-9

    1. Montreal Canadiens (Hockey team)--Biography. 2. Hockey players--Québec (Province)--Montréal--Biography. 3. Montreal Canadiens (Hockey team)--History. 4. Hockey Hall of Fame. I. Hockey Hall of Fame II. Title.

GV848.M6P62 2008   796.962092'271428   C2008-903639-5

Honoured Canadiens

HOCKEY HALL *of* FAME

Fenn Publishing Company Ltd.
Bolton, Ontario

Contents

Foreword

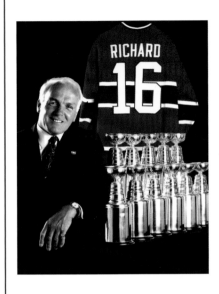

Like all kids growing up in Montreal, I dreamed of playing for the Canadiens. I was only six years old when my brother Maurice broke in with the team; I never thought I would get the chance to play with him, but I did. When he saw that I was about to make the team, he decided to play a little longer and I'm forever grateful that he did. I'll never forget that first training camp, or that first game.

There was just something about pulling on that famous sweater for the first time. I was fortunate enough to go on to win 11 Stanley Cups, yet nothing was like that first one. I was only 19 years old during my first season in the NHL, and to have it end with a Stanley Cup won alongside my brother was incredible. We ended up winning the Cup the next four years straight until Maurice retired in 1960.

The day I was inducted into the Hockey Hall of Fame in 1979 was something I'll never forget. Being there along with a player like Bobby Orr was pretty special since I was never even supposed to make it to the NHL in the first place. Everyone said I didn't have what it took, and that at only 5-foot-7, I was too small, but I still played in the NHL for 20 years.

The game has changed over the years, but what it takes to be a champion remains the same. Winning is all about teamwork and being there for each other. That's where it all began for the great Canadiens teams of the past, and I don't think that has changed in today's NHL. Without that bond between players, it's unlikely we would have enjoyed all the success we did. A team that sticks together, wins together.

The pressure to win that exists in Montreal was always there, but I didn't feel it. We had such confidence and faith in one another that nothing else really mattered. No matter how many great players we had on our teams, from Jean Béliveau and Maurice Richard, to Dickie Moore and Jacques Plante, no one was bigger than the club as a whole. We had one common goal, one mission. The Canadiens are the only team I ever played for, and the Canadiens sweater was the only one I ever knew. Nothing makes me prouder than the fact I was a member of such a storied organization, and I'm sure the 53 other men featured in these pages, if you could ask them today, would say the same thing.

Henri Richard
11-time Stanley Cup Champion

Introduction

When we were privileged enough to become majority owners of the Montreal Canadiens in January 2001, it was the realization of a lifelong dream to become associated with one of the greatest professional sports franchises in the world. Only the New York Yankees had won as many championships; no team, however, came close to having as many great players or builders from its past inducted in its respective sport's Hall of Fame.

At the time, the Canadiens' Centennial was not something at the forefront of my mind. Soon enough – as early as 2004, in fact – plans were already taking shape for a buildup to the 100th anniversary of our organization's founding on December 4, 1909. I can tell you that being a part of the ensuing events, initiatives, and celebrations has been a unique experience.

As we have paid special tribute to our glorious past over the recent seasons, I have been honoured to meet many of the men who helped establish the rich heritage we are blessed to salute today. Henri Richard, the greatest individual champion in all of pro sports, is but one of these, and the fact he continues to play a vital role for us as an ambassador is testimony to how special the Canadiens family truly is. Without his contributions and those of all his teammates past and present, along with the enduring support of our fans, our Centennial would be no more notable than a passing date on the calendar.

Words cannot express how fortunate we are to be associated with the Montreal Canadiens, and by extension, the unforgettable figures who have shaped their legacy. The men featured in these pages are legends who have realized one of the game's most significant achievements – earning immortality in the Hockey Hall of Fame – and we are incredibly proud that together they played a key role in helping build the first 100 years of our team's great history.

George N. Gillett, Jr.

George N. Gillett, Jr.
Team Owner

Comprising game-worn jerseys from such legends as Howie Morenz, Maurice Richard and Jean Béliveau, to Guy Lafleur, Bob Gainey, and Patrick Roy, the Centennial Hockey Collection™, an assortment of extremely rare Habs items belonging to a private collector, provides a unique look at 100 years of Canadiens hockey.

Howarth "Howie" Morenz

Centre 1923-24 to 1936-37

Morenz won the Stanley Cup three times during his 12-year career with the Canadiens, and the team missed the playoffs only once in that time.

Morenz was named the best hockey player for the first half of the 20th century, testament to both his skill and popularity.

"The Stratford Streak" possessed great puckhandling skill and a sizzling shot, but he was best remembered for his incredible speed.

By the time Howie Morenz was named the best hockey player for the first half of the 20th century, in 1950, he had been dead for 13 years. But his life was the stuff of legend, and although players of the early game differed and disagreed on many things, to a man they said Morenz was the greatest player of all time.

He went by several nicknames, including Mitchell Meteor, Canadien Comet, and Hurtling Habitant, but the one that was most popular and lasted longest was Stratford Streak. All the names pointed to Morenz's great speed, but he was a player who was the best in all aspects of the game. He had a sizzling shot; he was a great passer; he was the toughest player in the game; he had the heart of a lion and the disposition of a gentleman. And he could go from end-to-end and lift fans out of their seats like no one. He was the first real hockey star in the United States, and American media nicknamed him the "Babe Ruth of hockey," such was the impression he made and the influence he commanded.

Of course, Morenz was the star of the Montreal Canadiens for some 12 years, but the truth was that early

CANADIENS NUMBERS
HOWARTH "Howie" MORENZ
("The Stratford Streak")

b. Mitchell, Ontario, June 21, 1902   **d.** Montreal, Quebec, March 8, 1937
5'9"   165 lbs.   centre   shoots left

	REGULAR SEASON					PLAYOFFS				
	GP	G	A	Pts	Pim	GP	G	A	Pts	Pim
1923-24 ♟	24	13	3	16	20	6	7	3	10	10
1924-25	30	28	11	39	46	6	7	1	8	8
1925-26	31	23	3	26	39	—	—	—	—	—
1926-27	44	25	7	32	49	4	1	0	1	4
1927-28	43	33	18	51	66	2	0	0	0	12
1928-29	42	17	10	27	47	3	0	0	0	6
1929-30 ♟	44	40	10	50	72	6	3	0	3	10
1930-31 ♟	39	28	23	51	49	10	1	4	5	10
1931-32	48	24	25	49	46	4	1	0	1	4
1932-33	46	14	21	35	32	2	0	3	3	2
1933-34	39	8	13	21	21	2	1	1	2	0
1936-37	30	4	16	20	12	—	—	—	—	—
TOTALS	460	257	160	417	499	45	21	12	33	66

Morenz died before his time, and the Canadiens immediately retired his number 7, a number which was never worn by any other after he played his first game with the Habs.

Howarth "Howie" Morenz

Centre 1923-24 to 1936-37

Morenz battles for a loose puck in front of the New York Rangers' net.

in his life he wanted nothing to do with professional hockey. He started playing the game as a goalie, but in his first meaningful game he allowed 21 goals and was promptly made into a rover by his coach in Stratford. He quickly displayed an uncanny ability to put the puck in the net, and it wasn't long before word trickled to the Canadiens that a star was playing in Stratford.

The Morenz family had moved from Mitchell to Stratford, and in 1917 Howie tried to join the army. His mother found him at a recruiting station and apprised

the people in charge that the 18-year-old before them was really only 15 years old. They returned to Stratford, and Howie started to play more and more hockey.

Cecil Hart travelled there to meet Morenz, and with a $400 enticement he was able to convince the young player to commit to the Canadiens for the 1923-24 season. Just before training camp, though, Morenz changed his mind. He walked into Léo Dandurand's office, put the $400 on his desk, and asked for the contract back. Dandurand assured the player all would be well and that under no circumstances would the contract be nullified, and Morenz went on to have a brilliant career.

Morenz played on a line with Aurèle Joliat and Billy Boucher in his rookie season and the team won the Stanley Cup. The next year, Morenz scored 28 goals in 30 games and took the team to the Cup finals before losing to the Victoria Cougars.

Arguably his finest season was 1927-28 when he led the league in goals, assists, and points (33, 18, and 51, respectively) and was named winner of the Hart Trophy. Equally impressive was the 1930-31 season when Morenz led the league with 51 points, won the Hart Trophy, and led the team to its second straight Stanley Cup. Morenz scored the Cup-winning goal in those 1931 playoffs to make that season even more memorable.

Or perhaps it was the previous season that was his finest when he scored 40 goals in only 44 games. Regardless, Morenz was the most exciting and dominant player in the league for many seasons, but by the early 1930s he was slowing down. His leg speed wasn't the same, and his goal production had suffered. The Forum fans who had cheered him wildly thousands of times now started to boo him, and he was traded to Chicago on October 3, 1934, a trade that tore at his heart.

Morenz played dispirited hockey for two seasons with the Hawks and later New York Rangers, a faded version of his glorious past who was given little motivation to shine in cities where hockey wasn't appreciated with the same religious zeal as in Montreal. But when Cecil Hart became the Canadiens' general manager in 1936, one of his first moves was to re-acquire Morenz. Now 34, he nevertheless found his love for the game again and played like the Morenz of old.

Midway through that 1936-37 season, however, tragedy struck. In a home game against Chicago, Morenz roared down the right wing. He tried to get by Black Hawks defenceman Earl Siebert, who knocked him down, and Morenz fell awkwardly into the boards. These were the days when boards were truly boards—panels of wood—and Morenz's skate got caught between two sections of wood. His leg and ankle snapped in four places, and he was carried off and sent directly to hospital where doctors

saw firsthand the trauma Morenz's leg had suffered.

Six weeks later, Morenz was dead. He never left the hospital, and despite encouragement from thousands of well-wishers he knew that his career likely was over that night he was carried off. The Canadiens held his funeral in the Forum itself. Teammates were pall-bearers and hockey fans mourners. Some 50,000 people paid their last respects, and Montreal's streets were lined with upwards of 250,000 people. The team announced that no player would ever wear Morenz's number 7 again.

Morenz left this world with 271 goals and 472 points, both all-time records in the early days of the NHL. He both embodied a great hockey player and personified one.

Although Morenz played briefly for the Rangers and Black Hawks, his memory is forever etched as a Canadiens star.

Howarth "Howie" Morenz

Centre 1923-24 to 1936-37

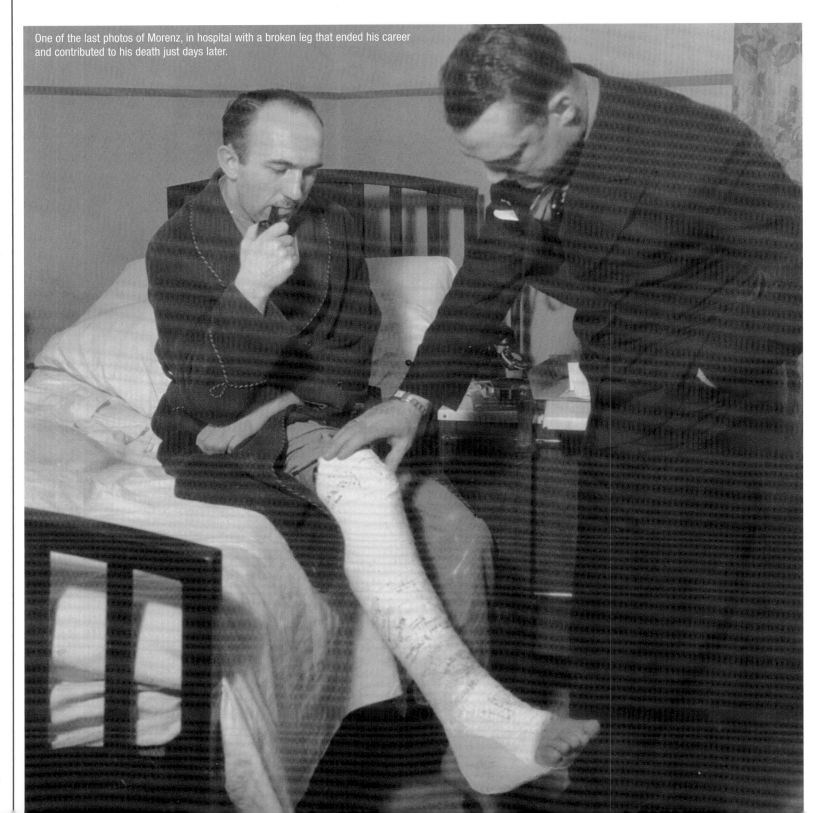

One of the last photos of Morenz, in hospital with a broken leg that ended his career and contributed to his death just days later.

He was larger than life in the eyes of his legions of fans, but he also lived up to that reputation through his play. In the modern age of television, internet, and photography, it might be easy to dismiss Morenz when compared to Howe, Orr, and Gretzky, but if laurels from opponents count for anything—and in hockey they do—the name Morenz fits in nicely along those more modern greats.

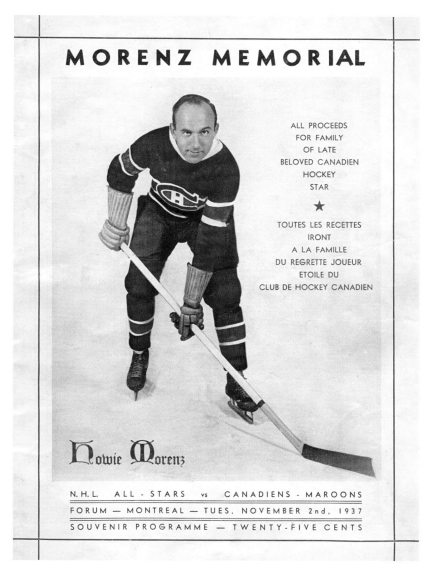

MORENZ MEMORIAL

ALL PROCEEDS
FOR FAMILY
OF LATE
BELOVED CANADIEN
HOCKEY
STAR

★

TOUTES LES RECETTES
IRONT
A LA FAMILLE
DU REGRETTE JOUEUR
ETOILE DU
CLUB DE HOCKEY CANADIEN

Howie Morenz

N.H.L. ALL-STARS vs CANADIENS-MAROONS
FORUM — MONTREAL — TUES. NOVEMBER 2nd, 1937
SOUVENIR PROGRAMME — TWENTY-FIVE CENTS

A Memorial Game was played in honour of Morenz shortly after his death, a chance for players and teams alike to honour one of the greats.

MYTH VS. MEDICINE

No one who was at the Montreal Forum on January 28, 1937, could have anticipated beforehand that they were going to watch Howie Morenz play his final game. No one who saw the terrible injury he suffered could have known that this was the last public appearance, so to speak, in his life. Yet six weeks later, the news was announced with despair, shock, and disbelief—Howie Morenz was dead. The night he suffered that fateful broken leg he was taken to St. Luke's Hospital in Montreal. Doctors sedated him and applied a cast, but Morenz's spirit was shattered beyond repair. It was clear his leg was going to be fine, but fine only in respect to daily life. He knew his playing career was over, and he could not come to terms with the news for which he had had no time to prepare. While he lay in his hospital bed, Morenz was besieged by visitors to the point that hospital staff had to curtail visits by friends and well-wishers. Morenz suffered a nervous breakdown and died several days later of a coronary embolism. His longtime friend and teammate, Aurèle Joliat, interpreted events not in the medical sense but in the symbolic sense, giving weight to Morenz's importance to the city of Montreal and the player's love for the game. Joliat said, simply, that Morenz had died of a broken heart. Indeed, with his spirit destroyed by the injury, his body was no longer willing.

Georges Vézina
Goalie 1910-11 to 1925-26

Vézina in full equipment, wearing two identical gloves in the era before a catching mitt and blocker were introduced.

At the turn of the 20th century, Chicoutimi was so far away from Montreal that it was hard to believe there was any connection at all between the tiny northern community and the cultural capital of Quebec. But in 1910, at the conclusion of their first professional season in the NHA, the Montreal Canadiens traveled around the province on what was called a barnstorming tour, a common way to let fans in smaller locales see their heroes play.

A young Vézina in the early days of his career with the Canadiens.

The Montreal goalie was Joe Cattarinich, and in front of him was a roster chock full of greats, from Newsy Lalonde to Jack Laviolette to Didier Pitre. The local Chicoutimi team was no match for the fledgling Habs, but the professional NHA team could not score on the 23-year-old goalie at the other end. When George Kennedy bought the Canadiens, Cattarinich urged him to sign the other goalie. That is how Georges Vézina came to play for the fabled Club de Hockey.

Vézina started the first game of the 1910-11 season for Montreal, and he played in every single game for the team—regular season and playoffs—for the next 15 seasons (plus one game). He was nicknamed the "Chicoutimi Cucumber" because of his calm and cool disposition, but he was better known for his abilities. Back home, he had not donned skates until he was 18 years old, playing goal all his teen years in boots.

For almost all his career, goalies were not allowed to fall to the ice, so the boots, born of financial hardship, proved an excellent method of training for Vézina. In those early days, he played at the local arena which was owned by his father, Jacques, and built by the famed Price brothers of Montreal.

Off ice, he was a gentle man who didn't smoke or drink to excess like many of his colleagues. He was revered by fans in Montreal and respected by opponents throughout the league. During his life, he and his wife produced an extraordinary

24 children, but many of them died at an early age. Still, it was his play in goal that made him the stuff of legend.

The consistency with which Vézina played during his career was nothing short of exceptional. He won two Stanley Cups with the Canadiens, the first in 1916 when they beat the Portland Rosebuds in the last game of a best-of-five series. This was the first championship for the team.

CANADIENS NUMBERS
GEORGES VÉZINA ("The Chicoutimi Cucumber")

b. Chicoutimi, Quebec, January 21, 1887   **d.** Chicoutimi, Quebec, March 27, 1926
5'6"   185 lbs.   goalie   catches left

		REGULAR SEASON						PLAYOFFS				
	GP	W-L-T	Mins	GA	SO	GAA	GP	W-L	Mins	GA	SO	GAA
1910-11	16	8-8-0	980	62	0	3.80	—	—	—	—	—	—
1911-12	18	8-10-0	1109	66	0	3.57	—	—	—	—	—	—
1912-13	20	11-9-0	1217	81	1	3.99	—	—	—	—	—	—
1913-14	20	13-7-0	1222	64	1	3.14	2	1-1-0	120	6	1	3.00
1914-15	20	6-14-0	1257	81	0	3.86	—	—	—	—	—	—
1915-16 ⚱	24	16-7-1	1482	76	0	3.08	5	3-2-0	300	13	0	2.60
1916-17	20	10-10-0	1217	80	0	3.94	6	2-4-0	240	29	0	4.80
1917-18	21	12-9-0	1282	84	1	3.93	2	1-1-0	120	10	0	5.00
1918-19	18	10-8-0	1117	78	1	4.19	10	6-3-1	656	37	1	3.38
1919-20	24	13-11-0	1456	113	0	4.66	—	—	—	—	—	—
1920-21	24	13-11-0	1441	99	1	4.12	—	—	—	—	—	—
1921-22	24	12-11-1	1469	94	0	3.84	—	—	—	—	—	—
1922-23	24	13-9-2	1488	61	2	2.46	2	0-2-0	120	4	0	2.00
1923-24 ⚱	24	13-11-0	1459	48	3	1.97	6	6-0-0	360	6	2	1.00
1924-25	30	17-11-2	1860	56	5	1.81	6	3-3-0	360	18	1	3.00
1925-26	1	0-0-0	20	0	0	0.00	—	—	—	—	—	—
NHL TOTALS	190	103-81-5	11,592	633	13	3.28	26	16-9-1	1,616	75	4	2.78

*1909-17=NHA

Georges Vézina

Goalie 1910-11 to 1925-26

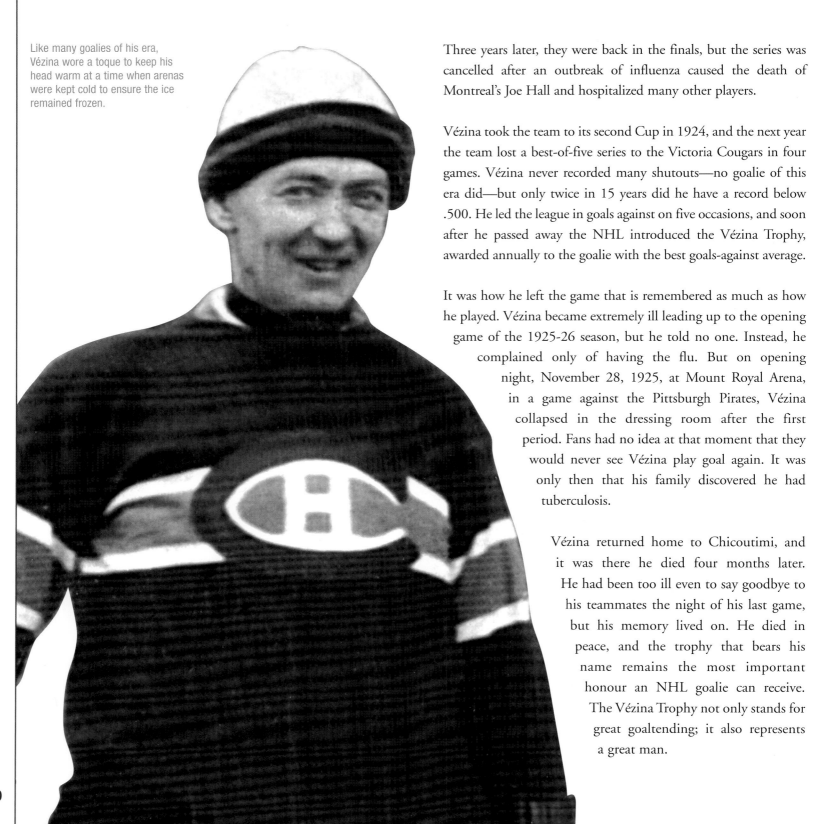

Like many goalies of his era, Vézina wore a toque to keep his head warm at a time when arenas were kept cold to ensure the ice remained frozen.

Three years later, they were back in the finals, but the series was cancelled after an outbreak of influenza caused the death of Montreal's Joe Hall and hospitalized many other players.

Vézina took the team to its second Cup in 1924, and the next year the team lost a best-of-five series to the Victoria Cougars in four games. Vézina never recorded many shutouts—no goalie of this era did—but only twice in 15 years did he have a record below .500. He led the league in goals against on five occasions, and soon after he passed away the NHL introduced the Vézina Trophy, awarded annually to the goalie with the best goals-against average.

It was how he left the game that is remembered as much as how he played. Vézina became extremely ill leading up to the opening game of the 1925-26 season, but he told no one. Instead, he complained only of having the flu. But on opening night, November 28, 1925, at Mount Royal Arena, in a game against the Pittsburgh Pirates, Vézina collapsed in the dressing room after the first period. Fans had no idea at that moment that they would never see Vézina play goal again. It was only then that his family discovered he had tuberculosis.

Vézina returned home to Chicoutimi, and it was there he died four months later. He had been too ill even to say goodbye to his teammates the night of his last game, but his memory lived on. He died in peace, and the trophy that bears his name remains the most important honour an NHL goalie can receive. The Vézina Trophy not only stands for great goaltending; it also represents a great man.

Vézina wore these skates for much of his career.

To honour Vézina's memory, the NHL introduced an eponymous trophy to be awarded annually to the goalie(s) who allowed the fewest goals over the course of a season.

THE VÉZINA TROPHY

The first winner of the trophy was Vézina's successor in the Montreal nets, George Hainsworth. He won it in 1927, and again the next two years, after which Boston's Tiny Thompson won it for the first of four times. In the 1940s, Montreal's Bill Durnan won it six times in seven years between 1943 and 1950 and then Jacques Plante also won it six times in a seven-year stretch (1955-62). Ken Dryden won the trophy five times in the 1970s. In 1981, the purpose of the award changed radically. It had gone simply by mathematical calculation to the goalie(s) who allowed the fewest goals (i.e., the best GAA), but starting in 1981 that winner(s) was given the Jennings Trophy. The Vézina was turned into an MVP trophy for goalies, the winner being decided by a vote by the NHL's general managers (one vote per team).

Aurèle Joliat
Left Wing 1922-23 to 1937-38

Small in stature but big in heart and competitiveness, Joliat was the very symbol of a Canadiens player during the 1920s and 1930s.

Bad luck got Aurèle Joliat from the gridiron to the rink, and fate got him from the west to the east. In the end, the best small player of his era wound up playing his whole hockey career with the Montreal Canadiens, winning three Stanley Cups and retiring as the highest scoring left winger in NHL history.

Joliat started playing serious hockey in Iroquois Falls in 1920, but the Flyers were an amateur team and he was offered $200 to play a game, thus rendering him a professional. Instead of pursuing a pro career,

CANADIENS NUMBERS
AURÈLE JOLIAT

b. Ottawa, Ontario, August 29, 1901   **d.** Montreal, Quebec, June 2, 1986
5'5"   136 lbs.   left wing   shoots left

| | REGULAR SEASON | | | | | PLAYOFFS | | | | |
	GP	G	A	Pts	Pim	GP	G	A	Pts	Pim
1922-23	24	12	9	21	37	2	1	0	1	11
1923-24	24	15	5	20	27	6	4	2	6	6
1924-25	25	30	11	41	85	5	3	0	3	21
1925-26	35	17	9	26	52	—	—	—	—	—
1926-27	43	14	4	18	79	4	1	0	1	10
1927-28	44	28	11	39	105	2	0	0	0	4
1928-29	44	12	5	17	59	3	1	1	2	10
1929-30	42	19	12	31	40	6	0	2	2	6
1930-31	43	13	22	35	73	10	0	4	4	12
1931-32	48	15	24	39	46	4	2	0	2	4
1932-33	48	18	21	39	53	2	2	1	3	2
1933-34	48	22	15	37	27	3	0	1	1	0
1934-35	48	17	12	29	18	2	1	0	1	0
1935-36	48	15	8	23	16	—	—	—	—	—
1936-37	47	17	15	32	30	5	0	3	3	2
1937-38	44	6	7	13	24	—	—	—	—	—
TOTALS	655	270	190	460	771	54	15	14	29	88

though, he went west to do farm work during harvest time, but he ended up playing football for the Regina Boat Club in Saskatchewan. Early in his career, however, he broke his right leg in three places, ending his football career almost before it began.

Things took another turn, though, when he ran into Bob Pinder, manager of the Saskatoon Sheiks hockey team. Pinder offered Joliat a contract to play hockey, and Joliat accepted. During one practise, however, Joliat was hit in that right leg by a shot from Rusty Crawford, forcing him to miss the entire year.

Prior to the start of the 1922-23 season, Joliat's luck changed for the better, once and for all. Pinder had heard that the Canadiens wanted to trade Newsy Lalonde. The great Newsy was past his prime and didn't get along well with teammate Sprague Cleghorn, so the Habs wanted to trade him. Pinder was also interested in trading Joliat for something, too, because Joliat, a top prospect, seemed to have a leg that wouldn't heal. The teams swapped players and the rest, as they say, is history.

Canadiens fans couldn't understand how this little Joliat could possibly take the place of the great Lalonde, but even in his first season little Aurèle showed what he was capable of doing. He scored 12 goals in 24 games and proved an adept stickhandler. As a kid, he had always played defence, but in Iroquois Falls he was moved to the left wing to take advantage of his shifty work with the puck. He was never known for a great shot, but in close he could deke a goalie into submission. He had to be quick with his hands, though, because he wasn't going to intimidate opponents with his size. Joliat was called the Mighty Atom because of his ability to slither around the

Aurèle Joliat
Left Wing 1922-23 to 1937-38

ice without being hit, but if he had to stand up for himself he was capable of doing just that, too.

In his second season, Joliat was put on a line with the great Howie Morenz and Billy Boucher. The trio dominated the league and took the Habs to a Stanley Cup win. Indeed, it was Joliat who scored the final goal against the Calgary Tigers in 1924 to win the trophy.

Joliat and Morenz stayed on the same line for 13 years, leading the Canadiens to two more Stanley Cup wins, in 1930 and 1931. Joliat was a great player and fine scorer, but he always played in the shadow of Morenz, which was fine by Aurèle. He considered Morenz the greatest player of all time. After Boucher retired in early 1927, the Joliat-Morenz tandem partnered with Art Gagne and later Nick Wasnie and Johnny Gagnon. In 1934, when Morenz was traded to Chicago, Joliat played on a line with Pit Lepine and Wildor Larochelle.

(l to r) Trophy presented by the Canadiens to Joliat to mark the occasion of his 500th NHL game, on February 8, 1934; Joliat's famous cap; a trading card of the day.

For four years, 1933-37, Joliat was the team's leading scorer. He was famous for wearing a black-peaked cap, and players often skated with distraction trying to knock it off his head. On the one hand, the efforts were worth it because Joliat would always stop to put it back on, and he became angry to the extreme when this happened. On the other, he played with renewed spirit and opposing players often regretted the sly move.

By the time he retired in 1938, Joliat had 270 goals to his credit in the NHL, making him the highest-scoring left winger to that date. He won the Hart Trophy in 1933-34 and was named to the First All-Star team once (1930-31), and the Second team three times (1931-32, 1933-34, and 1934-35).

Joliat played all of his 16 years with the Canadiens and was the all-time leading scorer for left wingers when he retired in 1938.

As much as his playing was the stuff of legend, his return to the ice in 1981 was the icing on the cake. The 79-year-old Joliat, skating in full equipment for the first time in 43 years, was the toast of Ottawa during a charity game, skating with a skill that belied his age. He even contributed a goal to his team's cause. Joliat talked of making a comeback, but just for one exhibition game, to let the modern players know they had nothing on the oldtimers who played 60 minutes a game for a couple of thousand dollars a season. The body may have grown old, but the spirit remained undiminished.

COMEBACK AT AGE 79

On January 30, 1981, the Ottawa Oldtimers played the NHL Oldtimers in a charity game at the Ottawa Civic Centre. The proceeds from the game went to the Parkinson's Disease Society, and playing for Ottawa was none other than Aurèle Joliat. He was two pounds heavier than his playing weight of 136 and was happy to clarify for posterity that he stood 5'5" and not 5'6" as most record books credited him. Other players that night included Henri Richard, Phil Goyette, and Claude Provost—as well as honourary referees Maurice Richard and Red Storey—but it was the 79-year-old Joliat who wowed the 8,000 fans with a smooth stride and competitive nature that no 79-year-old could be expected still to possess. Joliat wore his trademark black cap, and he wore the same skates he had used the last time he played—in 1938 with the Canadiens!

William Northey
Builder

Northey was at the forefront of the development of hockey in Montreal, starting with the Westmount Arena for which he assisted building.

While the Allan Cup was long considered the equal to the Stanley Cup, it was at Northey's suggestion the trophy be instituted.

It is quite unfathomable to consider what hockey would have been like had William Northey not played such an important role in its development through the game's early years, particularly the difficult transition from amateur to professional play in the early 1900s.

A superb athlete in many sports, Northey knew he wanted to spend his life in athletics but also knew he could make a greater contribution off the field of play, as it were, than on it. He moved to Montreal in 1893, and it was there he spent the balance of his life, shaping hockey in that city and around the country. Northey was the secretary-treasurer of the Montreal AAA when that organization decided to build an arena

devoted entirely to hockey. The Westmount Arena opened on December 31, 1898, ushering in a new era for the sport.

In 1900, it was at Northey's suggestion that hockey games be changed from two periods of play (a hand-me-down rule from soccer) to three periods. The next year, he suggested teams play six men aside instead of seven. This wisdom was not shared by everyone, but Northey cleverly got his way by pointing out to team owners that one less player on ice meant one less salary to pay.

By 1906, professional hockey had crept into the amateur game. It was Northey who oversaw the reformation of the ECAHA (Eastern Canadian Amateur Hockey Association), and in 1914 he oversaw the creation of the Canadian Amateur Hockey Association (CAHA), a governing body that would deal with all amateur hockey in the country. Today, that body is called Hockey Canada, and it is the strongest national hockey body in the world.

In 1924, Northey organized the Canadian Arena Company and sought

Northey's influence and prominence led to many invitations such as this by the IOC to a state dinner in London.

to build a new arena exclusively for the Canadiens. Although he wanted a 12,500-seat structure, he could not convince the financial backers that such a capacity was needed and a smaller arena called the Forum was built with a scaled-down capacity of 9,700. The Forum endured some 70 years and saw more Stanley Cup victories than any other arena in hockey history.

WILLIAM NORTHEY

b. Leeds, Quebec, April 29, 1872
d. Montreal, Quebec, April 9, 1963

THE ALLAN CUP

By 1908, amateur hockey in Canada was in tatters. Most of the serious hockey teams in the country were becoming professional, feeling they needed to attract the top stars to survive and knowing the only way to do that was through salaries. Teams in the ECAHA called upon Northey to reorganize the league, and to this end his first move was to call Sir Montagu Allan to donate a trophy specifically for amateur hockey since the Stanley Cup was being won more and more by professional teams. Allan agreed only if Northey oversaw every aspect of the new silverware, and the result was a more unified structure right across the country with one common goal—to win the Allan Cup. This new trophy was as important as the Stanley Cup for decades, and although it is no longer in the same class, it is still competed for by amateur leagues across Canada every spring.

Edouard "Newsy" Lalonde

Centre 1909-10 to 1921-22

One of the leading scorers of his day, Newsy Lalonde had eight seasons of at least 22 goals in an era when he never played more than 24 games in a year.

Lalonde started playing hockey in the early years of the 1900s when pro leagues were starting to supplant amateur ones. Prior to 1909, when the Canadiens were formed and Lalonde first played in Montreal, he was a star who accepted offers from all over the country.

In 1909-10, Newsy performed double duty. As a member of the Canadiens, he led the NHA in scoring with 16 goals in just six games in the league's first year. The Canadiens, however, didn't qualify for the NHA playoffs, so he signed with Renfrew after the regular season to try to help that team win the Stanley Cup. On March 17, 1910, Lalonde scored nine goals in a game against Cobalt, a remarkable achievement even for his day. In 1911-12, the Patrick brothers signed him for the

Famous for wearing a peaked cap wherever he played, Newsy Lalonde was one of the great stars of the years leading up to the formation of the NHL and beyond. Although he was the highest paid player in both hockey and lacrosse, and ventured from team to team with little apparent loyalty, he fell in love with Montreal and played the vast majority of his career with the Canadiens. He later coached the team, and once he left the game professionally remained a fixture at the Forum for decades until his death.

CANADIENS NUMBERS
EDOUARD "Newsy" LALONDE

b. Cornwall, Ontario, October 31, 1888   **d.** Montreal, Quebec, November 21, 1971
5'9"   168 lbs.   centre   shoots right

	REGULAR SEASON					PLAYOFFS				
	GP	G	A	Pts	Pim	GP	G	A	Pts	Pim
1909-10	6	16	—	16	40	—	—	—	—	—
1910-11	16	19	—	19	63	—	—	—	—	—
1912-13	18	25	—	25	61	—	—	—	—	—
1913-14	14	22	5	27	23	2	0	0	0	2
1914-15	7	4	3	7	17	—	—	—	—	—
1915-16	24	28	6	34	78	4	3	0	3	41
1916-17	18	28	7	35	61	5	2	0	2	47
1917-18	14	23	7	30	51	2	4	2	6	17
1918-19	17	22	10	32	40	10	17	22	39	9
1919-20	23	37	9	46	34	—	—	—	—	—
1920-21	24	33	10	43	36	—	—	—	—	—
1921-22	20	9	5	14	20	—	—	—	—	—
NHL TOTALS	99	124	41	165	181	12	21	24	45	26

*1909-17=NHA

Vancouver Millionaires on the west coast, and Newsy once again led the league in scoring, this time with 27 goals in just 15 games.

But it was with les Canadiens that he is most remembered during the team's years at the Westmount Arena, which was always packed when Lalonde played. Fans would cheer Newsy's every move, and his scoring was a sight to behold. He returned to the Canadiens in 1912, and over the next two years scored an incredible 47 goals in just 32 games. He missed most of 1914-15 with an injury, but Lalonde led the NHA in goals in 1915-16 with 28, and in the playoffs he helped the team defeat the Portland Rosebuds 2-1 in the final game of a best-of-five to win the Stanley Cup.

This proved to be the only championship of Lalonde's career, but the very next year, the last of the NHA, he had 28 goals in just 18 games. Lalonde stayed with the Habs when the new NHL was formed in December 1917, and in that inaugural season he continued his scoring exploits by recording 23 goals in just 14 games. Perhaps his finest seasons, though, were 1919-20 and 1920-21. By this time the NHL had established itself as the dominant league in the country, but Lalonde remained its premier scorer. He had 70 goals in only 47 games in those two seasons, second to none for finding the back of the net.

Lalonde led the NHL in points twice and goals once, and he was on the 1919 team that went to the Cup finals against Seattle, only to have the series cancelled because of the flu pandemic and the death of teammate Joe Hall, a one-time, longtime nemesis.

Newsy was traded to the Saskatoon Sheiks prior to the 1922-23 season by owner Léo Dandurand, and the player was, at first, furious. Lalonde was well established in Montreal and had no desire to move, but Dandurand had the chance to acquire a young player named Aurèle Joliat and was not going to pass up the chance. What Dandurand cunningly did on Lalonde's behalf was guarantee that Lalonde would be paid the same salary with the Sheiks for the next two years as he had been paid in Montreal, a gesture that helped Lalonde get over the insult

of being traded far from home.

After retiring in 1927, Lalonde went into coaching and returned to Montreal in this capacity in 1932. He stayed for two and a half years, but the team had little success in the Stanley Cup playoffs and he was replaced by Dandurand midway through the 1934-35 season.

It's hard to fathom today, but Lalonde was even more famous for his lacrosse play than for hockey, and he was paid far better for the former than latter. He played some 20 years as a pro, and in 1950 he was named Canada's greatest lacrosse player for the first half of the century. He claimed to enjoy the sport more, too, because it was played in the summer, out of doors.

THE NEWSPAPER STORY

Edouard Lalonde got his nickname because as a small lad he worked for the local *Cornwall Freeholder* newspaper. He lived with his parents just down the road from the paper's offices, and his father worked a cobbling business from home. Later in life, Lalonde became the top-paid athlete in both hockey (winter) and lacrosse (summer), and he was famous for signing with the highest bidder in many circumstances. What few people knew was that the first time Lalonde had a substantial sum of money, he returned to Cornwall and bought the building in which his parents lived and operated the cobbling business, giving it to his mother and telling her she would own the building for as long as she lived.

Joe Malone
Forward 1917-18 to 1923-24

One of the bigger and stronger players in the game, Joe Malone was almost impossible to check and a gentleman at all times.

In an era of stick swinging, violent brawls, and almost inhuman intimidation, Joe Malone was a sporting giant on the ice. He was called "Phantom" because no one knew where he was on the ice until he had the puck on his stick. A moment later, it was often in the net.

Malone was, above all, a goal scorer. He was large, but skated straight up and forcefully, and it was this quality that probably ensured other bullies in the game left him alone. When he had the puck, he was hands down the best stickhandler in the game, and although not the swiftest player, he was deceptively fast. More to the point, though, when he decided to let go a shot, he took his time, aimed with purpose, and more often than not scored. He was also adept at faking a shot to draw the goalie out of his net.

It was in 1908 that Malone joined his hometown team, the Quebec Bulldogs, and it was with that team he remained most of the next nine years, scoring at will and establishing himself as the best scorer in the game. The Bulldogs won consecutive Stanley Cups in 1912 and 1913. In the former, Malone had five of the team's 17 goals in defeating Moncton by scores of 9-3 and 8-0. The next year, Malone had nine goals in a single game of the Cup challenge against the Sydney Miners, a 14-3 win

CANADIENS NUMBERS
JOE MALONE

b. Quebec City, Quebec, February 28, 1890   **d.** Montreal, Quebec, May 15, 1969
5'10"   150 lbs.   forward   shoots left

| | REGULAR SEASON | | | | | PLAYOFFS | | | | |
	GP	G	A	Pts	Pim	GP	G	A	Pts	Pim
1917-18	20	44	—	44	30	2	1	0	1	3
1918-19	8	7	2	9	3	5	5	0	5	0
1922-23	20	1	0	1	2	2	0	0	0	0
1923-24	10	0	0	0	0	—	—	—	—	—
TOTALS	58	52	2	54	35	9	6	0	6	3

Malone finished his career winning a Cup with the Canadiens, in 1923-24.

followed by a 6-2 win to retain control of the Cup. During the 1912-13 regular season, Malone scored 43 goals in just 20 games.

When the NHL was formed before the start of the 1917-18 season, the Bulldogs opted not to play that year and Malone was claimed by the Montreal Canadiens. He was forced to play left wing because the Canadiens had the great Newsy Lalonde at centre, but the adjustment was seamless. His first year was a record-setting one. He scored 44 goals in a mere 20 games, an average of more than two goals per game, still the best ratio of all time in the NHL. All the while he played with his trademark sportsmanship and clean play, endearing himself to fans of the game.

This 1917-18 season is difficult to quantify and compare with today's game. Malone regularly played close to 60 minutes of every game, and the style of play was more like soccer than hockey of the modern era. That is, he would play like crazy for brief spurts and then skate lazily for other periods to recover. Today, line changes ensure fresh players are on the ice at all times and players do their recovering on the bench. Malone also played at a time when goalies were not allowed to fall to the ice. Nevertheless, no one else scored at such a rate, so his exploits, on that merit, can be compared to any era.

Malone played the next season with the Canadiens as well but missed much of the season because of a badly sprained ankle. After that, he returned to Quebec when the Bulldogs decided to play in the NHL, and again he led the league with 39 goals in 24 games. From 1920 to 1922, Malone played for the Hamilton Tigers which had acquired many Bulldogs in a fire sale. Malone was also a coach and manager, and he finished his career back in Montreal, playing parts of two seasons before calling it quits for good.

A LAST HURRAH

Joe Malone returned to the Canadiens in 1922 after being traded by Hamilton. The once great scorer had lost a step and was working almost full-time as a tool maker (which is why he had been exempt from service during the First World War), and he missed several road games as a result. The next year, he was beset by both a throat ailment and by an even more formidable foe—youth. Howie Morenz was starting out with the Canadiens, and it didn't take long for everyone to realize, Malone included, that Morenz was the way of the future. Malone retired halfway through the season, and his number 9 sweater was left hanging for Maurice Richard to claim two decades later.

Sprague Cleghorn

Defence 1921-22 to 1924-25

Cleghorn played with Cyclone Taylor on the Renfrew Millionaires before joining the Canadiens.

Like Red Horner or Eddie Shore a generation later, Sprague Cleghorn had two sides to his legend on ice. On the one hand, he was a brilliant rushing defenceman; on the other, he was a player for whom there were no limits to fighting. In an era of tough players, though, Cleghorn was the toughest and the most skilled.

Cleghorn won three Stanley Cups, first with the Ottawa Senators in 1919-20, then with the Senators again a year later, and, finally, with the Montreal Canadiens in 1923-24. He played four full seasons with the Habs during the prime of his career and later joined the Boston Bruins for three years to close out his NHL career.

Born in Montreal, he and brother Odie played for the Montreal Wanderers for several years in the NHA. But when that league disbanded and re-launched as the NHL in 1917, the Wanderers' arena burned down and Sprague ended up with the Senators and Odie with the Canadiens. It wasn't until 1921 that the siblings re-united with the Canadiens, but when they did they were a fearsome, brilliant pair by anyone's standards.

It was back in 1910 that Sprague made the change from forward to defence while playing alongside the great Cyclone Taylor with the

CANADIENS NUMBERS
SPRAGUE CLEGHORN

b. Montreal, Quebec, March 11, 1890   **d.** Montreal, Quebec, July 11, 1956
5'10"   190 lbs.   defence   shoots left

| | REGULAR SEASON | | | | | PLAYOFFS | | | | |
	GP	G	A	Pts	Pim	GP	G	A	Pts	Pim
1921-22	24	17	9	26	80	—	—	—	—	—
1922-23	24	9	8	17	34	1	0	0	0	7
1923-24	23	8	4	12	45	6	2	2	4	2
1924-25	27	8	10	18	89	6	1	2	3	4
TOTALS	98	42	31	73	248	13	3	4	7	13

Renfrew Millionaires. The pair was legendary for their end-to-end rushes, and by the time Cleghorn had retired in 1928 only Harry Cameron had scored more goals from the blueline. Indeed, Sprague scored five goals in one game, on December 27, 1913, while playing for the Wanderers.

Cleghorn's career was in doubt when he missed the entire 1917-18 season with a badly broken leg. He made a full recovery, though, and by the time he joined the Canadiens in 1921 he was with a team destined for glory. In his first season, he scored 17 goals in 24 league games, an unheard of total for a blueliner, and he also led the league in penalty minutes with 80. Backed by the great Georges Vézina, the team won the Stanley Cup in 1924. By this time, Cleghorn was Montreal captain and his teammates included several future hall of famers, notably Howie Morenz, Aurèle Joliat, and Joe Malone.

The next year, the team returned to the Stanley Cup playoffs but lost a best-of-five finals to the Victoria Cougars in four games. Before the start of the next season, Cleghorn was sold to the Boston Bruins for cash, and three years later he retired from the game to pursue a coaching career.

Sprague was most effective when he played alongside his brother, Odie, and the bond between the two was so strong that they passed away just days apart.

One of the many players in the league who combined skill and toughness, Cleghorn was among the leaders in both categories.

BROTHERS FOREVER

Sprague Cleghorn was only 66 when he died in hospital from complications after being hit by a car while walking to work. The events utterly destroyed the spirit of brother, Odie. The two had played together much of their lives and lived together, or near each other, as well. Odie was so overcome by grief that on the morning he was supposed to go to Sprague's funeral, he never woke up. He was discovered by their sister, with whom Odie had been living, in bed, and was laid to rest three days after Sprague.

Herb Gardiner

Defence 1926-27 to 1928-29

The Montreal Canadiens enjoyed a double reward in the early spring of 1924. In the first place, they defeated the Calgary Tigers 6-1 and 3-0 to win the Stanley Cup. In the second place, they were so impressed by one of the Tigers, defenceman Herb Gardiner, they later signed him to a contract.

Gardiner's story is utterly compelling if not extraordinary. It started in 1908 when he played senior hockey for his hometown Winnipeg Victorias. The next year he played in a local bankers' league, as far away from the professional ranks as possible. For the better part of the next nine years Gardiner was out of hockey altogether.

Gardiner's rise to prominence was all the more remarkable given that during his youth he was out of the game entirely for nine years.

Gardiner did not make his NHL debut until 1926 when he was 35 years old, testament to his enduring skills.

INDUCTED 1958

From 1910-14 he worked as a surveyor for Canadian Pacific Railway, and in 1914 he enlisted in the war. He served overseas with the 2nd C.M.R. in Flanders and France, rising to the rank of Lieutenant, but in 1918 he was wounded and sent home. Gardiner continued to contribute to the war efforts with Lord Strathcona's Horse until the end of the war. It was only then that he picked up a hockey stick again.

Gardiner played in Calgary for the next seven years, first with the Wanderers and then the Tigers, but when he joined the Canadiens in 1926, at age 35, he reached the greatest heights of his career. As an NHL "rookie," Gardiner played every minute of every game and won the Hart Trophy as the league's most valuable player. The Canadiens lost to Ottawa in the semi-finals of the playoffs, though, to end Gardiner's chance of winning a Stanley Cup. The next year he was almost as impressive as the Habs lost only eleven times in 44 games, but again the team came up just short in the playoffs, this time to the local rivals, Maroons.

In 1928-29, the Habs loaned Gardiner to Chicago for the balance of the year, but they recalled him toward the end of the regular season so he could help with the playoffs. Unfortunately, Boston swept the best-of-five in three games and Montreal sold him to the Bruins soon after.

After his playing days were over, Gardiner became a coach and executive, settling in Philadelphia in the Can-Am league.

CANADIENS NUMBERS
HERB GARDINER

b. Winnipeg, Manitoba, May 8, 1891   **d.** Philadelphia, Pennsylvania, January 11, 1972
5'10"   190 lbs.   defence   shoots left

	REGULAR SEASON					PLAYOFFS				
	GP	G	A	Pts	Pim	GP	G	A	Pts	Pim
1926-27	44	6	6	12	26	4	0	0	0	10
1927-28	44	4	3	7	26	2	0	1	1	4
1928-29	7	0	0	0	0	3	0	0	0	2
TOTALS	95	10	9	19	52	9	0	1	1	16

A COACH IN THE MAKING

Although the Boston Bruins acquired Gardiner from Montreal, they never got him into a game. Instead, they sold his rights to the Philadelphia Arrows of the Can-Am league, and Gardiner happily moved to Pennsylvania where he spent most of the next seven years as coach (although he did play a handful of games in emergency situations). Gardiner later joined the inspection staff of Frankford Arsenal. He passed away in Philadelphia in 1972 after a lengthy illness during his retirement.

Donat Raymond
Builder

Donat Raymond was a founder of the Canadian Arena Company, the driving force behind the construction of a new arena known as the Forum.

The connection between Donat Raymond and the Montreal Canadiens began long before either party even knew it. Raymond was an avid hockey fan who held box seats at the Westmount Arena, where the team played in the NHA and later, along with the Montreal Wanderers, the NHL.

When the Arena burned down, Montreal had no great building for hockey, and Raymond sought to spur a growth in the game by giving his city a venue of which to be proud. To that end, he helped form the Canadian Arena Company in 1923, and Raymond was named president. He then worked tirelessly to secure financing for a 9,700-seat arena, and on opening night, November 29, 1924, his dreams came true.

Raymond did not—could not—rest on his laurels, though. Although the new Montreal Forum was spectacular and the most modern hockey

rink in the world, the two teams—Canadiens and Maroons—were hardly playing up to the building's quality. The 1930s were marked by flagging attendance and poor performances on ice, the lone exceptions being intra-city games between the two teams which produced sell-outs in the seats and a bitter rivalry on the ice. The Maroons didn't survive the 1930s, but the Canadiens, of course, did. It was Raymond who almost single-handedly kept the team financially afloat, and the fortunes of the Canadiens changed forever when Dick Irvin left Toronto to coach the Habs.

After that, the team started winning, and Raymond could relax as it won the Stanley Cup with greater frequency. He remained president of the Company until 1957 when the team was bought by Senator Hartland Molson.

Raymond was a supporter of the team during the lean years as the Canadiens went from empty stands to sold-out crowds, largely thanks to his perseverance and loyalty to the team.

DONAT RAYMOND

b. St. Stanislas de Kostka, Quebec, January 3, 1880
d. Montreal, Quebec, June 5, 1963

MORE THAN JUST HOCKEY

Donat Raymond made his mark in Quebec first in the hotel business, and it was his success in this venture that led to his influence in the financial world of Montreal. He was elected to the Senate as a Liberal on December 20, 1926, but his successes did not end there. Raymond was also an accomplished breeder, and his horses won three King's Plates (in 1914 with Irish Heart, 1923 with King Wave, and 1930 with Span).

Sylvio Mantha
Defence 1923-24 to 1935-36

Mantha won his first Stanley Cup in his rookie season, 1923-24, and won twice more during his illustrious career.

When Mantha was named captain in 1926, he was just 24 years old, one of the youngest ever to hold the responsibility.

Although he was a defenceman his entire NHL career, Sylvio Mantha played forward earlier in his hockey life and, as a result, was a fine rushing defenceman when he got to the Montreal Canadiens in 1923. Not only did he become an instant star with the team, he was joining a lineup that included Howie Morenz, Aurèle Joliat,

Georges Vézina, captain Sprague Cleghorn, and coach Léo Dandurand. Mantha's rookie season ended the night of March 25, 1924, when the Canadiens defeated the Calgary Tigers 3-0 to win the Stanley Cup. His timing could not have been better.

The next year Mantha was again instrumental in taking the team to the

Stanley Cup playoffs, but this time the team fell just short, losing to the Victoria Cougars in four games of a best-of-five series played entirely in Vancouver. It was to be several years before the Habs won the Cup again, but the team routinely finished in first place in the Canadian Division. These were the years when the NHL was a ten-team league split between Canadian and American Divisions, the former consisting of the two Montreal teams—Canadiens and Maroons—and Ottawa, Toronto, and the New York Americans. The American Division consisted of Boston, Detroit, Chicago, New York Rangers, and Pittsburgh Pirates or Philadelphia Quakers.

Despite being just 24 years old, Mantha took over from Billy Coutu as the team's captain in 1926, a responsibility he carried with pride until 1935 when he was also named playing-coach (except 1932-33 when goalie George Hainsworth was captain). Mantha took the team to back-to-back Stanley Cup wins in 1930 and 1931, defeating Boston in two straight games of a best-of-three finals in the former and Chicago in the deciding game of a best-of-five the next year. In 1930, Mantha scored in both finals' games. He also has the distinction of scoring the first goal in the new Boston Garden, on November 20, 1928. It was the only goal of a 1-0 Montreal win in the arena's first game.

CANADIENS NUMBERS
SYLVIO MANTHA

b. Montreal, Quebec, April 14, 1902   **d.** Montreal, Quebec, August 7, 1974
5'10"   178 lbs.   defence   shoots right

| | REGULAR SEASON | | | | | PLAYOFFS | | | | |
	GP	G	A	Pts	Pim	GP	G	A	Pts	Pim
1923-24 🏆	24	1	3	4	11	2	0	0	0	0
1924-25	30	2	3	5	18	6	0	1	1	2
1925-26	34	2	1	3	66	—	—	—	—	—
1926-27	43	10	5	15	77	4	1	0	1	0
1927-28	43	4	11	15	61	2	0	0	0	6
1928-29	44	9	4	13	56	3	0	0	0	0
1929-30 🏆	44	13	11	24	108	6	2	1	3	18
1930-31 🏆	44	4	7	11	75	10	2	1	3	26
1931-32	47	5	5	10	62	4	0	1	1	8
1932-33	48	4	7	11	50	2	0	1	1	2
1933-34	48	4	6	10	24	2	0	0	0	2
1934-35	47	3	11	14	36	2	0	0	0	2
1935-36	42	2	4	6	25	—	—	—	—	—
TOTALS	538	63	78	141	669	43	5	5	10	66

A TRUE MONTREALER

Sylvio Mantha was born in Montreal, died in Montreal, and spent almost his entire life in Montreal. He was raised in a house near Cote St. Paul Road and Ste. Clotilde St. and played for the Notre Dame de Grâce Juniors in 1918-19. From there he went to Verdun and then spent two years developing with the Imperial Tobacco Manufacturers' League. In 1922, Mantha joined the Northern Electric league and then played his most serious hockey with the Nationale, a senior team based in Montreal. It was there that Léo Dandurand discovered him and put him in the Canadiens lineup. Several years later, Sylvio's brother, Georges, also signed with the team and stayed with the Canadiens his whole career, some 13 years and 488 games. Sylvio later refereed and coached in Montreal and the surrounding areas for several years.

Frank Selke
Builder

General manager Frank Selke (far right) was always the first to congratulate his players for their stellar play.

From the time he became general manager of the Montreal Canadiens in 1946, to the time he retired in 1964, Frank Selke first helped revive a franchise, then built it into the greatest dynasty hockey has ever known, and, finally, left the city a legacy of a second dynasty in the years immediately following his retirement. Indeed, Selke is arguably the single most influential and successful person in the history of the franchise. When Selke left Toronto and arrived at the Forum in the fall of 1946, he was coming to a team that had had little success at the box office in the 1940s. Still, the team had a core of star players who represented the Canadiens' immediate future. Selke was also leaving a team that was about to win four Stanley Cups in five years (and had also won in 1942 and 1945), so he well knew what a winning organization should look like. What he saw in Montreal in 1946 wasn't it.

Selke poses with player Bob Gainey, who won the Selke Tropy its first four years of existence.

In his first four years, the team made it to the Stanley Cup finals only once. Selke, meanwhile, was busy building the team from the bottom up, improving its scouting and

FRANK SELKE

b. Berlin (Kitchener), Ontario, May 7, 1893
d. Rigaud, Quebec, July 3, 1985

GOODBYE TORONTO— HELLO MONTREAL

The departure of Frank Selke from Maple Leaf Gardens to the rival corridors of the Forum can be traced to one very specific incident. In 1941, Leafs' owner Conn Smythe left the team to do his part in Canada's war efforts. He left Selke, his right-hand man, in charge of all business operations, but he also wanted detailed updates for all goings on related to the club. Prior to the start of the 1943-44 season, though, Selke made a significant trade on his own. He sent Frank Eddolls to Montreal for the rights to youngster Ted Kennedy. The move enraged Smythe for several reasons. First, he was not consulted. Second, he was very high on Eddolls as a prospect. Third, he wasn't so keen on Kennedy. And fourth, most important of all, the trade turned out to be a move of staggering serendipity. The event caused a schism in their long and close friendship, but Selke realized he no longer wanted to be second in command. He believed he could run his own team, and when Montreal gave him the chance, he took it.

Frank Selke
Builder

Selke jokes with his great star, Maurice Richard, as the Rocket puts his signature on another contract.

adding farm teams and junior teams to its organization to create a comprehensive whole. By the early 1950s, his plan was starting to reap rewards, and by the mid-1950s he had a team that was second to none.

From 1951 to 1960, the team made it to the Cup finals every year, a ten-year streak of unprecedented success. Toronto and Detroit got the better of the Habs in the first half of the decade, but between 1956 and 1960, no team

could beat Les Canadiens. This streak of five Cups in a row is likely never to be broken and goes down as Selke's greatest achievement.

Coinciding with these victories was another important decision that fell to Selke. In the summer of 1955, coach Dick Irvin stepped down to leave a cavernous opening in the team's structure. Selke considered many candidates for the vital post but realized the key to the coach's success would be his ability to handle the team's greatest player, Maurice Richard. To that end, Selke saw no person better to take over than Toe Blake, a

former teammate and linemate of Richard who knew the Rocket as well as anyone. Selke's instincts were astute, and Richard led the team to five straight Stanley Cup victories.

Selke's finest attribute was his ability to see the big picture. Yes, a win on Saturday night was important, but not as much as the structure of the team and an intelligent plan for the future. To this end, even while he was in his prime and winning the Stanley Cup, he knew his day, like everyone's, would end at some point. He hired a young man named Sam Pollock who worked his way up through the system slowly and methodically, from scout to manager of the junior team to assistant to Selke himself. When Selke retired in 1964, Pollock was in his prime and ready to take over. As a result, Selke continued to watch his team win the sacred trophy for many years after his retirement.

Selke (left) and coach Dick Irvin share a moment. The two men were integral to the renaissance and domination of the Habs in the late 1940s and throughout the 1950s.

Well respected everywhere he went, Frank Selke always held his players' undivided attention.

George Hainsworth

Goalie 1926-27 to 1936-37

The great George Hainsworth did what few thought any man could do—replace Georges Vézina.

Even though he retired more than seven decades ago, Hainsworth's 94 regular-season shuouts remains third highest all-time.

CANADIENS NUMBERS GEORGE HAINSWORTH

b. Gravenhurst, Ontario, June 26, 1895   **d.** Gravenhurst, Ontario, October 9, 1950
5'6"   150 lbs.   goalie   catches left

	REGULAR SEASON						PLAYOFFS					
	GP	W-L-T	Mins	GA	SO	GAA	GP	W-L	Mins	GA	SO	GAA
1926-27	44	28-14-2	2,732	67	14	1.47	4	1-1-2	252	6	1	1.43
1927-28	44	26-11-7	2,730	48	13	1.05	2	0-1-1	128	3	0	1.41
1928-29	44	22-7-15	2,800	43	22	0.92	3	0-3-0	180	5	0	1.67
1929-30 🏆	42	20-13-9	2,680	108	4	2.42	6	5-0-1	481	6	3	0.75
1930-31 🏆	44	26-10-8	2,740	89	8	1.95	10	6-4-0	722	21	2	1.75
1931-32	48	25-16-7	2,998	110	6	2.20	4	1-3-0	300	13	0	2.60
1932-33	48	18-25-5	2,980	115	8	2.32	2	0-1-1	120	8	0	4.00
1936-37	4	2-1-1	270	12	0	2.67	—	—	—	—	—	—
TOTALS	318	167-97-54	19,930	592	75	1.78	31	13-13-5	2,183	62	6	1.70

After the forced retirement of Georges Vézina on November 28, 1925, because of tuberculosis, the Montreal Canadiens struggled to find a replacement for the best goalie in pro hockey. They tried Herb Rheaume and Alphonse "Frenchy" Lacroix, but neither was up to the task. Finally, on the recommendation of Newsy Lalonde, the team signed George Hainsworth who had most recently been playing for the Saskatoon Crescents. The Crescents played in the WHL, and when that league folded its players, including Hainsworth, were free agents to play where they could.

Hainsworth was not an obvious choice.

INDUCTED 1961

By the time he played his first game for the Canadiens he was 31 years old and entering his 15th year of senior or pro hockey. Additionally, he had spent his entire career in either the Ontario Hockey Association or the Western Hockey League, organizations not of comparable quality to the superior NHL.

Nevertheless, Hainsworth came to Montreal and proved a stunning success. Over the next seven years, he played all but two games for the team and led the league in several statistical categories during his tenure with the Habs. In his first season, 1926-27, Hainsworth played every game and led the league with 14 shutouts. He also won the newly-minted Vézina Trophy, given by the Canadiens owners in respect of their deceased goalie and to be awarded annually to the goalie or goalies on the team that allowed the fewest goals.

The next two years were remarkably similar. Hainsworth won the Vézina each of these seasons and had 13 and 22 shutouts, respectively, the latter figure coming in a 44-game season and which, to this day, remains a single-season record. These records, though, reflect the era as much as Hainsworth's brilliance. In these days, forward passing was not permitted in most areas of the rink, so scoring was minimal. To start the 1929-30 season, passing was allowed all over the ice and scoring rose while shutouts and goalie averages dropped and rose. Ironically, it was this 1929-30 season, when Hainsworth had "only" four shutouts (which still was tops in the league), that the Canadiens won the Stanley Cup for the first time since 1924.

Montreal won the best-of-three finals in a 2-0 sweep over Boston, a team that had defeated the Canadiens in all four regular-season games. The next year, the Canadiens repeated as Cup champs. Hainsworth played two more seasons for the Canadiens. In 1931-32, he lead the league in wins with 25 in just 48 games, but the year after he had a weak 18-25-5 record and the Habs traded him to Toronto for another goalie, Lorne Chabot. After three seasons and three games with the Leafs, he was released, but Hainsworth, now 41 years old, signed with Montreal to close out his career. He played four games with the Club de Hockey in 1936-37 before retiring.

Hainsworth's 94 career shutouts are third all-time behind Terry Sawchuk (103) and Martin Brodeur (96 and counting). His is an amazing story of having to replace a legend while himself becoming one.

A RECORD NEVER TO BE EQUALED

When George Hainsworth recorded 22 shutouts in one season, the 44-game schedule of 1928-29, he set a record that will surely never be broken. It was the culmination of three outstanding years to begin his career, having had 14 and 13 shutouts, respectively, in his rookie and sophomore seasons. Hainsworth played every minute of every game for the Canadiens in 1928-29, but what is doubly remarkable is that 15 of the team's games went into mandatory 10-minute overtime. Yet, still, he managed to earn a shutout in half his team's games. These were years when the NHL's rules regarding forward passing were changing. In 1928-29, forward passing was allowed only in the defensive and centre-ice areas. Forward passing inside the opposition blueline wasn't allowed until the next year at which time scoring around the league nearly doubled and recorded shutouts decreased substantially.

Joe Hall
Defence 1917-18 to 1918-19

He was called "Bad Joe" for most of his career, and with good reason. Hall was a vicious player with his stick, but he offset his temper with a fiery competitiveness and a skill that belied his sometimes reckless behaviour. By the time he died in a Seattle hospital, teammates and opponents could speak only to his abilities.

Although he was born in England, Hall arrived in Canada at age two with his parents and settled in Brandon,

Manitoba. It was there that he started playing hockey, and although he roamed around several leagues in Canada he settled down with the Montreal Shamrocks in 1909 when the National Hockey Association began.

Prior to the start of the NHA, Hall was with the Kenora Thistles in January 1907 when the small town wrested the Stanley Cup from the Montreal Wanderers. He had previously played for the Winnipeg Rowing Club in January 1903 when that team ventured to Ottawa to try to defeat the overpowering Silver Seven in an earlier Stanley Cup

Joe Hall was as "bad" as he was skilled, and he was both feared and revered for these contrasting characteristics.

challenge. The incumbent champions defeated the visitors 2-0 in the final game of a tense best-of-three.

Hall joined the Quebec Bulldogs the following year and remained in the provincial capital for the next seven years. He helped the Bulldogs to two straight Stanley Cup victories, in 1912 and 1913. In the former, he was one of the league's top scorers in the regular season, and in the latter he scored half his team's goals in the deciding 6-2 victory over the Sydney Miners in a two-game challenge.

These years were also marked by a ferocious rivalry with the Montreal Canadiens, notably fought between Hall and their top star Newsy Lalonde. In 1917, however, the Bulldogs withdrew from the new National Hockey League, which had replaced the NHA, and all the players were put into a draft for the NHL. Hall was selected by the Canadiens, and management made the irony greater by making Lalonde and Hall roommates.

In his first year with the team, 1917-18, the Canadiens didn't make it to the Cup playoffs, but the next year they did. The team traveled to Seattle to play a best-of-seven with the Metropolitans, but this series, in March 1919, was complicated by the worldwide influenza pandemic. Teams had split the first five games evenly (two wins each and one tie) when several

Montreal players had to be hospitalized. Joe Hall died on April 5, and the rest of the series was cancelled. No team was awarded the Stanley Cup that season.

Hall had signed a huge $600 contract with the Canadiens for the 1918-19 season (including a $100 bonus for winning the Cup), but the Spanish flu, which claimed the lives of some 675,000 people in the U.S. and more than 20 million worldwide, was too strong to allow Hall to collect. He left behind a wife, two sons, and a daughter.

THE CANCELLED SERIES

It started out as a North American series of historic proportions. The western and American Seattle Metropolitans faced the famed Montreal Canadiens in a best-of-seven series in Seattle, the winner claiming the Stanley Cup. The hosts romped to a 7-0 win in the first game, but the Habs fought back to even the series with a 4-2 win in game two. Again, Seattle took the lead after a 7-2 win, and the Mets held Montreal to a scoreless draw in game four. The fifth game saw Montreal win in overtime by a 4-3 score, a game which in some way might have decided the Cup. That result evened the series at two wins and a tie for each team, after which the series was cancelled because of the flu pandemic. But had Seattle won, it might well have been awarded the Cup because it was leading the series at the time of the cancellation. Jack McDonald was the hero for Montreal, scoring at 15:57 of overtime in that fifth and final game.

CANADIENS NUMBERS
JOE HALL

b. Staffordshire, England, May 3, 1882   **d.** Seattle, Washington, April 5, 1919
5'10"   175 lbs.   defence   shoots right

| | REGULAR SEASON | | | | | PLAYOFFS | | | | |
	GP	G	A	Pts	Pim	GP	G	A	Pts	Pim
1917-18	21	8	7	15	100	2	0	1	1	12
1918-19	17	7	1	8	89	5	0	0	0	17
TOTALS	38	15	8	23	189	7	0	1	1	29

Maurice "Rocket" Richard

Right Wing 1942-43 to 1959-60

The Rocket celebrates his 626th career point to become the NHL's all-time leading scorer.

It doesn't matter if other players have scored more goals or won more Stanley Cups. It doesn't matter that today's players are bigger and faster and shoot the puck harder, or the goalies better conditioned and more skilled. It doesn't matter that his last game came in 1960, almost half a century ago. There will never, ever be a player like Maurice "Rocket" Richard. More than any other NHLer, he was a social, even political figure, and perhaps as great as his hockey career was he was, first and foremost, a French-Canadian.

Richard is the most loved and revered player in Montreal Canadiens history. He was one of seven children. Hockey fans know of Henri, the much younger brother, but there were three other brothers—René, Jacques, Claude—and two sisters, Georgette and Marguerite. This was not a rich family, and times were tough for the kids. Later, when Maurice became the Rocket and the boy became a hockey sensation, his humble origins made it easy for the people of Quebec to identify with him. His success, on the other hand, was perhaps the single greatest inspiration for a generation of underclass citizens of the province, that rare beacon of

The Richard brothers were inseparable everywhere they went.

hope, that ray of pride that shines through the gloom of poverty and destitution with unwavering tenacity.

Richard first put on skates at age four, and like so many other boys across Canada he fell in love with hockey. Of course, Walter Gretzky is famous for building son, Wayne, a backyard rink, but back in the mid-1920s Mr. Onesime Richard also built a backyard rink for his

children. Maurice started to play organized hockey at age eleven in his neighbourhood. He was very good, and by the time he was in his late teens it was clear he was destined for greatness.

His entry into the NHL was by no means smooth, however, and his place in history was anything but assured

CANADIENS NUMBERS
MAURICE "Rocket" RICHARD

b. Montreal, Quebec, August 4, 1921   **d.** Montreal, Quebec, May 27, 2000
5'10"   170 lbs.   right wing   shoots left

	REGULAR SEASON					PLAYOFFS				
	GP	G	A	Pts	Pim	GP	G	A	Pts	Pim
1942-43	16	5	6	11	4	—	—	—	—	—
1943-44	46	32	22	54	45	9	12	5	17	10
1944-45	50	50	23	73	46	6	6	2	8	10
1945-46	50	27	21	48	50	9	7	4	11	15
1946-47	60	45	26	71	69	10	6	5	11	44
1947-48	53	28	25	53	89	—	—	—	—	—
1948-49	59	20	18	38	110	7	2	1	3	14
1949-50	70	43	22	65	114	5	1	1	2	6
1950-51	65	42	24	66	97	11	9	4	13	13
1951-52	48	27	17	44	44	11	4	2	6	6
1952-53	70	28	33	61	112	12	7	1	8	2
1953-54	70	37	30	67	112	11	3	0	3	22
1954-55	67	38	36	74	125	—	—	—	—	—
1955-56	70	38	33	71	89	10	5	9	14	24
1956-57	63	33	29	62	74	10	8	3	11	8
1957-58	28	15	19	34	28	10	11	4	15	10
1958-59	42	17	21	38	27	4	0	0	0	2
1959-60	51	19	16	35	50	8	1	3	4	2
TOTALS	978	544	421	965	1,285	133	82	44	126	188

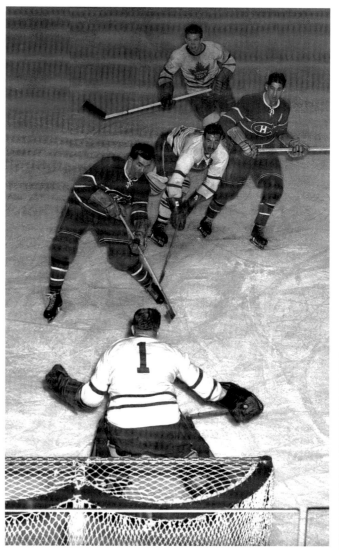

Richard swoops in on Toronto's Turk Broda.

Maurice "Rocket" Richard

Right Wing 1942-43 to 1959-60

Richard fights for the puck in the slot against the team's longtime rivals, the Maple Leafs

early on. During his last two years of amateur hockey, with the Montreal Sr. Canadiens, Richard was beset by injuries. He missed most of 1940-41 with a badly broken ankle and most of the next season with a broken wrist. Still, the NHL Canadiens signed him prior to the 1942-43 season, a move that looked like a mistake when Richard broke his ankle again in just the 16th game of his rookie season with the team. He missed the rest of the year, and the club was concerned that, great as his skills were, he was too brittle for a rough-and-tumble game like NHL hockey.

Richard proved the worriers wrong in 1943-44. He played 46 of the 50 scheduled games, scored 32 goals, and led the team into the playoffs with great promise. By the time the Canadiens had won the Stanley Cup, Richard was a hero and on his way to glory. He scored 12 goals in just nine post-season games, including five in the four-game sweep of Chicago in the finals. In game two, won by Montreal 3-1, Richard scored all three goals.

It was during this season that Maurice became the Rocket. Teammate Ray Getliffe was sitting on the bench watching the young star barrel up ice, tear in on goal with what would become his trademark "fire in his eyes," and score. Getliffe remarked that Richard looked like a rocket. Sportswriter Dink Carroll, standing behind the bench, heard the remark and used it in his story, and the name became the most popular identifier of Richard for the rest of his life.

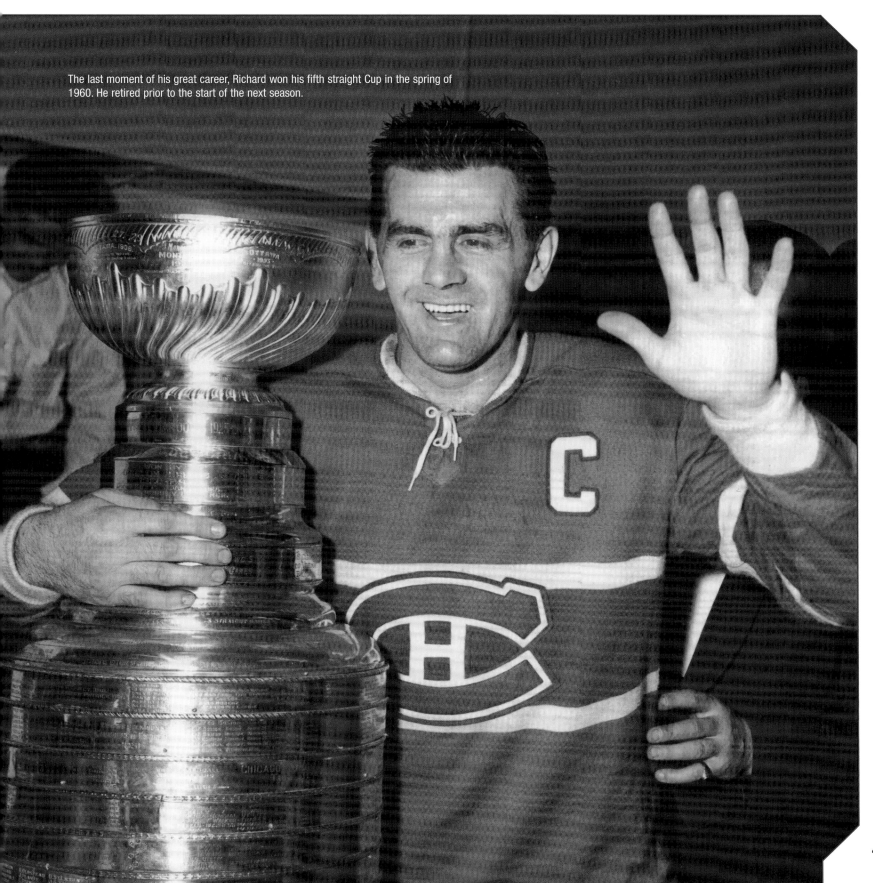

The last moment of his great career, Richard won his fifth straight Cup in the spring of 1960. He retired prior to the start of the next season.

Maurice "Rocket" Richard

Right Wing 1942-43 to 1959-60

Big things were expected of Richard the next year, but no one could have expected how big Richard would get. The first signs of record-breaking greatness came the night of December 28, 1944, a home game against Detroit. Richard had spent the day moving, and he even suggested to coach Dick Irvin he wouldn't be able to play, such was his fatigue. Irvin told him to do his best, and Richard responded with an NHL record eight points (including five goals) in a 9-1 win over the Red Wings.

As the 50-game schedule was drawing to a close, Richard was approaching the NHL record of 44 goals in a season, set by Joe Malone in 1917-18 in a 20-game season. In truth, the game and rules had changed so much that to compare eras and records from Malone's days to Richard's was unfair—a record was a record. Richard not only equaled that mark, he set a new standard for scorers when, on March 18, 1945, he scored his 50th goal of the season against Boston's Harvey Bennett.

The 50 goals-in-50 games remained the very basis for great scorers until it was equaled by Mike Bossy of the New York Islanders more than 30 years later and then surpassed by Gretzky in 1981-82 when he scored 50 times in the first 39 games of the season. Gretzky ended that season with 92 goals, a record that might stand even longer than Richard's original achievement.

Armed with his intimidating stare, Richard was never one to back down from a fight, going toe-to-toe with the Rangers' Ivan Irwin.

The Canadiens didn't win the Cup that year, but they did win again the next season. Richard had only 27 goals in the regular season, but he again led all playoff scorers with seven goals as the Habs swept Chicago in four games straight and then won the Cup in a five-game series against the Bruins.

Richard was establishing himself as the best in the game for several reasons. First, he was a rare example of a left-handed shot who played the right wing. By playing the "off wing," he was able to drive hard to the goal while having a better angle to shoot the puck (i.e., the puck was closer to the middle of the ice than the boards). The position also catered to his love of driving to the net, more or less defining his style of play out of necessity.

While Richard relaxes on the boards, teammate Jean Béliveau skates onto the ice.

He was also a rare example of a pure scorer. No one ever said he was a great passer or backchecker. His skill and his career rested on his ability to score. Of course, in order to do this, he also had to create space for himself and stand up for himself, and he was known never to shy away from either a fight or from swinging his stick at an opponent, if that's what it took to earn his opponents' respect.

THE FIRST TO 500

It doesn't matter how many players achieve the 500-goal milestone, the first to have done so will always be Maurice Richard. On the night of October 19, 1957, he arrived at the Forum to face goalie Glenn Hall and the Chicago Black Hawks with a career total of 499 goals to his credit. Late in the first period, Ian Cushenan of the Hawks was penalized for holding Richard, and coach Toe Blake put out arguably the best power-play unit in the history of the game. Richard hopped off the bench to join Jean Béliveau, Dickie Moore, and Doug Harvey on defence. The other defensive position was taken by forward Bernie Geoffrion. Moore brought the puck into the Hawks' end and fired a pass down low to Béliveau, stationed to Hall's left. He made a quick pass to the back side of the goalie, and Richard one-timed the shot past Hall, who had earlier made two sensational stops on the Rocket to prevent number 500. On this shot, he wasn't able, and Richard scooped the history-making puck out of the net.

Maurice "Rocket" Richard

Right Wing 1942-43 to 1959-60

Richard celebrates his historic 500th career regular-season goal, the first player in NHL history to achieve the great milestone.

Toronto goalie Turk Broda is no match for Richard in this one-on-one confrontation at Maple Leaf Gardens.

Such was Richard's unprecedented popularity that the team actually accorded him a special night of honour on February 17, 1951, less than a decade into his career and nearly a decade before he was to retire. It was as if the need to celebrate his career was bursting at the seams to such a degree that the team simply couldn't wait until his final game or season to acknowledge his value to the Canadiens' history.

Richard remained healthy for many seasons, but he missed several weeks in 1951-52 with a mysterious stomach ailment which doctors couldn't accurately diagnose. Richard was sent to Florida for rest, and by the time the playoffs were at hand he was healthy again. Although the Canadiens lost to Detroit in the finals, it was a goal by Richard in the semi-finals against Boston that is still considered one of the greatest playoff moments of all time. The series went the full seven games, and in the middle period of that deciding game with the score 1-1, Léo Labine of the Bruins knocked Richard unconscious with a clean but ferocious check.

Richard revived and returned to the game, feeling groggy. With less than four minutes left in the third period, though, he made a solo dash past two Bruins before beating Sugar Jim Henry with a shot. Billy Reay added an empty-net goal to make the final score 3-1, but Richard was the hero. The photograph of a humbled Henry, head bowed and shaking Richard's hand after the game, remains one of the great hockey images.

The next year, on November 8, 1952, Richard became the all-time leading goalscorer when he notched his 325th career goal, surpassing Boston's great Nels Stewart. He remained the all-time scorer for eleven years, during which time he upped the record total to 544.

The pivotal moment in Richard's career came the night of March 13, 1955. In a game in Boston, all hell broke loose

Maurice "Rocket" Richard

Right Wing 1942-43 to 1959-60

and Richard ended up clubbing Bruins' defenceman Hal Laycoe over the head with his stick. In the ensuing melee, he also punched linesman Cliff Thompson. NHL president Clarence Campbell suspended Richard for the final three games of the regular season and all of the play-offs. Four nights later, in the team's first game since the suspension, in Montreal, Campbell was in attendance as the Canadiens played host to Detroit. During the first intermission, fans ignited smoke bombs and began rioting in the Forum, and Campbell ordered the game forfeited to the Red Wings.

Fans spilled into the streets and continued their riotous behaviour, joined by thousands more not at the game. The shocking night of violence was so horrifying that Richard himself went on radio in Montreal to quell the disturbance. The event had both a hockey and social importance. In the case of the game, Richard had been leading the league in scoring, but in the final three games teammate Bernie Geoffrion surpassed Richard and won the Art Ross Trophy. It was the closest Richard ever came to winning the scoring race, and Geoffrion was booed mercilessly by his hometown fans as he passed Richard on the final weekend of play. In the playoffs, Detroit beat Montreal in a bitter seven-game finals that any Canadiens fans would say would have had a different result had Richard been in the lineup.

In social terms, Richard had made it clear that in his mind this suspension was not about violence in the game. It was about an English-Canadian president wielding power over a French-Canadian player. The social context of the English defeating the French and treating them with subservience was what the general French population could relate to. The fact that the incident took place during an NHL game hardly mattered. Richard became a hero, not for the NHL, not even for the Canadiens, but for French-Canadians. He made it clear that he was a French-Canadian

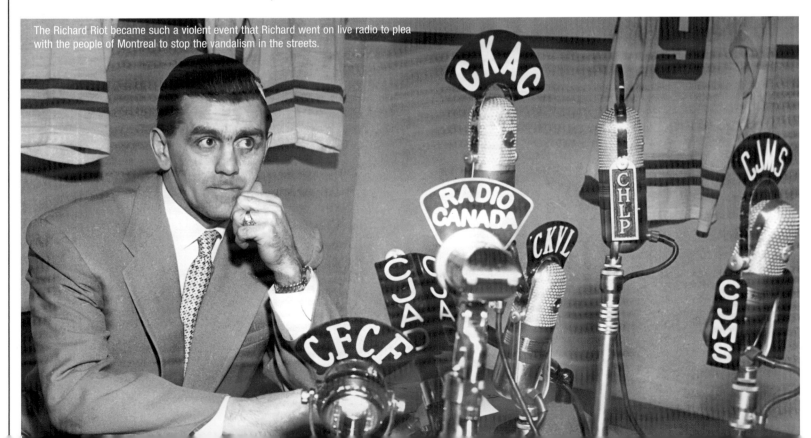

The Richard Riot became such a violent event that Richard went on live radio to plea with the people of Montreal to stop the vandalism in the streets.

first and last, and he made it clear that, in his mind, Campbell used his power to extinguish these values.

In the end, of course, Campbell's suspension stood, and the attacks against Laycoe and Thompson were never condoned or excused. But Richard's pride and honour raised his status far above hockey superstar. After the riot, Richard still had five good years of hockey left to give, and these were among his most memorable years. He was named team captain in 1956 and won the Cup in each season he held the role. The previous year his brother, Henri, had joined the team and given Maurice renewed interest in the game.

On October 19, 1957, Richard became the first player in NHL history to reach 500 career goals. Just a short time later, he suffered a bad injury to his Achilles tendon and missed the rest of the season, leaving his career in doubt. He came back the next year, though, only to hurt his ankle and miss several weeks again. His final season, 1959-60, saw the team win its fifth straight Stanley Cup, and although Richard collected his final playoff goal puck he did not retire right away. Indeed, he attended training camp for the 1960-61 season, and it was only then that he realized he was a step slower, a year older, and in no position to add anything to his legacy on ice.

Richard finished with 544 career goals, the all-time record until Gordie Howe bettered the mark. He was hustled into the Hockey Hall of Fame a year later, the usual five-year waiting period waived for the Rocket. As the years passed, he was never far from the Forum, symbolically or physically. However, the night of March 11, 1996, might well have been his single greatest memory, even though he was now 75 years old and many decades past his last game. On this night, the Forum closed, and the Canadiens brought back almost all of their living legends. The last player introduced was Maurice Richard, and as tears filled his eyes and he raised his arms begging the fans to stop standing, stop cheering, stop clapping, they renewed their homage to their hero over and over for eleven minutes. Only then could it be said the Forum had been given a proper farewell.

In the case of Richard, time does not diminish memory, and in 1998 the NHL introduced the Maurice Richard Trophy to be given annually to the top goal scorer in regular season play. The first winner was Anaheim's Teemu Selanne, and at the awards ceremony in Toronto in June 1999, Richard himself gave the Finnish superstar the eponymous trophy. It was the first and only time Richard was able to do so. He passed away May 27, 2000, and like Howie Morenz some three-quarters of a century earlier, Richard was given a funeral that perhaps was unmatched in Quebec history. His body lay in state at the new Bell Centre, and thousands of fans filed through to pay their last respects. Hundreds of thousands of fans lined the route from the arena to the cemetery to honour their hero, a man of humble origin who rose to prominence, a man proud of his heritage and his culture, the first truly French-Canadian symbol of pride. And he was a pretty good hockey player as well.

"Hat trick" or "tour de chapeau," call it what you will. The Rocket recorded many a great night during his illustrious career.

Jack Laviolette

Although he was born in Belleville, Ontario, Jack Laviolette lived all his adult life in Montreal. And why wouldn't he? After signing with the Montreal Shamrocks in 1907, he played the rest of his career in that city and became a pioneering member of the new Montreal Canadiens when the team debuted in 1909.

Laviolette played two years with the Montreal Shamrocks, a member of the ECAHA (East Coast Amateur Hockey Association). But in the fall of 1909, the ECAHA met strong opposition from a new league, the NHA (National Hockey Association). Laviolette was wooed from the Shamrocks by the fledgling Canadiens and named playing manager and captain, the inaugural leader in team history, thus starting his pro career at age 30.

Laviolette wore his share of different Canadiens sweaters over the course of his career.

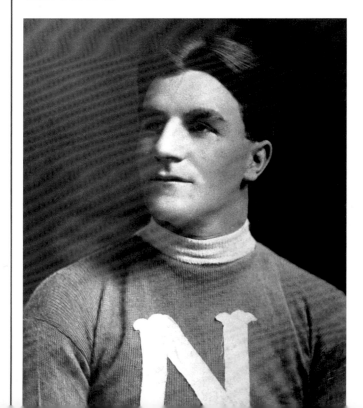

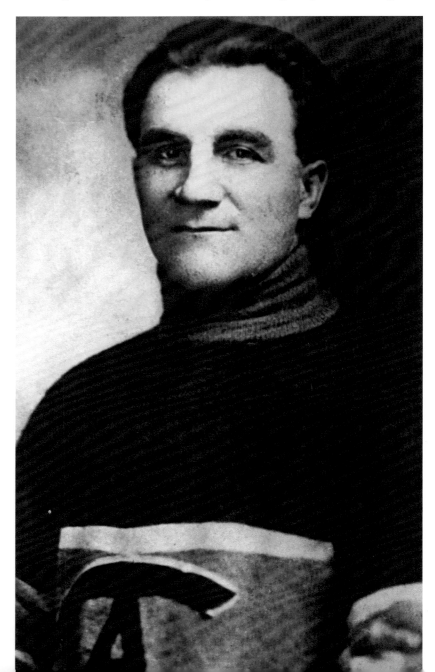

His dual roles with the team earned him a salary of $5,000, a colossal sum for the day. Indeed, the owners of the team, T.C. Hare and Ambrose O'Brien, gave Laviolette free rein to organize the team as he saw fit.

He started as a defenceman partnered with Didier Pitre, and he later played with Newsy Lalonde. The three soon played together as a forward line, and such was the skating ability of these players—their end-to-end rushes, their speed and skill—that the team came to be known as the Flying Frenchmen, a name that has been used periodically ever since to define a high-scoring or entertaining Montreal team.

The Canadiens won their only Stanley Cup during the NHA era in 1915-16 after defeating the Portland Rosebuds by a 2-1 score in game five of the best-of-five series, the first time a fifth game had been played in Cup competition. All games were played in Montreal, and Laviolette

earned his only championship in the process. It was also the first Cup win for the Canadiens franchise, today the winningest team in Stanley Cup history.

In 1917, the NHA disbanded and re-formed under the name NHL (National Hockey League). Laviolette was a spare by this point in his career, but he was forced out of the game altogether after an unfortunate accident in the summer of 1918. He enjoyed race-car driving in the off-season and had planned on touring a new car across Quebec. However, he got into an accident and had to have his right foot amputated.

His last game on skates occurred in 1921 at the Mount Royal Arena when a benefit game was played in his honour. An artificial foot was made for him, and he worked the game as a referee.

CANADIENS NUMBERS
JACK LAVIOLETTE

b. Belleville, Ontario, July 27, 1879   **d.** Montreal, Quebec, January 9, 1960
5'11"   170 lbs.   defence/forward   shoots right

	REGULAR SEASON					PLAYOFFS				
	GP	G	A	Pts	Pim	GP	G	A	Pts	Pim
1909-10	11	3	0	3	26	—	—	—	—	—
1910-11	16	0	0	0	24	—	—	—	—	—
1911-12	17	7	0	7	10	—	—	—	—	—
1912-13	20	8	0	8	77	—	—	—	—	—
1913-14	20	7	9	16	30	2	0	1	1	0
1914-15	18	6	3	9	35	—	—	—	—	—
1915-16	18	8	3	11	62	4	0	0	0	6
1916-17	17	7	3	10	24	6	1	2	3	9
1917-18	18	2	1	3	6	2	0	0	0	0
NHL TOTALS	18	2	1	3	6	2	0	0	0	0

*1909-17=NHA

LACROSSE STAR

Jack Laviolette was also a sensational lacrosse player and is an inductee in Canada's Sports Hall of Fame for his career in that sport. He played with the Nationale Club and with Montreal AAA, and his teammates included legends of the game such as Johnny Howard, Gord and George Finlayson, and Andy Hamilton. More important, though, Laviolette played on the Nationale with Didier Pitre and Newsy Lalonde, his hockey teammates with the Canadiens. Their careers culminated in 1910 when they traveled to British Columbia to try to wrest the Minto Cup from the New Westminster Salmon Bellies.

Ambrose O'Brien
Builder

It was a series of extraordinary events which made the name Ambrose O'Brien so prominent and important in the development of professional hockey and in the creation of the Montreal Canadiens hockey club.

O'Brien owned a hockey team in Renfrew in the early 1900s, but this was a very good team playing unworthy opponents. O'Brien, like any player or executive today, dreamed of winning the Stanley Cup, not some local Northern Ontario championship. So, he applied for admission to the ECAHA (Eastern Canadian Amateur Hockey Association). The ECAHA rejected his petition, and at the same time it expelled the Montreal Wanderers. O'Brien met with those owners and decided to form a

new league called the National Hockey Association (NHA). To give this new league credence, six teams were established, four of which were financed by O'Brien and his father, who had acquired great wealth through mining and the railway.

In addition to Renfrew and the Wanderers, the NHA included teams in Cobalt and Haileybury. The sixth team was called the Montreal Canadiens, financed by O'Brien on condition it would be turned over to investors once these could be found. The league played for the O'Brien Cup, a trophy later used by the NHL in 1917 after it replaced the NHA. These league champions either were awarded or could challenge for the coveted Stanley Cup.

Ironically, the ECAHA was then hit with the withdrawal of the Quebec

O'Brien almost single-handedly financed the new National Hockey Association, forerunner to the NHL.

O'Brien failed to win a Stanley Cup with the Renfrew Millionaires, but he did manage to bring the Montreal Canadiens into this world in 1909.

INDUCTED 1962

Bulldogs and Ottawa Senators, the latter applying to the NHA and gaining admission. This left the once-powerful amateur league with only two teams, forcing its disbandment.

The six-team NHA became the best league in Canada, and O'Brien was determined to get the Stanley Cup for his Renfrew team. He signed Lester and Frank Patrick, Cyclone Taylor, Marty Walsh, and Fred Whitcroft, all stars of the day, and their cumulative salaries led to the team being nicknamed the Millionaires.

Alas, the team never won the Cup, and O'Brien's beloved dream ended soon after in ironic fashion. The Patrick brothers moved to Vancouver to form their own breakaway league, and like O'Brien, lured players to the west with promise of great salaries. They themselves had been able to afford the development of the Pacific Coast Hockey League because of money they earned from O'Brien playing in the NHA!

The O'Brien Trophy was the championship award for the winners of the NHA playoffs.

In 1917, the NHA was disbanded and O'Brien returned to private business. But thanks to him, the ECAHA gave way to the NHA and, finally, the NHL. In reality, the creation of the NHA started the Montreal Canadiens on their way to great fame and glory.

AMBROSE O'BRIEN

b. Renfrew, Ontario, May 27, 1885
d. Ottawa, Ontario, April 25, 1968

A FRENCH TEAM FOR MONTREAL

While the ECAHA had expelled the Montreal Wanderers from its league, O'Brien believed there were enough French-Canadian players—and fans—in Montreal to support a team made up solely of French-speaking players. To that end, he introduced the Canadiens to the NHA. The roster in 1909-10 included Jack Laviolette, Newsy Lalonde, Didier Pitre, Richard Dickette, Art Bernier, Albert Millaire, Edgar Leduc, and Edgar Chapleau. Their first game of the season was played January 5, 1910, when the Canadiens defeated Cobalt, 7-6. After one year under the ownership of O'Brien, he sold the team to George Kennedy for the sum of $7,500. Kennedy owned the team until his death in 1921, after which it was sold by his widow to the trio of Léo Dandurand, Joe Cattarinich, and Louis Letourneau. In September 1935, the Canadian Arena Company took possession of the team.

Didier Pitre

An original member of the Canadiens in 1909, Pitre played nearly every pro game of his career with the Canadiens before retiring in 1923.

Pitre (right) helped lead the Canadiens to the team's first Stanley Cup in 1915-16.

He played by his own rules, on and off the ice, but in his day Didier Pitre was the highest scoring, best paid player in the game. He weighed in at just over 200 pounds and was a smooth skater for a big man, but it was his ferocious shot that made him the stuff of legend. Pitre was credited with shattering several sections of boards behind enemy goals from shots that sailed wide, and although this seems a stretch today it must be remembered in the 1910s boards were made of wood and were, no doubt, of varying quality and condition.

Pitre began his career playing professionally for the Montreal Nationale in 1903. The next year, he moved on to the American Soo in the IHL, the first pro league ever established. He moved around for a few years, but in 1909 he settled with the Canadiens and started a career that saw him play 13 of the next 14 years with the team in the

NHA and NHL. The lone exception was the 1913-14 season when he traveled west to play for the Vancouver Millionaires. Indeed, Pitre was the first player the Montreal Canadiens ever signed when the team was formed in 1909.

Pitre began on defence for Montreal alongside Jack Laviolette. The pair were such gifted skaters they were dubbed the Flying Frenchmen and two years later they moved up to play alongside Newsy Lalonde as a forward unit. The trio led the Canadiens to their first Stanley Cup, in 1915-16. The Canadiens defeated the Portland Rosebuds 2-1 in the deciding game of the best-of-five series played entirely in Montreal.

This was to be the only Cup of Pitre's career, although he did play in the 1919 finals which were cancelled because of the influenza pandemic. Although Pitre was loved by the fans and was equally a sensation on ice, he endured rough times during the last years of his career. When Léo Dandurand took over as part owner of the team in 1921, he wanted to instill

a new mindset in his players, one which was easily implemented among the younger players but less so with the veterans from another, pre-war era.

Dandurand demanded both loyalty and discipline from his players. Pitre was accommodating in the former but not so much in the latter. He never adhered to a training regimen and happily stayed out late having fun, but this was never a concern because the next night he would always be the best player on the ice. Nevertheless, although Pitre was the top player in hockey, he lost much of his salary in dribs and drabs over the season through fines. Indeed, the Canadiens actually had a meeting to determine whether they should suspend Pitre. They believed if he were

the highest paid player he should play commensurately better than his teammates.

In the end, Pitre's skills were such that he remained with the team until 1923 when he was 38 years old. He retired as one of the greatest early stars of the Canadiens, and he settled in Sault Ste. Marie, Michigan, where he continued to play for several years while working as a truck driver. Pitre died at just 50 years of age after an attack of acute indigestion.

CANADIENS NUMBERS
DIDIER PITRE

b. Valleyfield, Quebec, September 1, 1883   **d.** Sault Ste. Marie, Michigan, July 29, 1934
5'11"   185 lbs.   forward/defence   shoots right

	REGULAR SEASON					PLAYOFFS				
	GP	G	A	Pts	Pim	GP	G	A	Pts	Pim
1909-10	12	10	—	10	5	—	—	—	—	—
1910-11	16	19	—	19	22	—	—	—	—	—
1911-12	18	27	—	27	40	—	—	—	—	—
1912-13	17	24	—	24	80	—	—	—	—	—
1914-15	20	30	4	34	15	—	—	—	—	—
1915-16	24	24	15	39	42	5	4	—	4	18
1916-17	21	21	6	27	50	6	7	—	7	32
1917-18	20	17	—	17	29	2	0	1	1	13
1918-19	17	14	5	19	12	10	2	6	8	3
1919-20	22	14	12	26	6	—	—	—	—	—
1920-21	23	16	5	21	25	—	—	—	—	—
1921-22	23	2	4	6	12	—	—	—	—	—
1922-23	22	1	2	3	0	2	0	0	0	0
NHL TOTALS	127	64	28	92	84	14	2	7	9	16

*1909-17=NHA

BECOMING A CANADIEN

Didier Pitre was a prize catch in December 1909 when he was at the height of his powers. He was on his way to the train station to travel to Montreal when he was pursued by both Canadiens' manager Jack Laviolette and Montreal Nationale representatives as well (of the Federal Amateur Hockey League). The Nationale got there first, and Pitre signed a contract on the spot for a whopping $1,100. But when Laviolette arrived, Pitre signed again—this time for $1,700! The two teams took each other, and Pitre, to court to resolve the double-contract dilemma. In the end, the judge decided it was up to Pitre to choose a team. Pitre went with the Canadiens, a new team that had yet to play a game. On the opening night of the season, January 5, 1910, Pitre was not only in the lineup—he scored the winning goal in overtime of a 7-6 game. The contest, played at the Jubilee Rink (natural ice) in Montreal was against the Cobalt Silver Kings.

Léo Dandurand
Builder

Dandurand bought the Canadiens with Joe Cattarinich and Louis Letourneau and soon transformed the team into the high-scoring team that came to be called the Flying Frenchmen.

Leo Viatuer Joseph Dandurand came to Montreal in 1905 when his parents sent him to St. Mary's College. He became an ardent and successful athlete, notably in hockey, baseball, and lacrosse, and he maintained an interest in the business of sports long after his abilities had been exhausted on the field of play.

In 1909, Dandurand started an involvement in the real estate market and soon branched out to the wholesale tobacco industry. In 1913, along with friend and partner Joe Cattarinich, he became promoter for the Kempton Park racetrack in Laprairie.

On December 4, 1914, Dandurand represented a local Montreal hockey team at a meeting in Ottawa during which the Canadian Amateur Hockey Association was founded. Dandurand had established and played for the St. Jacques Hockey Club and had earned a reputation as a sound businessman, and it was for this reason he had been extended an invitation. The CAHA became the governing body for all amateur hockey in the country, and Dandurand soon left his mark. He initiated a rule which forbade more than two penalties to occur simultaneously, thereby eradicating the common situation of the day that often saw multiple penalties leave teams playing two men a side.

Dandurand (fourth from left, in hat) was not just an owner; he was a passionate fan of the game who loved the Canadiens like anyone else in the city.

His greatest coup came in late 1921 when he, Catttarinich, and Louis Letourneau purchased the Montreal Canadiens. Whereas Cattarinich was known as the "quiet one," Dandurand was a loud and boisterous promoter ready to put his name, face, and voice into any situation to help promote his interests. To that end, he became coach and general manager of the Canadiens, and during his five-year tenure the team went from bland misfortune to roaring success.

Dandurand signed only players who could skate and score, players who could lift fans out of their seats with a great rush and lead the team to victory. The Canadiens came to be known as the Flying Frenchmen, and under Dandurand's guidance the team won the Stanley Cup in 1924 by sweeping Vancouver and Calgary in the playoffs.

In addition to owning the Habs, Dandurand was a successful businessman and sports lover who later brought the Alouettes football team to Montreal.

He and Cattarinich at one time owned some 17 racetracks across North America, and Dandurand further entrenched his name in Montreal's sporting history by establishing the Montreal Alouettes football team in 1946. Under his aegis, the team flourished in Big Four football and won the Grey Cup in 1949.

LÉO DANDURAND

b. Bourbonnais, Illinois, July 9, 1889
d. Montreal, Quebec, June 26, 1964

NOT AN EASY PURCHASE

The sale of the Montreal Canadiens wasn't as straightforward as history shows. After owner George Kennedy passed away in late 1921, his widow put the team up for sale and three interested parties came forward. One group from Ottawa was fronted by NHL president Frank Calder; another was the owners of the Mount Royal Arena, led by Tom Duggan; the third was the trio of Dandurand, Joe Cattarinich, and Louis Letourneau. On the day Mrs. Kennedy met the groups, Dandurand and friends were at a racetrack in Cleveland and had to be represented by Cecil Hart. Duggan marched into the office, dropped ten one-thousand dollar bills on the table, and announced this was his offer. Hart left the room, called Cleveland, and returned with an offer of $11,000. Duggan refused to get into an auction, stomped out of the room, and left the ownership of the club to Dandurand, Cattarinich, and Letourneau.

Tommy Gorman
Builder

Although Tommy Gorman was a general manager for the Montreal Canadiens only six years, what he accomplished during that time remains a remarkable contribution to the team's history.

For starters, by 1940 the Canadiens had not won the Stanley Cup in nine years. Indeed, they hadn't even been to the finals in that time. The war was raging in Europe and players from all teams had left the NHL to contribute overseas, but Gorman quickly assembled a team that won the Cup in just his fourth season. That roster of 1943-44 included Toe Blake, Maurice Richard, Elmer Lach, and Bill Durnan, and was coached by Dick Irvin. All but Blake came to Montreal through Gorman's ingenuity. Two years later, Gorman's team won the Cup again.

Gorman was not just a genius with players; he knew how to get the most out of the team itself. He was a tireless promoter of the Canadiens, calling them "the greatest team in the world," with a defiance that belied their mediocre position when he first assumed duties. By the time he left, in 1946, his declaration could not be refuted. Additionally, he was known for his humour and his ability to get along with the French media, even though his French was no more sophisticated than "oui" and "non."

Gorman struck the perfect balance between astute businessman and hockey genius, bringing great players to the Habs but also drawing full houses to the Forum.

Gorman's tour of duty in the NHL started with Ottawa, moved to the New York Americans and Chicago, and finished in Montreal, first with the Maroons and finally the great Habs.

He not only took a non-playoff team and turned it into a champion, he took a team that played before half-empty houses and turned it into a "sold right out" venture night in, night out.

Gorman's hiring was a sage move by the Canadiens. He started in the working world at age nine, as a page boy in the House of Commons, in 1895. He later became a newspaperman in Ottawa, rising to editor of the *Citizen*. In 1917, he scraped enough money together to become part owner of the Ottawa Senators and was a founder of the National Hockey League. Gorman's success with the team was extraordinary—the Senators won three Stanley Cups in four years (1920, 1921, 1923), but

he sold his stake in the team in 1925 to start the New York Americans. Gorman later managed Chicago to a Stanley Cup (1934), and a year later managed the Montreal Maroons to their second and final NHL Cup victory as well.

Success followed Gorman throughout his life, both in hockey and horseracing, his other lifelong passion. He later won an Allan Cup in Ottawa, but his ability to promote the game, the teams, and the players, made him a special person for the Canadiens and the NHL.

Gorman was responsible for six Stanley Cup wins during his career, the final two with the Canadiens, in 1944 and 1946.

TOMMY GORMAN

b. Ottawa, Ontario, June 9, 1886
d. Ottawa, Ontario, May 15, 1961

OLYMPIC GOLD

Although Gorman won six Stanley Cups during his career, one of his proudest accomplishments came long before his life in hockey began. In 1908, he was a member of Canada's lacrosse team that played in the Olympics in London, England. Only two teams competed (Great Britain was the other), and Canada won the one-game, gold-medal showdown by a 14-10 score. Gorman received his medal from the Prince of Wales, who later became King George V. The next year, Gorman was recruited by the Regina Capitals as they tried to wrest the Minto Cup from the great New Westminster Salmon Bellies. Alas, Gorman et al. were unable to do so, and he went on to pursue a career in journalism.

Bill Durnan
Goalie 1943-44 to 1949-50

Durnan strays far from his crease to play the puck before a Leafs' forward can get to it, a move not uncommon during the Original Six days.

CANADIENS NUMBERS BILL DURNAN

b. Toronto, Ontario, January 22, 1916   **d.** Toronto, Ontario, October 31, 1972
6'   190 lbs.   goalie   catches right

| | REGULAR SEASON | | | | | PLAYOFFS | | | | | |
	GP	W-L-T	Mins	GA	SO	GAA	GP	W-L	Mins	GA	SO	GAA
1943-44	50	38-5-7	3,000	109	2	2.18	9	8-1	549	14	1	1.53
1944-45	50	38-8-4	3,000	121	1	2.42	6	2-4	373	15	0	2.41
1945-46	40	24-11-5	2,400	104	4	2.60	9	8-1	581	20	0	2.07
1946-47	60	34-16-10	3,600	138	4	2.30	11	6-5	720	23	1	1.92
1947-48	59	20-28-10	3,505	162	5	2.77	—	—	—	—	—	—
1948-49	60	28-23-9	3,600	126	10	2.10	7	3-4	468	17	0	2.18
1949-50	64	26-21-17	3,840	141	8	2.20	3	0-3	180	10	0	3.33
TOTALS	383	208-112-62	22,945	901	34	2.36	45	27-18	2,871	99	2	2.07

Durnan enjoys a goalmouth chat with Maurice Richard after practice.

Durnan chats with Toe Blake in the dressing room.

It wasn't a long career that made goaltender Bill Durnan remarkable; rather it was virtually constant success for several years that earned him his Hockey Hall of Fame honours. Indeed, Durnan played only 383 regular-season games in the NHL—all with the Montreal Canadiens—over just seven full seasons (1943-50). But during that time he won the Vézina Trophy six times and led the team to two Stanley Cups—the first in 1944 to cap a tremendous rookie season, the second two years later.

Durnan didn't play his first NHL game until he was 27 years old, but it was a knee injury in his teens that prevented him from starting much earlier with his hometown Maple Leafs. Durnan suffered the injury at age 16 and was slow to recover. The Leafs, figuring he was damaged goods, gave up on him and Durnan ended up playing for the Kirkland Lake Blue Devils for four seasons (1936-40). He had moved north primarily to play softball (he was an outstanding pitcher), his other great love, but in the

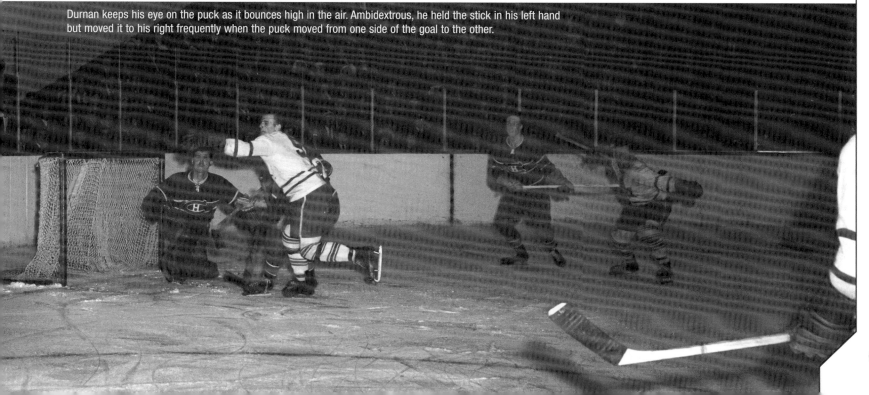

Durnan keeps his eye on the puck as it bounces high in the air. Ambidextrous, he held the stick in his left hand but moved it to his right frequently when the puck moved from one side of the goal to the other.

Bill Durnan
Goalie 1943-44 to 1949-50

Durnan plays the puck to the side of his goal. The two big bulbs in the bottom of the photo are the goal lights which attached to the top of the goal judge's cage behind the net.

winter he joined the Blue Devils and enjoyed renewed success in goal. The Blue Devils were assembling an excellent team in the Northern Ontario Hockey Association, and in Durnan's last year the team won the Allan Cup by defeating the Calgary Stampeders.

This championship earned him a shot with the Montreal Royals in the superior Quebec Senior Hockey League, and from there the Canadiens inherited his talents. Len

Peto signed him to the Royals, but Peto was also part of the Canadiens' front office and made sure Durnan was given a chance with the Habs in due course. In retrospect, Durnan's rookie season was extraordinary, but the day by day happenings were less glamorous. Durnan was replacing the popular French-Canadian Paul Bibeault, and whenever he allowed a goal on home ice fans would shout Bibeault's name derisively in Durnan's direction. The taunts never abated, even after several years with the team, and it was in part from the stress and expectations that Durnan's career was so short.

When Durnan joined the Canadiens in the fall of 1943, he joined a team that featured Maurice Richard, Toe Blake, and Elmer Lach. Better known as the Punch Line, this was one of the highest scoring lines in the game. Yet it was Durnan's goaltending that proved the difference in the playoffs. The Habs beat the Leafs in five games in the semi-finals and then swept the Black Hawks in four straight to win the Stanley Cup. Along the way, Durnan allowed just 14 goals in nine games and stopped Virgil Johnson on a penalty shot in the final game, the first penalty shot in the Cup finals in Canadiens' history.

Durnan led the NHL in victories four times, and four times during his career he played the entire schedule of games for the Canadiens.

He credited much of his success to his ambidextrous play. Durnan used two gloves that looked like big oven mitts, and he switched his stick from hand to hand depending on which side of his goal the puck was. As a result, he always had a better angle to the shooter and was always in perfect position. During one stretch of play, he recorded a shutout sequence of 309:21 in March 1949, including four straight shutouts, a record which stood more than half a century. Durnan is also remembered as the last goalie to captain a team, an honour he shared with Toe Blake during the 1947-48 season.

Adversaries on ice but bonded by mutual respect off, Durnan and Toronto's Turk Broda shake hands after a memorable playoff series in 1948.

TWO HANDS ARE BETTER THAN ONE

Durnan credited his ambidextrous skills to an early coach. Steve Faulkner coached Durnan in a church league in Toronto and convinced the young goalie to move his stick as he moved his body. Faulkner taught Durnan how to switch the stick from one hand to the other. It wasn't easy at first because the boy was so young and the stick seemed so heavy. But Faulkner kept after Durnan and gradually the stick became lighter and he could switch it more or less effortlessly.

Despite the difficulty in learning the skill, Durnan saw the advantages quickly. A goalie can move his hand a lot faster than he can move his body. As a result, when a goalie can use both hands, he always has an open hand guarding the wide part of the net.

Albert "Babe" Siebert

Forward/Defence 1936-37 to 1938-39

Few players in Montreal Canadiens history arrived with the team in mid-career and had the instant impact that Babe Siebert had when he joined the Habs to start the 1936-37 season. The 32-year-old had been in the league eleven years and won two Stanley Cups, the first as a rookie with the crosstown Maroons in 1925-26, the second seven years later with the New York Rangers.

Siebert arrived a little older and slower than in his prime, but in respect of the passage of time he moved from the wing to defence and in so doing extended his career by several seasons. With the Maroons, he played on the famous "S Line" with Hooley Smith and Nels Stewart, but in Boston he teamed with Eddie Shore on the blueline and became an all-star defenceman.

At both forward and defence, Siebert was known for his pure physical strength, whether preventing a goal or barreling down ice with the puck.

In 1936, Cecil Hart returned as coach of the sagging Canadiens. He had only two deals in mind—bring back Howie Morenz and acquire Babe Siebert. He accomplished both, and the results were instantaneous. Siebert was awarded the Hart Trophy in his first year with the Canadiens, and the team also had an impressive run in the playoffs. Siebert played two more excellent years and then retired to take over as coach for the 1939-40 season, but before he had a chance to step behind the bench, tragedy struck.

(below) Program from the Memorial Game after the death of Siebert; (right) Siebert's contract with the Canadiens for the 1928-29 season.

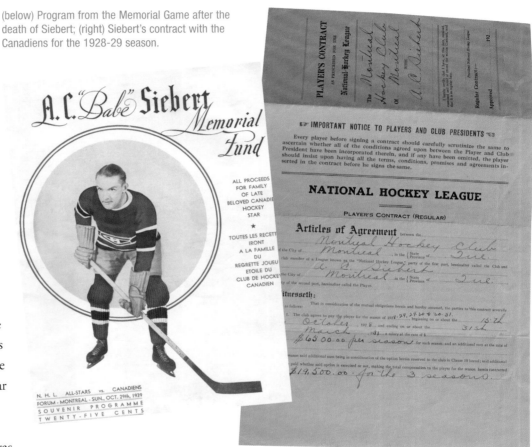

CANADIENS NUMBERS
ALBERT "Babe" SIEBERT

b. Plattsville, Ontario, January 14, 1904   **d.** St. Joseph, Ontario, August 25, 1939
5'10"   182 lbs.   forward/defence   shoots left

| | REGULAR SEASON | | | | | PLAYOFFS | | | | |
	GP	G	A	Pts	Pim	GP	G	A	Pts	Pim
1936-37	44	8	20	28	38	5	1	2	3	2
1937-38	37	8	11	19	56	3	1	1	2	0
1938-39	44	9	7	16	36	3	0	0	0	0
TOTALS	125	25	38	63	130	11	2	3	5	2

Vacationing with family before the start of a new season, Siebert drowned while swimming after an inflated inner tube his daughters, Judie and Joan, had lost control of while playing in the water. His death was doubly difficult for his wife. For years she had been an invalid, unable to walk on her own, but she never missed a home game. Babe was famous for carrying her to her rinkside seat before each game, and after he showered and dressed after playing 60 minutes of intense hockey, he returned, picked her up in his arms, and carried

her to their car to go home together.

Nurses, medical expenses, and hospital bills claimed much of Siebert's income, but he never complained and continued to play with a determination that inspired his wife and was, in turn, an inspiration to him. His teammates were saddened by his death, both on account of the player he was but more important because of the person he was.

Not only was he a great hockey player, Siebert was a greater man, a devoted husband to his incapacitated wife, and a loving father to his children for whom he gave his life.

THERE PASSED A MAN

Babe Siebert was so well respected by players around the league, both on and off the ice, that they banded together to play a charity all-star game in support of his widow. The game took place at the Forum in Montreal on October 29, 1939, and raised $15,000 for Mrs. Berne Siebert and her children. It featured the Canadiens against a team of all-stars, almost all of whom went on to the Hockey Hall of Fame: Eddie Shore, Dit Clapper, Frank Brimsek, and Bobby Bauer (all of Boston); Syl Apps and Gord Drillon (Toronto); Syd Howe and Ebbie Goodfellow (Detroit); Neil Colville and Art Coulter (Rangers) among the stars. They won the game 5-2 before a crowd of 6,000. Apps was the big star, scoring once and adding three assists. Montreal's goals were scored by René Trudel and newly-acquired Earl Robinson. Memorializing Siebert, *Montreal Star* writer Elmer Ferguson noted Siebert's resolve and pride, on ice and off, finishing by saying simply, "There passed a man."

Hector "Toe" Blake

Left Wing 1934-35 to 1947-48

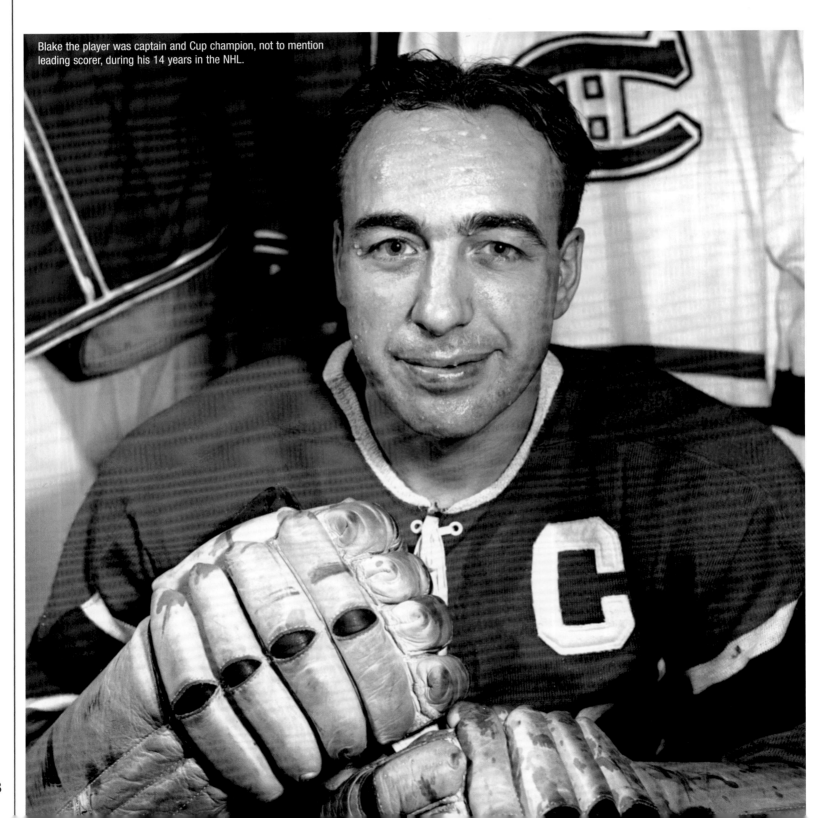

Blake the player was captain and Cup champion, not to mention leading scorer, during his 14 years in the NHL.

There is, quite simply, no one who has had the combined playing and coaching career of Toe Blake. He was inducted into the Hockey Hall of Fame as a player, but he could have been re-inducted as a builder several years later. Winning eight Stanley Cups as a coach is pretty good proof for the latter category.

As a boy, he had a sister who pronounced his name "Hectoe" and over time this got shortened to "Toe." He played his first serious hockey in Sudbury in 1932 when the Wolves won the Memorial Cup, although he played only a few games, spending the majority of the year with Falconbridge. It was the beginning of a career full of championships. Blake moved down to Hamilton to play senior hockey with the Tigers, a great relief to him because work— even with skates and stick—was hard to come by during the Depression.

It was there that the Montreal Maroons took notice of him. Blake played a handful of games with the team in the 1934-35 season, during which time the Maroons won their second and final Stanley Cup. But although he was a fine prospect the Maroons were in dire need of a goalie. They traded Blake, Ken Gravel, and Bill Miller to the crosstown Canadiens for Lorne Chabot, and the rest, as they say, is history. The balance of Blake's professional life passed in Montreal, and his successes were unmatched.

Blake was a fiery left winger with a bad temper when he first joined the team, but coach Cecil Hart managed to get him to contain and channel that emotion to more resourceful ends. Not surprisingly, the more Blake stayed out of the penalty box, the more effective a player he became. He led the league in points in 1938-39 and won the Hart Trophy as well with 24 goals and 47 total points (Sweeney Schriner of the New York Americans was second with 44 points). Soon, journalists were calling Blake the "Old Lamplighter" in awe of his scoring exploits. A year later, in 1940, Blake took over from Walt Buswell as captain, a role he maintained until his last game in the league.

In the early 1940s, Blake found a second life playing on a line

Hector "Toe" Blake

Left Wing 1934-35 to 1947-48

Blake (right) talks to his linemate and right winger, Maurice Richard, after a game, the intensity still set in the Rocket's stare.

with newcomers Maurice Richard and Elmer Lach. Coach Dick Irvin used the Punch Line to the fullest, and the trio was the highest-scoring combination in the NHL. In one five-year stretch (1942-47), Blake averaged 26 goals and 57 points and the team won two Stanley Cups, in 1944 and 1946. In both those victories, it was Blake who scored the Cup-winning goal. Blake was also named to the league's end-of-season All-Star team three times. In 1944-45, Lach, Richard, and Blake finished 1-2-3 in scoring, a rare feat even during the Original Six era. Teammates and foes alike were astounded that Blake won the Lady Byng Trophy in 1945-46, the mirror opposite to his play as a rookie.

By the time the 1947-48 season began, Blake knew the end of his playing days was near. Indeed, he entered the season with one thing in mind—Bill Cowley's NHL all-time points record. Cowley, the great Boston Bruins forward, had retired in the spring of 1947 with 548 career points to his credit. Blake was just 45 points behind Cowley to start the year, and if all went well there was every reason to expect he'd better this mark well before the end of the season.

True to form, Blake was having another fine year, but on the night of January 11, 1948, in a game against the New York Rangers, his career came to an end. He suffered a badly broken ankle and missed the rest of the season, and when he was given the opportunity to coach Buffalo in the AHL the next year he abandoned his dream of becoming the leading scorer in favour of establishing himself in a second career as a "bench boss."

In that first season as coach, Blake filled a dual role by remaining a player as well for part of the year. The next season he was head coach in Valleyfield, a team in the Quebec Senior Hockey League which featured Jean Béliveau and the Quebec Aces. Blake learned the ropes in the QSHL for nearly four years, and in 1955 the ultimate position opened for him.

After 15 years with the Canadiens, coach Dick Irvin left the team in the summer of 1955 to lead the Chicago Black Hawks. In Montreal, the opening created an enormous challenge. General manager Frank Selke offered the job to Blake because he felt Blake, more than anyone, could control Maurice Richard. The two had been longtime teammates, and—Selke reasoned—if Blake couldn't harness the team's star player, nobody could.

CANADIENS NUMBERS
HECTOR "Toe" BLAKE

b. Victoria Mines, Ontario, August 21, 1912   **d.** Montreal, Quebec, May 17, 1995
5'10"   165 lbs.   left wing   shoots left

	REGULAR SEASON					PLAYOFFS				
	GP	G	A	Pts	Pim	GP	G	A	Pts	Pim
1934-35	8	0	0	0	0	1	0	0	0	0
1935-36	11	1	2	3	28	—	—	—	—	—
1936-37	43	10	12	22	12	5	1	0	1	0
1937-38	43	17	16	33	33	3	3	1	4	2
1938-39	48	24	23	47	10	3	1	1	2	2
1939-40	48	17	19	36	48	—	—	—	—	—
1940-41	48	12	20	32	49	3	0	3	3	5
1941-42	48	17	28	45	19	3	0	3	3	2
1942-43	48	23	36	59	26	5	4	3	7	0
1943-44 🏆	41	26	33	59	10	9	7	11	18	2
1944-45	49	29	38	67	25	6	0	2	2	5
1945-46 🏆	50	29	21	50	2	9	7	6	13	5
1946-47	60	21	29	50	6	11	2	7	9	0
1947-48	32	9	15	24	4	—	—	—	—	—
TOTALS	577	235	292	527	272	57	25	37	62	23

Hector "Toe" Blake

Left Wing 1934-35 to 1947-48

Coach Blake, wearing his trademark fedora, stands behind the bench watching play.

THE GOOD HUSBAND

Of course, Toe Blake's competitive spirit cannot be questioned, but his private life was an even greater challenge. His wife, Betty, was equally vigorous in life. They married in 1934 after being introduced in Hamilton by Tigers teammate Max Bennett, who was their best man at the wedding. Betty was with Toe through every part of his career, but during the 1967-68 season she became very sick. After the Cup triumph on May 11, 1968, while players celebrated, fans poured into the streets, and media went crazy, Blake left the Forum quickly to be with his wife in hospital. This was a major factor in his decision to retire that year, and just three years later Betty passed away.

Blake (centre) wore his favourite fedora everywhere he went.

The hiring was genius, and Blake's efforts were equally successful. He did, indeed, know just how to handle the temperamental Richard, but he also knew how to coach the rest of the highly-skilled team as well. Blake led the Canadiens to a Stanley Cup in his first year behind the bench, but he didn't stop there. The team won five Cups in a row (1955-60) and became the most successful dynasty in hockey history.

Blake remained behind the bench for 13 years, winning the Stanley Cup eight times during that period. His teams had an extraordinary regular-season record of 500-255-159 in 914 games, and in the playoffs Blake's record was 82-37 in 119 career games. His remarkable ability to coach a team loaded with talent set him apart, while maintaining the team's tried-and-true method of breaking players in slowly.

Blake was famous for his calm demeanor behind the bench, standing tall, sporting his trademark fedora as he organized the team like a conductor would an orchestra. He was, however, not the most popular coach, known as a taskmaster and a man who relentlessly pushed even the greatest players to be better. They often didn't like him during the season, but they all enjoyed the Stanley Cup parties hosted almost annually at Blake's Tavern, a downtown Montreal pub run by the coach.

By the time he retired in 1968, Blake had won three Stanley Cups as a player and eight as a coach. He retired as a player second on the all-time scoring list, and when he left the bench his was a record for most wins and championships as a coach. In truth, there is no legend to whom Toe Blake can be properly compared.

After winning three Stanley Cups as a player, Blake guided the Canadiens to eight more Cups as the team's head coach.

Coach Toe Blake was a master motivator, a man who knew how to get the most from his players, a coach who understood the importance of tactics to victory.

Émile "Butch" Bouchard

Defence 1941-42 to 1955-56

Bouchard's casual smile during this photo shoot presents sharp contrast to his intense gaze during games.

It is impossible to compare the life and times of Butch Bouchard to any player today. Bouchard started skating only at age 16, an age today when most aspiring pros already have agents and sponsors. Yet, just four years after putting on a pair of skates for the first time, Bouchard was playing for the Montreal Canadiens. Determination and circumstance were what got him there.

Bouchard grew up in virtual poverty, and he had to rent skates each time he wanted to play hockey. He made up for a lack of money and a late start by pursuing the game with unmatched tenacity. A large teenager, he

lifted weights and kept himself in impeccable shape year 'round. To offset his dire financial situation, he established an apiary farm and sold honey by the thousands of pounds, allowing him to support himself and his family.

Indeed, it was his job as an apiarist that prevented him from qualifying to fight during the war (he was deemed an irreplaceable farmer). Instead, he played hockey for Verdun in the evenings, and soon the Habs took notice of his play. Coach Dick Irvin signed Bouchard to a

CANADIENS NUMBERS
ÉMILE "Butch" BOUCHARD

b. Montreal, Quebec, September 11, 1920
6'2"   205 lbs   defence   shoots right

| | REGULAR SEASON | | | | | PLAYOFFS | | | | |
	GP	G	A	Pts	Pim	GP	G	A	Pts	Pim
1941-42	44	0	6	6	38	3	1	1	2	0
1942-43	45	2	16	18	47	5	0	1	1	4
1943-44 🏆	39	5	14	19	52	9	1	3	4	4
1944-45	50	11	23	34	34	6	3	4	7	4
1945-46 🏆	45	7	10	17	52	9	2	1	3	17
1946-47	60	5	7	12	60	11	0	3	3	21
1947-48	60	4	6	10	78	—	—	—	—	—
1948-49	27	3	3	6	42	7	0	0	0	6
1949-50	69	1	7	8	88	5	0	2	2	2
1950-51	52	3	10	13	80	11	1	1	2	2
1951-52	60	3	9	12	45	11	0	2	2	14
1952-53 🏆	58	2	8	10	55	12	1	1	2	6
1953-54	70	1	10	11	89	11	2	1	3	4
1954-55	70	2	15	17	81	12	0	1	1	37
1955-56 🏆	36	0	0	0	22	1	0	0	0	0
TOTALS	785	49	144	193	863	113	11	21	32	121

Captain Bouchard accepts the Cup after the Habs beat Boston 4-1 in a best-of-seven series in 1953.

Émile "Butch" Bouchard

Defence 1941-42 to 1955-56

contract and sent him to Providence midway through the 1940-41 season, but it was at the following training camp that Bouchard made his greatest impression.

Coach Dick Irvin was looking for new blood for a team that had nearly failed to survive the 1930s, and Bouchard proved to be just the man. He showed up to his first training camp in peak condition and promptly set to dishing out one rock solid bodycheck after another, infuriating his teammates who typically used training camp to work their way slowly into shape. Bouchard made the team, remaining on the Canadiens blueline for the next 15 years and 785 regular-season games.

Although his weakness was his skating, Bouchard was also smart enough to acknowledge as much and work out a solution. For him, that meant playing defensive hockey, and paired with the rushing Doug Harvey, that

Bouchard (right) chats with teammate Ken Reardon.

wasn't too difficult to accomplish. Bouchard also used his immense size and strength to his advantage, and he was renowned not for starting fights but breaking them up.

Under coach Irvin, the Canadiens quickly developed into a team that made the Canadiens legendary. By the mid-to-late 1940s, "firewagon hockey" was in full swing in Montreal. Irvin had a great goalie in Bill Durnan, a great tandem on the blueline in Bouchard and Harvey, and a

group of mostly young forwards who started to tear up the league. Maurice Richard, Elmer Lach, and Toe Blake—the Punch Line—comprised the top-scoring line in the NHL.

Bouchard had his finest years during this time. He was named to the First All-Star team in three straight years (1944-45 to 1946-47) and also played in six All-Star Games. He was part of four Stanley Cup-winning teams

Bouchard was among the hardest hitters in the game.

ONE LAST YEAR

By the time the 1955-56 training camp opened, Butch Bouchard was ready to retire. But incoming coach Toe Blake, a longtime teammate of Bouchard's, convinced the ageing defenceman to hang in there for one more year through the transition of coach Dick Irvin to Blake. Despite a banged-up body, notably a bad knee, Bouchard agreed. Blake played him more than either imagined, but by the playoffs the tank was empty. Bouchard didn't play a minute of the team's 4-1 series win in the semi-finals, and he didn't dress for the first four games of the Stanley Cup finals against Detroit. But with the Canadiens coming home and leading the series 3-1, coach Blake dressed Bouchard for game five. The defenceman sat on the bench for the first 59 minutes, but with the Habs winning 3-1 Blake tapped his warrior blueliner on the shoulder and told him to take a shift. The next time the captain returned to the bench, he was holding the Stanley Cup. This was Butch Bouchard's final moment as an NHL player.

Émile "Butch" Bouchard

Defence 1941-42 to 1955-56

in Montreal. In his 15 seasons, Bouchard played in the Cup finals nine times. His style of play, however, took its toll on his body. He missed most of the 1948-49 season with a leg injury, and he seemed capable of playing with pain that would hospitalize most anyone else.

When Toe Blake retired in 1948, the players elected Bouchard captain, and he remained in that capacity until his own retirement eight seasons later. He took the job of captaining the team with the same seriousness he had devoted to everything else related to his career. He mentored the younger players, inspired the older ones, and was a father or brother off ice to his teammates as situations dictated. Years later, Jean Béliveau credited Bouchard with showing him

what it meant to be Montreal's captain, everything from how to act on the players' bench during the game to what clothes to wear on off days.

In all, Bouchard won the Stanley Cup four times. The first came in 1943-44, his third season; the second in 1945-46; and, the last two as captain, 1952-53 and 1955-56.

Ever the entrepreneur, Bouchard had something to go to once he was done with playing the game. He had long ago sold his apiary business and soon after opened Chez Émile Bouchard, a fine dining restaurant in downtown Montreal that was a hot spot for years. It was this combination of industry and imagination that got him to where he was, so it was only appropriate that these qualities carried him through his post-playing days as well.

Bouchard (far right) won the Cup four times with Montreal, twice in the early stages of his career, twice toward the end while he was captain.

(l to r) Ken Reardon, Bill Durnan, and Butch Bouchard won a Stanley Cup together as teammates in 1945-46.

Elmer Lach

Centre *1940-41 to 1953-54*

Lach played his entire career with the Habs and might well have been called the best player in the league if not for legendary teammate Maurice Richard.

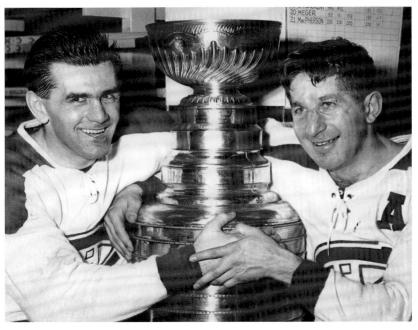

Lach (right) and Maurice Richard hold that which they fought for a year to win—the Stanley Cup.

The Punch Line caught standing still. Right winger Maurice Richard (left), Lach (middle), and veteran Toe Blake formed the most dynamic threesome of the mid-1940s, an offensive threat in every game and every shift.

It's difficult to know which is the more impressive aspect of Elmer Lach's career. There is his extraordinary list of injuries which he endured during his 14 seasons with the Canadiens, his only NHL team. Or, there is his passing and playmaking. Perhaps it is the fact that when he retired in 1954, he was the all-time points leader in the annals of the NHL. Or perhaps it is the compliment paid to him by coach Dick Irvin who called him a "four-way player."

Irvin argued that while some players are great on offense and others great on defence, Lach is great in both directions as well as from side to side. In other words, Lach was a complete player, a Selke Trophy winner before the trophy ever existed. But, Lach also would have been the first multiple winner of the Masterton Trophy, such were the recoveries he made from various injuries.

Lach's career started slowly. In 1940-41 he had only seven goals, and the year after his season ended the night of the first game. In the opening contest he broke his elbow so badly doctors feared he'd not only never play again but that he'd never have full use of his elbow. They were half right, but that's because although they understood x-rays they didn't understand the spirit of Lach. He was able to return to only 60 per cent of his range of motion in that elbow, but he went on to score 18 goals the next year playing on a line with Maurice Richard and Toe Blake.

Called the Punch Line, this threesome dominated the NHL game for several years. Richard was the scorer, of course, and Blake was a scorer and playmaker both. Lach could put the puck in the net, but his forte was the perfect pass. For him, however, passing wasn't just a matter of looking for an open man and firing the puck that way. Lach was a brilliant skater and a fearless one as well, thus accounting for his ability to get clear of an opponent and also to be hammered by same periodically. One way or another, Lach was one determined player, and by the time he retired he had assisted on 159 of Richard's 384 goals, a remarkable total, really. Further, Lach and Richard had almost identical points-per-game averages over their careers.

There was nothing Lach couldn't do. He was a master on the faceoff and one of the first true practitioners of the saucer pass. He could move the puck from side to side but also check from side to side (as per Irvin's wisdom). He could score when given the chance, make the pass

CANADIENS NUMBERS
ELMER LACH

b. Nokomis, Saskatchewan, January 22, 1918
5'10"   165 lbs.   centre   shoots left

| | REGULAR SEASON | | | | | PLAYOFFS | | | | |
	GP	G	A	Pts	Pim	GP	G	A	Pts	Pim
1940-41	43	7	14	21	16	3	1	0	1	0
1941-42	1	0	1	1	0	—	—	—	—	—
1942-43	45	18	40	58	14	5	2	4	6	6
1943-44 ♟	48	24	48	72	23	9	2	11	13	4
1944-45	50	26	54	80	37	6	4	4	8	2
1945-46 ♟	50	13	34	47	34	9	5	12	17	4
1946-47	31	14	16	30	22	—	—	—	—	—
1947-48	60	30	31	61	72	—	—	—	—	—
1948-49	36	11	18	29	59	1	0	0	0	4
1949-50	64	15	33	48	33	5	1	2	3	4
1950-51	65	21	24	45	48	11	2	2	4	2
1951-52	70	15	50	65	36	11	1	2	3	4
1952-53 ♟	53	16	25	41	56	12	1	6	7	6
1953-54	48	5	20	25	28	4	0	2	2	0
TOTALS	664	215	408	623	478	76	19	45	64	36

Elmer Lach
Centre 1940-41 to 1953-54

when a teammate was open, and the more he played the more he learned. Although he was never the captain of the Canadiens, he was always looked to as one of the team's leaders.

Lach's finest years came during the war. In 1943-44, he finished fifth in scoring, and the team won the Cup by sweeping Chicago in four straight games. The next year Lach finished in top spot in the scoring race. Ironically, he had 26 goals and 54 assists. The number two man was

Richard who had 50 goals and 23 assists, just the reverse ratio of goals to assists. This was the historic year Richard scored 50 goals in 50 games, and while he got much deserved credit for reaching the historic plateau, there is little doubt he couldn't have done it without Lach. Critics agreed, for while Richard's 50-in-50 made the headlines, it was Lach who was chosen Hart Trophy winner at season's end.

The next year, Lach led the league in assists with 34 and the Habs won their second championship in three years, this time defeating Boston in five games. He won his second scoring title in 1947-48 (in the days

Willing to do whatever it took to win, Lach was always ready to sacrifice his body to make a play.

before the Art Ross Trophy was handed out), this time by the slimmest of margins. His 61 total points was one better than Buddy O'Connor of the Rangers. In 1951-52, Lach again led the NHL with 50 assists, and in 1953 he won his third and final Stanley Cup with the team. He retired the next year with 623 points in 664 games (Richard had only a few more points than Lach after the same number of NHL games).

The injury list would make the average person squeamish just by reading it let alone having to endure it. In addition to the smashed elbow, Lach broke his jaw twice (excruciatingly, in the same place), fractured

his skull, broke his cheekbone and thumb and several fingers at various times, suffered torn ligaments in his knee, a serious gash on his leg when defenceman Bob Goldham accidentally stepped on it, and broke his nose badly from an errant high stick in a goalmouth scrum. And this doesn't count the more routine severed arteries, facial cuts, and general trips to the medic for stitchwork. By the time Lach retired at age 36, he was an old 36 with nothing left to give. But that which he had given to the Canadiens and the NHL was enough to earn him distinction among teammates and peers, friends and adversaries. And that is a reward any player would gladly accept on his way out of the NHL.

Lach is hoisted by Maurice Richard (left) and Butch Bouchard after scoring the Stanley Cup-winning goal in overtime against the Bruins in 1952-53.

ALL-TIME SCORER

Playing on a line with Maurice Richard and Toe Blake was great so long as you weren't interested in fame and glory. For although Elmer Lach was as important as his two linemates, he was never going to be talked about in the same breath as Richard, whose personality and scoring records were the stuff of legend, or Blake, whose record of success was almost without parallel. Yet, despite all his injuries, Lach retired at the end of the 1953-54 season as the player with the most total points and assists in NHL history. He passed Bill Cowley for points on February 23, 1952, when he recorded his 549th point, and he also bettered Cowley's assist mark of 353 (finishing with 408). Of course, Richard surpassed Lach for points two years later, but this doesn't diminish the under-stated greatness of Lach himself.

Ken Reardon

Defence 1940-41 to 1949-50

Ken Reardon was far more than just tenacious; he was ferocious, a player whose survival seemed to depend on every shift and every stride he took on ice.

Even by standards of the Original Six, the war between Ken Reardon and Cal Gardner was one rooted in an indescribable competitive spirit, even hatred, that continued until both men went to the grave decades after their playing days were over.

The feud began during the 1947-48 season while Reardon, a lifelong member of the Canadiens, was high-sticked by Gardner (at the time with the Rangers) in the mouth, requiring 14 very painful stitches. Gardner and Reardon brawled a short time later after the former had been traded to Toronto, and both were fined and suspended for the ugly, stick-swinging incident. Reardon, though, vowed further revenge for the stitches, and this earned him a date with league president Clarence Campbell who demanded a $1,000 peace bond from Reardon, refundable if the player did not follow through on threats to get Gardner.

Time passed, Reardon received his money back, and then late in the 1949-50 season Reardon leveled Gardner with a shoulder check that broke the Leafs' player's jaw. When informed of the injury, Reardon

CANADIENS NUMBERS
KEN REARDON

b. Winnipeg, Manitoba, April 1, 1921   d. St. Sauveur, Quebec, March 15, 2008
5'10"   180 lbs.   defence   shoots left

	REGULAR SEASON					PLAYOFFS				
	GP	G	A	Pts	Pim	GP	G	A	Pts	Pim
1940-41	34	2	8	10	41	3	0	0	0	4
1941-42	41	3	12	15	93	3	0	0	0	4
1945-46	43	5	4	9	45	9	1	1	2	4
1946-47	52	5	17	22	84	7	1	2	3	20
1947-48	58	7	15	22	129	—	—	—	—	—
1948-49	46	3	13	16	103	7	0	0	0	18
1949-50	67	1	27	28	109	2	0	2	2	12
TOTALS	341	26	96	122	604	31	2	5	7	62

INDUCTED 1966

Reardon watches the front of his net while defending against the rival Maple Leafs.

deadpanned, "It couldn't have happened to a nicer guy." The feud continued until the day they retired, and carried on off the ice until the day they passed away.

This was how Reardon played every night. Like many defencemen of the day, he was not a good skater and was not blessed with a great shot or intricate stickhandling ability, but he was a warrior on the blueline and a fierce competitor who inspired those around him by his play.

Reardon came by his passion honestly. He was one of four children orphaned after both parents died just a year apart, and the children went to live with an uncle on the outskirts of Winnipeg. Ken found it almost impossible to work (as a CNR telegraph messenger) and play hockey, so

he had to give up the game he loved. The family moved to a small town in British Columbia the next year, and it was only when Ken was 17 that he was able to play in a league again.

That was 1937, and two years later the Rangers put him on and later took him off their reserve list. Paul Haynes of the Canadiens gave him a tryout, and in 1940 Reardon was on the blueline of the re-building Montreal Canadiens. He was teamed with Jack Portland, but his big break came the next year when coach Dick Irvin made Butch Bouchard his partner. Reardon thrived with the great defenceman, but after only one year he left the

Ken Reardon

Defence 1940-41 to 1949-50

team to join the army, a decision that cost him three years of his career.

At first, Reardon was stationed in Ottawa and was able to play hockey. He was on the Ottawa Commandos team that won the Allan Cup in 1943, one of the finest amateur teams in Canadian history. He was assigned to the 86th Bridge Company and served overseas, earning a certificate of merit from Field Marshall Montgomery for his role in building a bridge to help troops advance, all the while under fire.

After being discharged in 1945, Reardon re-joined the Canadiens as if time had stood still. Indeed, he was named to the Second All-Star team for 1945-46 and helped the team to a Stanley Cup (Montreal had won two years earlier while Reardon was in England during the war). He played for four more years and was named to the NHL's First or Second All-Star team twice each.

Of course, Reardon's hard-hitting style of play frequently got the better of him even as he got the better of his opponents. There was no gear other than first gear for him, no speed other than top speed, no letting up in the first or last minute of a game or season. His career was a list of injuries and by the time he retired in 1950, he was only 29 years old, but his body was battered and bruised far beyond his years.

Nevertheless, the career of Ken Reardon was exceptional in quality even though it was short. He played only seven full seasons, but he was one of the best defensive defencemen in the game and a fearless competitor.

THE INJURY LIST

Even though he played only seven full seasons, Ken Reardon never played a full schedule in any of those. His hellbent physical play lay more than one opponent low, but it also caused him several long stretches on the trainer's table. In one memorable collision with Toronto's Bill Barilko, Reardon suffered a broken shoulder and fractured fibula and missed six weeks of the 1948-49 season. He was cracked over the head more than once in a brawl, suffered numerous broken bones, and was stitched up countless times. He was once charged with assault for going into the stands to battle a fan who had enraged him, but charges were dropped and Reardon came out battling the next game. Same as always.

Reardon (left) with goalie Bill Durnan and defence partner Émile Bouchard consistently shut down opposing team's top offensive stars.

Reardon's career lasted only seven NHL seasons, in part because it was interrupted by war service, in part because he played with a physical force that took its toll on his body.

Tom Johnson

A weak skater as a teen, Johnson worked on defensive play, eventually becoming a Hall of Famer with the Canadiens.

Johnson watches as goalie Jacques Plante smothers the puck.

Johnson may not have had the offensive skills teammate Doug Harvey had, but he was a rock inside his own blue line, making precious few errors over the course of his career.

INDUCTED 1970

It was late January 1951, halfway through Tom Johnson's rookie season, that the Montreal Canadiens knew they had a great defenceman. The 22-year-old, who had played most of the previous three seasons in the minors, clashed with Toronto captain Ted Kennedy. They fought on the ice; they fought in the penalty box; and, they fought again on the ice. Johnson was not going to give an inch to the Leafs' great captain, and in the process he made it clear to his teammates and management he was willing to do anything and everything to win. That season, he accrued some 128 penalty minutes, a large total, indeed, for the time. Although he didn't win the Calder Trophy at year's end—that honour went to

Detroit goalie Terry Sawchuk—Johnson distinguished himself as one of the fiercest newcomers to the NHL.

Johnson had been coveted by the Leafs when he was playing in Winnipeg, but Frank Selke moved to the Canadiens as general manager and lured him away. As a teen, Johnson was big and strong, but he had one great weakness—he could barely skate. Selke put him in the minors, and by the time he made it to the team in October 1950 Johnson was ready for the big league.

CANADIENS NUMBERS
TOM JOHNSON

b. Baldur, Manitoba, February 18, 1928   **d.** Falmouth, Massachusetts, November 21, 2007
6'   180 lbs.   defence   shoots left

| | REGULAR SEASON | | | | | PLAYOFFS | | | | |
	GP	G	A	Pts	Pim	GP	G	A	Pts	Pim
1947-48	1	0	0	0	0	—	—	—	—	—
1949-50	—	—	—	—	—	1	0	0	0	0
1950-51	70	2	8	10	128	11	0	0	0	6
1951-52	67	0	7	7	76	11	1	0	1	2
1952-53	70	3	8	11	63	12	2	3	5	8
1953-54	70	7	11	18	85	11	1	2	3	30
1954-55	70	6	19	25	74	12	2	0	2	22
1955-56	64	3	10	13	75	10	0	2	2	8
1956-57	70	4	11	15	59	10	0	2	2	13
1957-58	66	3	18	21	75	2	0	0	0	0
1958-59	70	10	29	39	76	11	2	3	5	8
1959-60	64	4	25	29	59	8	0	1	1	4
1960-61	70	1	15	16	54	6	0	1	1	8
1961-62	62	1	17	18	45	6	0	1	1	0
1962-63	43	3	5	8	28	—	—	—	—	—
TOTALS	857	47	183	230	897	111	8	15	23	109

Johnson gets physical at the crease, clearing away an enemy forward in textbook fashion.

Tom Johnson

Johnson puts the check on Frank Mahovlich, ensuring his goalie, Jacques Plante, doesn't even have to make a save on the play. Johnson won the Norris Trophy in 1958-59.

Of course, today Johnson is a member of the Hockey Hall of Fame, but for most of his playing days he was under-rated. This was because he lived in the shadows of Doug Harvey, a more flamboyant player and a defence-man with great offensive ability. But Johnson was a rock on the blueline and opponents knew they stood little chance in getting around him or making him look bad on a play.

Indeed, Johnson was renowned for two things. One, he

could strip an onrushing forward of the puck without making contact, thus enabling him to pass right away and create a counter-attack of great effectiveness as the opposition was still moving toward the Montreal goal while the puck was heading up ice.

Two, Johnson had what almost amounted to a trick defensive play. He would allow players to move around him to the outside, along the boards, but then he would spin to the inside, skate directly to his own goal, and cut the player off on the second confrontation before the player could take a shot or make a good pass. On the one hand, it was a successful way

to recover from being beaten; on the other, it was an effective way of keeping play to the outside, away from his goal.

While Harvey was the team's power-play quarterback, Johnson was the leader for the team's penalty-killing unit. He was a master at getting the puck from a scrum of players in the corner, and he was also known as a pinpoint passer. Ironically, the Norris Trophy came Johnson's way only once during his career, 1958-59. A glance at his statistics reveals that although Johnson averaged about three goals a year and, at best, 20 total

points, that Norris-winning season saw him score ten times and add 29 assists. The reason was simple. Harvey missed a good portion of the year with injury, and during that time coach Dick Irvin promoted Johnson to the power play where he proved remarkably adept. His scoring increased dramatically, and people around the league took greater notice of his talents. This was the only year during an eight-year period that Harvey himself did not win the Norris Trophy.

The look of intensity is writ large on the face of Johnson as he catches a breath on the bench during a break in the action.

AN ALL-STAR FOR A REASON

Tom Johnson played in eight All-Star Games during his career. These were played during an era when the Stanley Cup champion tackled a "best of the rest" team in a game played at the start of the season. Johnson played in six of the games because that's how many Cups he won with the Habs, but he also played in two other games because he was among the league's best defencemen. While Doug Harvey received most of the praise on the team, Johnson was surrounded by many other hall of famers, notably Rocket Richard, Jean Béliveau, Bernie Geoffrion, and Dickie Moore. No wonder the media and fans didn't have much time for a guy named Johnson. Yet, year after year, there he was, on the blueline, always appreciated by, if no one else, his coach and goalie. And that's all that mattered to the boy from Baldur, Manitoba, who had trouble skating and didn't see an indoor arena until he was 18 years old!

Jean Béliveau
Centre 1950-51 to 1970-71

Although Jean Béliveau wore the "CH" on his sweater for every one of his 1,125 regular-season games, he was, more than a Canadiens forward, an ambassador for the game itself. That is, if someone wanted to know what a hockey player was, he would need only to find out about Béliveau to get the perfect answer. As a player, "Le Gros Bill" could pass and shoot and score, skate and backcheck and play physically. As a captain, he was the very epitome of leader; and, as a man his conduct was just,

(l to r) Henri Richard, Jean Béliveau, John Ferguson, and Yvan Cournoyer enjoy a pop in the dressing room after a game.

Béliveau goes in alone on Toronto goalie Johnny Bower. The two played against each other more than 100 times during their careers.

exemplary, and the very ideal of sporting. Jean Béliveau was truly the most perfect hockey player to skate through the game.

His was a love affair that began early on. When he was five, Jean received a present of a pair of skates from his father, and the passion for sliding on the ice never abated from the moment he put those first pair of skates on. Jean played and practiced every chance he got, and it was clear from a very early age that his father had simply been a proxy between the boy and divine right. He was born to be a hockey player and destined for greatness.

Jean played first in Victoriaville and later in Quebec City, his time in the latter city of historic importance. He played with the junior Citadelle from 1949-51, overlapping with his transition to the senior league and the Quebec Aces which began in his last year with the Cidadelle. Béliveau

was the toast of the town. The fans in Quebec City fell in love with him as a player and man, and the Colisée was sold out for his every game. He led the junior league in scoring in his second season, and he led the senior league in goals and points in his two final seasons before moving up to the NHL.

But while Béliveau was enjoying a spectacular career with the Aces, the Montreal Canadiens were longing to get him into their NHL lineup. Béliveau saw no reason to change. He loved Quebec City and was being paid as well as what the Canadiens offered. He didn't want to leave, plain and simple. The Canadiens owned his rights and called him up twice. In 1950-51, he appeared in two NHL games, recording a goal and an

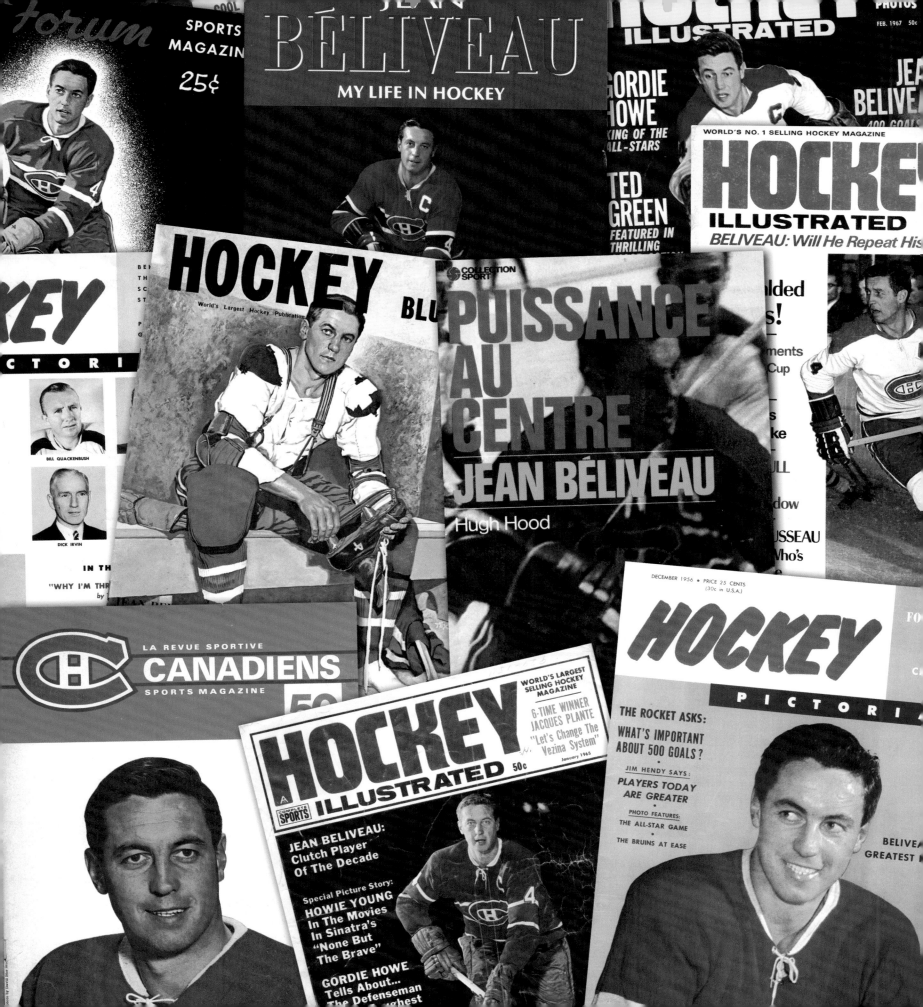

Jean Béliveau
Centre 1950-51 to 1970-71

Béliveau celebrating one of his ten Stanley Cup championships over the course of his 20-year career. The only other player in NHL history to hoist the Cup more often was teammate Henri Richard, who won the Cup eleven times. Béliveau also has his name on the Cup seven times as a member of the Habs' executive.

assist. In 1952-53—now bigger, stronger, and faster—he scored five goals in three games. He was, hands down, the best player in the world not playing in the NHL.

What did the Canadiens do? They bought the entire Quebec league and

CANADIENS NUMBERS
JEAN BÉLIVEAU ("Le Gros Bill")

b. Trois Rivières, Quebec, August 31, 1931
6'3"   205 lbs.   centre   shoots left

	REGULAR SEASON					PLAYOFFS				
	GP	G	A	Pts	Pim	GP	G	A	Pts	Pim
1950-51	2	1	1	2	0	—	—	—	—	—
1952-53	3	5	0	5	0	—	—	—	—	—
1953-54	44	13	21	34	22	10	2	8	10	4
1954-55	70	37	36	73	58	12	6	7	13	18
1955-56	70	47	41	88	143	10	12	7	19	22
1956-57	69	33	51	84	105	10	6	6	12	15
1957-58	55	27	32	59	93	10	4	8	12	10
1958-59	64	45	46	91	67	3	1	4	5	4
1959-60	60	34	40	74	57	8	5	2	7	6
1960-61	69	32	58	90	57	6	0	5	5	0
1961-62	43	18	23	41	36	6	2	1	3	4
1962-63	69	18	49	67	68	5	2	1	3	2
1963-64	68	28	50	78	42	5	2	0	2	18
1964-65	58	20	23	43	76	13	8	8	16	34
1965-66	67	29	48	77	50	10	5	5	10	6
1966-67	53	12	26	38	22	10	6	5	11	26
1967-68	59	31	37	68	28	10	7	4	11	6
1968-69	69	33	49	82	55	14	5	10	15	8
1969-70	63	19	30	49	10	—	—	—	—	—
1970-71	70	25	51	76	40	20	6	16	22	28
TOTALS	1,125	507	712	1,219	1,029	162	79	97	176	211

made it a professional league. Béliveau's contract called for him to play for the Canadiens if ever he turned pro, so he couldn't play pro for the Aces without being in breach of contract. He signed the most lucrative deal in NHL history in 1953, the day before the All-Star Game, which was the starting point for the season. Béliveau was paid $20,000 a year for five years, and, of course, he was worth every penny.

In his rookie season Béliveau missed several weeks with an injury and finished with only 13 goals in 44 games. The year after his offensive abilities came to the fore. He scored 37 times and played the full 70 games. Great a start as this was, however, he was very aware that opponents were taking advantage of his kind nature. He was being pushed and bumped in a way players would never dare touch Gordie Howe or Ted Kennedy, so in his third year Béliveau fought back.

In that season, 1955-56, he accrued 143 penalty minutes, but he also led the league with 47 goals and 88 points and took the team to his first Stanley Cup. He also led the league in playoff goals (12) and points (19). Although he was a consistent and high scorer most of his career, this proved to be the only time he won the Art Ross Trophy. The next year he played just as tough and finished with 84 points en route to his second Cup, and thereafter he was able to ease up on his physical play. The best way to ensure he was left alone was to fight and fight well, and he did that for long enough for opponents to realize it wasn't worth their while.

Béliveau led the league in goals in 1958-59 with 45, and over the first seven seasons of his career he was averaging nearly a point and a half a game. He also won five Stanley

Jean Béliveau

Centre 1950-51 to 1970-71

Cups in that time. The last of these came in 1959-60 after which captain Maurice Richard retired. Doug Harvey was given the "C" for the next year, after which there was little doubt Béliveau would be the next captain. Over the next ten seasons he wore the "C" with a class and dignity that was the very personification of the role.

Just as Jacques Plante tried to understand the art of goaltending, Béliveau dissected the role of a captain and then applied this knowledge to the position. He believed a captain had three functions: to be a leader in the dressing room; to be a communicator between players and management; and, to be a role model for fans. He lived every day of his captaincy aware all the time of these roles.

It was under his guidance that the Canadiens won four more Stanley Cups in the 1960s, winning every year between 1965 and 1969 with the exception of 1967 when they lost to the Maple Leafs in a six-game finals. During this time Béliveau suffered through the only unpleasant time of

Béliveau combined brilliant stickhandling, a great touch, and determined physical play to become one of the game's greatest players.

his life in Montreal. He incurred an eye injury thanks to the stick of Stan Mikita, and although he played through the pain and discomfort, his performance remained at a high level. He recovered fully, though, and fans returned to cheer him on. On March 3, 1968, in a game at the Olympia in Detroit, Béliveau became just the second player to reach the 1,000-point mark when he scored a goal in his 911th game. Gordie Howe had been the first to reach that mark some eight years earlier.

In his final season, 1970-71, Béliveau reached another great scoring milestone when he notched his 500th career goal. It came on February 11, 1971, against Minnesota, and he was only the fourth man to reach this mark after Maurice Richard, Howe, and Bobby Hull. Béliveau was also named to the First All-Star team six times and the Second team four times during his career. He won the Conn Smythe trophy in 1965 for his great playoff performance, the first year the trophy was presented. He also played in 13 All-Star Games.

A NIGHT OF HONOUR

By the time the 1970-71 season was in full swing, it was clear to Jean Béliveau that this, his 20th season with the Canadiens, was to be his last. Approaching his 40th birthday, his love for the game had not diminished, but he was getting tired. As a result, the Canadiens planned for a special night of honour for "Le Gros Bill," and March 24, 1971, prior to a game against Philadelphia, was the chosen date. The half-hour ceremony featured a plethora of gifts and kind words, but for the captain the *coup de grace* was a cheque for $155,855 for the Jean Béliveau Fund for underprivileged children. He was joined on ice by his wife, Elise, and 13-year-old daughter, Hélène, and once the honour was over and the teams got down to business, the 17,154 Forum fans were treated to an entertaining 5-3 win by the home side. Despite thousands of letters and telegrams to play one more year, Béliveau did, indeed, retire at season's end—after winning his tenth Stanley Cup, no less.

Jean Béliveau

Boston goalie Gerry Cheevers has a look at the two greatest number 4's of all time—Montreal's Jean Béliveau and Boston's Bobby Orr—as they jostle for position.

In retirement, Béliveau remained true to the Canadiens and worked with the team in a variety of positions, but his priority was to promote the team and the league. His extraordinary charisma and character, and the dignity with which he played the game and carried himself off ice, ensured he was not just a Canadiens player but an NHL player. And, he was not just a gentleman but a winner of the finest order.

Only teammate Henri Richard has won the Stanley Cup more often (eleven times to Béliveau's ten). Today, like a dignitary or former prime minister, Béliveau can be seen at most Montreal home games at the Bell Centre, looking not much different from the man who retired in 1971.

The Stanley Cup parade was a seemingly annual event in Montreal. Here Jean Béliveau rides in a car to celebrate the 1969 victory, a 4-0 series sweep of St. Louis.

Bernard Geoffrion

Right Wing 1950-51 to 1963-64

Geoffrion holds three pucks to celebrate another hat-trick performance.

Bernard "Bernie" Geoffrion was given the nickname "Boom Boom" while playing junior hockey in Laval. Charlie Boire, a writer with the *Montreal Star*, assigned the moniker to Geoffrion not so much because of his hard shot as the double sound Boire thought he heard when the player unleashed one of his patented slapshots. The first "boom" was the sound of the stick hitting the puck, and the second "boom" was of the puck hitting the boards.

Of course, the nickname was apt because Geoffrion did have the hardest shot in the game. He didn't invent the slapshot—it had been in use since the early 1900s in one form or another—but he certainly perfected the art of that shot. It required, after all, a special technique in the windup and follow-through, as well as pure strength, timing, and skill to get open

Geoffrion finds himself with the puck in front of the Toronto goal, singlehandedly taking on Johnny Bower and the entire Leafs' team!

on ice for long enough to let the shot go. Few players could master the shot in the early days, but Geoffrion practiced it every day until it became the most impressive and successful part of his arsenal.

Of course, if Geoffrion had played for another team or in another era, he would have been more famous than he was. But if he had played elsewhere or at another time, he might not have been as successful on ice because he was on a Montreal team that had more success than any other in NHL and Stanley Cup history. Indeed, Geoffrion holds two NHL records that surely will never be broken. He played in the Stanley Cup finals for ten straight seasons (1951-60) and appeared in 106 consecutive Stanley Cup finals' games. No other player on those great Montreal teams of the 1950s can say as much, nor can any player from any other team in any other era.

Yet Geoffrion played with Maurice Richard and Jean Béliveau and Doug Harvey and was usually overshadowed by those superstars. When he came to the Canadiens toward the end of the 1950-51 season, he was a highly-rated rookie from whom great things were expected by management. He delivered as promised. Geoffrion won the Calder Trophy in 1951-52 thanks largely to scoring 30 goals in 67 games. The next year he led the league in playoff goals with six and helped the team to a Stanley Cup, the first of six for Boom Boom.

He reached one plateau in 1954-55, but it was layered in controversy which had little to do with himself. Geoffrion was leading the league in goals and among the league leaders in points, but with just a few days left in the season Maurice Richard overtook him. Richard, however, went wild in a game in Boston and was suspended for the rest of the year by NHL

The ever-popular "Boom Boom" graced the cover of every major hockey publication during his career.

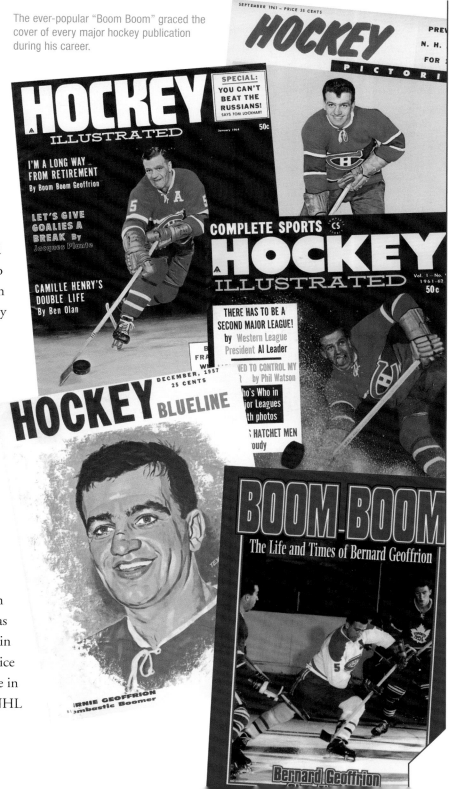

Bernard Geoffrion

Right Wing 1950-51 to 1963-64

president Clarence Campbell. Geoffrion was able to pass Richard and win the scoring title by a single point (75 to 74). Geoffrion was booed mercilessly by the home crowd when he passed Richard, however, and many fans believed he should have stopped scoring in order to give what was rightly Richard's.

The incident left lasting scars between the player and fans in large part because Richard, despite his many great glories during his lengthy career, never won the Art Ross Trophy. Two years later, Geoffrion earned praise and admiration for what was, by any definition, a miraculous comeback. During practice in late January 1958, Geoffrion collided harmlessly with teammate André Pronovost and collapsed to the ice.

A TRIBUTE AND MOURNING

The night of March 11, 2006, was supposed to be one of pure joy. The Canadiens were at home to play the Rangers, and pre-game ceremonies were held to honour Boom Boom Geoffrion and retire his number 5 to the rafters. Unfortunately, the great scorer had passed away early that very morning at his home in Atlanta, victim to a stomach cancer doctors could not entirely remove. Nevertheless, Boom Boom had wanted the proceedings to go on without him. That night his wife of 54 years, Marlene, and his children Danny, Bob, and Linda, many of his grandchildren, and several former teammates appeared on the Bell Centre ice to take part in the moving ceremony which concluded with a moment of silence for the departed Geoffrion. A number 5 banner with a black band was raised slowly to the rafters where it met up with Howie Morenz's number 7 near, but not at, the top. Symbolically, the two numbers were then raised together where they assumed their final positions side by side. Marlene was Morenz's daughter, and she was not only the child of a legend but the wife of one as well.

Geoffrion tries a wraparound on his backhand against Chicago. He won the Art Ross trophy as the league's leading scorer twice while playing for the Canadiens.

He was seen by team doctors and then rushed to hospital where he underwent emergency surgery for a ruptured bowel in his abdomen. He had his last rites read to him, and after his condition stabilized doctors told him his career might be over. Six weeks later, Geoffrion was back on the ice, and a few weeks after that he was holding the Stanley Cup for the fourth time in his career.

The previous season Geoffrion battled through another serious injury, this a shoulder separation that forced him out of 28 games. Yet he came back and led the league with a record eleven playoff goals and 18 playoff points to bring another Cup to Montreal. The Cup-clinching game was a 5-3 win over Boston. Boom Boom scored two goals,

Geoffrion was a star scorer, but he was also defensively responsible, here coming back to his own crease to check a player and prevent a scoring chance.

Bernard Geoffrion

Right Wing 1950-51 to 1963-64

"Boom Boom" makes a great deke in a game against Toronto.

including the winner, and added an assist.

For all of these successes, it might be that the 1960-61 season was the one Geoffrion would want to be remembered for above all others. As that season drew to a close, one of the most dramatic races in league history was playing out. Toronto's star left winger Frank Mahovlich was scoring at a record pace and

Geoffrion was not far behind. No one had scored 50 goals in a season since Maurice Richard in 1944-45, but now two players were certain to achieve the magic number. The only questions were who would do it first and who would finish with the most. Geoffrion was the answer on both counts.

Mahovlich suffered a terrible scoring slump in the final dozen games and finished with 48 while Geoffrion scored his 50th in his 62nd game

(the team's 68th game of the season). He went goalless on the final weekend in his attempt to establish a new record, but he became the first player since the Rocket to score 50 in a season. He was named Hart Trophy winner for this historic season which also saw him win the Art Ross Trophy for his 95 points, one shy of the all-time single season record held by teammate Dickie Moore, in 1958-59.

Because of Richard and then Gordie Howe, Geoffrion was named to only one First All-Star team, but by the time he retired in 1964 after 14 seasons with the Canadiens only two players had scored more goals than his 371—Howe and Richard. Geoffrion made a comeback in the late 1960s and upped his goals total to 393 after two seasons with the Rangers, and even by 1972 he was fifth on the all-time scoring list. He later made an unsuccessful attempt at coaching his beloved Canadiens, and he had the pleasure of seeing his son, Danny, play for him and the team, but Geoffrion will be remembered for his sensational scoring, his incredible string of playoff success, and his toughness. He didn't have the magic of Richard or the personality of Béliveau, but he had the stick of those great players. And, as any goal judge will repeat by rote—a goal is a goal.

CANADIENS NUMBERS
BERNARD GEOFFRION ("Boom Boom")

b. Montreal, Quebec, February 16, 1931   d. Atlanta, Georgia, March 11, 2006
5'9" 166 lbs. right wing shoots right

| | REGULAR SEASON | | | | | PLAYOFFS | | | | |
	GP	G	A	Pts	Pim	GP	G	A	Pts	Pim
1950-51	18	8	6	14	9	11	1	1	2	6
1951-52	67	30	24	54	66	11	3	1	4	6
1952-53	65	22	17	39	37	12	6	4	10	12
1953-54	54	29	25	54	87	11	6	5	11	18
1954-55	70	38	37	75	57	12	8	5	13	8
1955-56	59	29	33	62	66	10	5	9	14	6
1956-57	41	19	21	40	18	10	11	7	18	2
1957-58	42	27	23	50	51	10	6	5	11	2
1958-59	59	22	44	66	30	11	5	8	13	10
1959-60	59	30	41	71	36	8	2	10	12	4
1960-61	64	50	45	95	29	4	2	1	3	0
1961-62	62	23	36	59	36	5	0	1	1	6
1962-63	51	23	18	41	73	5	0	1	1	4
1963-64	55	21	18	39	41	7	1	1	2	4
TOTALS	766	371	388	759	636	127	56	59	115	88

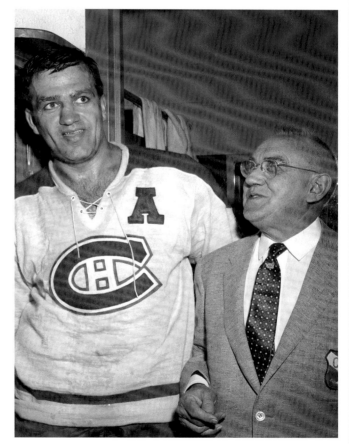

Geoffrion and his general manager, Frank Selke, enjoy a moment in the dressing room. Selke was the man who brought "Boom Boom" to the team.

Doug Harvey

Defence 1947-48 to 1960-61

Later called the Bobby Orr of his era, Doug Harvey was the greatest defenceman of his generation, a six-time Stanley Cup champion who won the Norris Trophy seven times (once while also coaching the New York Rangers, in 1961-62).

The Harvey-Orr comparison, however, is inaccurate in many ways. Orr was by far the better skater, and Harvey was better in his own end. Harvey played in an era when three goals a game almost guaranteed a win, while Orr played with the Boston Bruins, a team that set scoring records year after year. Harvey was more a passer than a scorer, and Orr was legendary for his scoring exploits as a defenceman. The comparison is most apt as regards two attributes. Both were skilled at moving the puck up ice, and, most important of all, both controlled the game when they were on the ice.

Harvey knew what to do when he had the puck. When the little black disc was on his stick, he was calm and intelligent where others panicked and made mistakes. He never went end-to-end the way Orr did. What Harvey was good at, though, was gaining possession of the puck and, in an instant, understanding what was happening. He knew where his teammates were; he knew what his opponents were thinking. As a result, Harvey invariably did the right thing—move the puck quickly, skate with it, make a perfect pass while in full flight.

If there is a kind of play that made Harvey famous it was his ability to skate with the puck quickly to his blueline and then hit a teammate with a pass before the far blueline. He maximized the ice and avoided offsides, and in an era when the two-line pass was forbidden he made the most of the ice to create offence.

As a kid, he was a multi-sport athlete, a great halfback and punter in football, a heavyweight boxing champion in the army during the Second World War, a fine hitter on the ball diamond. But being a Montrealer and growing up in Notre Dame de Grace, he was, first and foremost, a hockey player.

It was during the war years that Harvey started playing serious hockey

Harvey and teammates have an animated conversation with a referee during a stoppage in play.

In textbook style, Harvey keeps himself between the opponent and the goal and with a simple pokecheck clears the puck from harm's way.

Harvey was simply the best of the best among defencemen, both with the puck and without.

A BIG MISTAKE—A BIGGER RECOVERY

The 1960 Stanley Cup playoff run for Montreal was an historic one. The team's victory was its fifth in a row, a record unmatched to this day, and it was accomplished in dominating fashion—a four-game sweep of Chicago followed by a similar result against the Leafs. The series against the Hawks, however, took two turns, the first the result of a horrible gaffe by Doug Harvey, the second an incredible recovery by the defenceman. Montreal had won game one by a 4-3 score at the Forum, and the Canadiens seemed well on their way to another close win in game two playing controlled hockey with the lead, as they often did. As the game reached its conclusion, the Habs led 3-2 and were playing with confidence. But late in the game Harvey lost the puck at his blueline to Red Hay, and Hay went in alone and beat Jacques Plante to tie the score and send the game into overtime. Feeling horrible in the dressing room prior to the start of the fourth period, Harvey apologized to his teammates and promised to make amends. At 8:38 of the OT, he did just that, scoring the winning goal and giving the Habs a 2-0 stranglehold on the series. It was only his sixth playoff goal in 111 games, but it may well have made the difference in the team's quest for five straight Cups.

Harvey won the Norris Trophy seven times in an eight-year span, in part because of his brilliant rushes but also because of his near-perfect play inside his own blueline.

Doug Harvey

Defence 1947-48 to 1960-61

Harvey's number 2 was retired by the Canadiens in 1985.

Harvey chases down a loose puck during a game against the Blackhawks.

with the Montreal Royals, first in junior and then senior. In the latter, he helped the team win the 1947 Allan Cup, and the next year he started an NHL career with the Canadiens that had "hall of fame" stamped on it almost from the first day he played.

Harvey very quickly fit in on a soon-to-be powerful Montreal team. While there was the fiery scorer in Maurice Richard and the gentlemanly leadership of Jean Béliveau, Harvey led the team on ice and loosened the players up off it. In an era when a rant from coach Dick Irvin or Toe Blake was terrifying, Harvey often lightened the atmosphere with a bon mot to deaden the pain of the coach's wrath (but not its effect).

It was his calm that most players admired. Playing at the highest level was never easy, but Harvey made it seem so because he never got nervous before a game or flustered during it. Irvin and Blake loved having him in the lineup

because Harvey could play either left or right defence as well as anchor the power play and kill penalties.

In his 20 years in the NHL, Harvey never scored more than nine goals in any year, but his passing ability was the root of his skill as an offensive force. He proved that an offensive defenceman didn't necessarily have to score regularly but instead contribute to the team's offence through skating and puck movement. He was adept at keeping the puck inside the opposition blueline, making the transfer from defence to offence with speed and expertness, and other tactics which contributed to the team's goalscoring.

Most important, of course, was the team's impeccable record. Harvey never missed the playoffs during his 14 seasons with the Canadiens, winning six Stanley Cups and appearing in another five finals' series.

Harvey made history in 1961-62. He had won the Norris Trophy with the Canadiens the previous year, and before the 1961-62 season he was traded to the Rangers for Lou Fontinato and became New York's

playing coach. The Rangers finished in fourth place and qualified for the playoffs, and Harvey had another outstanding season on the blueline. This resulted in another Norris Trophy honour. Harvey remains the only player in NHL history to win an individual player trophy while coaching a team and the only player to win consecutive Norris Trophies with different teams.

Although Harvey enjoyed his season on Broadway, he hated the responsibility of coaching. After a career as a freewheeler, the onus of being responsible for an entire team was too great and he resumed playing with the team without the dual capacity of coach. Harvey played several years in the minors hoping for one more shot at the NHL, and he got that with St. Louis and coach Scotty Bowman who knew Harvey firsthand from his own time in the Montreal system.

By the time he retired in 1969, Harvey had been named to ten First All-Star teams and played in 13 All-Star Games. A legend on the blueline, his place in the game is forever established, and for anyone who wants to know more about his achievements, one only need to look at the many engravings of his name on the Stanley Cup.

CANADIENS NUMBERS
DOUG HARVEY

b. Montreal, Quebec, December 19, 1924   **d.** Montreal, Quebec, December 26, 1989
5'11"   187 lbs.   defence   shoots left

	REGULAR SEASON					PLAYOFFS				
	GP	G	A	Pts	Pim	GP	G	A	Pts	Pim
1947-48	35	4	4	8	32	—	—	—	—	—
1948-49	55	3	13	16	87	7	0	1	1	10
1949-50	70	4	20	24	76	5	0	2	2	10
1950-51	70	5	24	29	93	11	0	5	5	12
1951-52	68	6	23	29	82	11	0	3	3	8
1952-53	69	4	30	34	67	12	0	5	5	8
1953-54	68	8	29	37	110	10	0	2	2	12
1954-55	70	6	43	49	58	12	0	8	8	6
1955-56	62	5	39	44	60	10	2	5	7	10
1956-57	70	6	44	50	92	10	0	7	7	10
1957-58	68	9	32	41	131	10	2	9	11	16
1958-59	61	4	16	20	61	11	1	11	12	22
1959-60	66	6	21	27	45	8	3	0	3	6
1960-61	58	6	33	39	48	6	0	1	1	8
TOTALS	890	76	371	447	1,042	123	8	59	67	138

Harvey, like many of Montreal's greatest players, was accorded his own night of glory at the Forum to honour his legendary career.

Hartland Molson
Builder

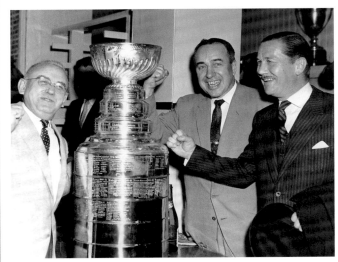

Molson celebrates a Stanley Cup victory with Frank Selke (left) and Toe Blake (centre).

Although Hartland Molson never played in the NHL, his contributions to the game and to the Montreal Canadiens made him a worthy inductee to the Hockey Hall of Fame in 1973 and an Officer of the Order of Canada in 1995.

The son of Colonel Herbert Molson, one of the founders of the Canadian Arena Company, which ran the Canadiens, Hartland was a graduate of Royal Military College. His university career reached its zenith in 1926 when his team from Kingston played in the Memorial Cup finals before losing to the Calgary Canadiens. He also took his RMC team to the university football title. After graduating, Molson spent a year in Paris and worked in business upon his return, mostly with Molson Brewery. In 1933, shortly after becoming a chartered accountant, he founded and ran the Dominion Skyways airline.

(l to r) Guy Lafleur, Hartland Molson, Jean Béliveau, and Maurice Richard enjoy each other's company.

During the Second World War, Molson enlisted in the army and rose in rank as far as captain. In 1940, he was shot down by the Germans during a mission in the Battle of Britain and was invalided home, but he was awarded the Order of the British Empire for his contributions to Canada's war efforts. He flew with the famous No. 1 Fighter Squadron, one of the most important units for the Allies during the war.

Molson worked his way up the ranks within the Molson Company and the Canadiens. On September 24, 1957, he and brother, Thomas, bought the Canadiens from Senator Donat Raymond. Over the years,

Hartland Molson worked his way up the ranks to oversee the Canadiens during their greatest days, winning the Stanley Cup six times in eleven years.

Hartland Molson became team president and chairman of the Canadian Arena Company before leaving in 1968. Under his auspices the team won six Stanley Cups.

His tenure was marked by enormous change and improvement within the NHL. Molson's business acumen was salient in developing the NHL Pension Fund, and he worked tirelessly to help grow the funds needed for building the Hockey Hall of Fame in 1961 in Toronto. During the 1960s, Molson realized that the NHL's most successful team needed the most modern arena, and to that end oversaw the complete refurbishing of the Forum. Steel beams, which obstructed many a view, were eliminated, and seating capacity increased to make it the biggest—and most modern—arena in the league.

HARTLAND MOLSON

b. Montreal, Quebec, May 29, 1907
d. Montreal, Quebec, September 28, 2002

PLAYING IN EUROPE

After graduating from RMC, Molson took a one-year appointment at the Banque Adam in Paris, France. During that time, he played on a team called the Paris Canadians and made several international appearances with that group. His most famous teammates were Clarence Campbell, who later became the president of the NHL in 1947, and Billy Bell, a former Stanley Cup winner with the Montreal Canadiens. The three were stars throughout Europe and impressed fans everywhere with their speed and skill.

Dickie Moore

Left Wing 1951-52 to 1962-63

Overcoming injuries and playing with a dedication that impressed even the toughest NHL veterans, Dickie Moore carved a niche for himself over a 12-year career with the Montreal Canadiens that earned him six Stanley Cup wins, six All-Star Game appearances, and two Art Ross Trophy honours as the league's top scorer.

Moore was one of ten siblings growing up in Montreal. Although most of the children were active, it was his sister, Dolly, who was the best athlete in the family. She was a star in track-and-field and nearly qualified for the Olympics. Dickie ("Richard" to his family) was hit by a car when he was 12 years old and lucky not to have

suffered permanent injuries. The incident, however, only foreshadowed his NHL career, which, while remarkable, was often hampered by bodily damage.

By the time he reached his mid-teens, Moore was becoming a fine young hockey player. He played junior for the Montreal Royals for two years, winning the Memorial Cup with the team in 1949 and again the next year with the Montreal Jr. Canadiens. His older brother, Jimmy, also played for the Royals, and together the boys were a handful for the coach, Tag Miller, who worried about their overly physical style of play.

By the time they won the Memorial Cup, Dickie was considered by Canadiens general manager Frank Selke to be a top prospect, and the

Moore celebrates winning his first Stanley Cup with teammates, in 1952-53.

Left winger Moore (front, right) celebrates one of his six Stanley Cup victories with the Habs during a career marked by injury and incredible recovery.

Dickie Moore

Left Wing 1951-52 to 1962-63

player was transferred to the superior Jr. Canadiens the next year where he helped the team win the Canadian junior championship again. In 1951-52, Moore played for the Royals in the Quebec senior league, and he continued to improve as the level of play got tougher.

THE HISTORIC GAME

Montreal finished the 1958-59 regular season with 91 points, best in the league. Second-place Boston had just 73 points, so when the Canadiens travelled to Madison Square Garden on March 22, 1959, for the final game of the 70-game schedule, there was little at stake for the team. But for Dickie Moore, it proved to be one of the most important games of his career. He was leading the league in scoring with 94 points, and right behind him was teammate Jean Béliveau with 88 points. It wasn't likely that Béliveau was going to get six more points than Moore on the final day, so "Diggin' Dickie" was pretty much assured of the Art Ross Trophy. In the first period, though, both Moore and Béliveau had a goal and assist, and in the third Béliveau added a second goal to finish with 91 points. Moore's two points gave him 96 for the year, breaking the previous single-season mark of 95 held by Gordie Howe. It wasn't until 1965-66 that the record was broken, by Chicago's Bobby Hull, who did what Moore had done and improved it by one point. Hull finished with 97 points on the year, but for seven seasons Moore's 96 points was the all-time best mark for one season of play.

He averaged well over a point a game and earned a call-up to the Canadiens where he continued his torrid pace. Moore had exactly 33 points in 33 games, including 18 goals, in his first season with the team.

And then the injuries started, and over the next two seasons he played just 31 games. Moore hurt one knee badly and missed several weeks, then injured both knees which cost him even more time. He also suffered a horrible injury to his collarbone which required surgery, a special harness, rehab, and stitches to connect his shoulder to his torso. Yet during these two years Moore managed to recover in time for the playoffs both years, winning a Cup in 1953 and losing the next year in the finals. In that 1954 loss to Detroit in seven games, Moore led all scorers in both points and assists (13 and eight, respectively).

CANADIENS NUMBERS
DICKIE MOORE

b. Montreal, Quebec, January 6, 1931
5'10"   168 lbs.   left wing   shoots left

| | REGULAR SEASON | | | | | PLAYOFFS | | | | |
	GP	G	A	Pts	Pim	GP	G	A	Pts	Pim
1951-52	33	18	15	33	44	11	1	1	2	12
1952-53	18	2	6	8	19	12	3	2	5	13
1953-54	13	1	4	5	12	11	5	8	13	8
1954-55	67	16	20	36	32	12	1	5	6	22
1955-56	70	11	39	50	55	10	3	6	9	12
1956-57	70	29	29	58	56	10	3	7	10	4
1957-58	70	36	48	84	65	10	4	7	11	4
1958-59	70	41	55	96	61	11	5	12	17	8
1959-60	62	22	42	64	54	8	6	4	10	4
1960-61	57	35	34	69	62	6	3	1	4	4
1961-62	57	19	22	41	54	6	4	2	6	8
1962-63	67	24	26	50	61	5	0	1	1	2
TOTALS	654	254	340	594	575	112	38	56	94	101

Despite wearing a cast for much of 1957-58, Moore led the league with 84 points.

Moore (left) was a popular fixture in the Habs dressing room, well-liked by teammates and coaches alike.

Moore played most of the next year but wasn't very effective, recording 36 points in 67 games (consider he scored 33 points in 33 games as a rookie). But for the next five years, the Canadiens won the Cup and Moore was playing the best hockey of his career. He played left wing on a line with Maurice and Henri Richard, and often switched to the right side or centre depending on injuries.

One of the more spectacular seasons of play in NHL history was Moore's in 1957-58. He led the league in scoring with 84 points and in goals with 36, fine achievements on their own merit. But what was truly amazing was that he achieved these numbers while wearing a cast to protect a broken left wrist for more than half the season! It was this kind of single-minded devotion to the team that inspired those around him and helped the Canadiens win the Cup five times in a row (1955-60).

The next year, 1958-59, Moore was healthy for the full season and led the league in points and assists (96 and 55) and again helped the team win the Cup. Not surprisingly, he also led the playoffs in points and assists as well (17 and 12 in eleven games).

In all, Moore averaged nearly a point a game during his dozen years with the team. He later made two comebacks after retiring in 1963. The first was with Toronto a year later and the second with the expansion St. Louis Blues in 1967-68 for 27 games, but Moore's legacy lies entirely with his time in Montreal. He was not only part of six Cup teams, he was the very embodiment of what it takes to win, and had the Bill Masterton Trophy been around in his day, Moore would have unquestionably won it once, if not twice.

But perhaps his greatest night came on November 12, 2005, long after his playing days. That night, he and Yvan Cournoyer shared the honour of having their number 12 retired to the rafters of the Bell Centre. Jean Béliveau, a teammate of both men, was one of the guest speakers at centre ice during the pre-game ceremonies, and ever after no one would wear the number made famous by Moore.

Doug Harvey looks on as Moore drinks from the Stanley Cup.

Joe Cattarinich
Builder

(l to r) Cattarinich, Letourneau, Dandurand owned the Canadiens from 1921 to 1935.

Out of a passion for sports, a keen business sense, and impeccable timing, Joe Cattarinich rose from the ranks of book-keeper to owner of the Stanley Cup champion Montreal Canadiens.

Cattarinich went to school in Lévis, Quebec, across the river from Quebec City, and got his first job as a book-keeper with a ship-building company. His skills as a lacrosse player, however, were too great to ignore and he soon moved to Montreal to pursue a career in that sport. He sold sporting goods in the daytime and played for the highly-regarded Nationale AAA team at night. He remained with that team for five years as an amateur and then another eight years as a professional, and it was

out of this last association that he helped the Nationale establish a pro hockey team, the first in Canada.

Cattarinich played with the team from 1909 to 1914, and it was during this time that he met Léo Dandurand, a successful businessman in the tobacco industry. The two developed interests together, primarily buying horseracing tracks around the continent, and their partnership climaxed on November 3, 1921, when they, along with Louis Letourneau, purchased the Montreal Canadiens for $11,000. The club had become available when previous owner, George Kennedy, passed away suddenly.

One of the "Three Musketeers," Joe Cattarinich helped bring three Stanley Cups to Montreal in eight seasons (1923-31).

Under the auspices of the "Three Musketeers," the Canadiens acquired several star players and became known as the Flying Frenchmen. These players included Aurèle Joliat, Howie Morenz, and Newsy Lalonde, along with goalie Georges Vézina. Indeed, Cattarinich was a goalie with the Nationale back in 1910 until one game when the team played Chicoutimi. Cattarinich was so awed by the performance of the opposing goalie that he quit and urged his own manager, Jack Laviolette, to sign that puckstopper, who turned out to be Vézina. The Nationale, in turn, made Cattarinich a director, and Vézina played every game for the Canadiens between 1910 and 1925.

The team won the first Stanley Cup for this ownership group in 1924, and again in 1930 and 1931. Letourneau sold his stake in the team in 1931, and Cattarinich and Dandurand remained owners for four more years until financial pressures forced them to sell the team for $165,000.

JOE CATTARINICH

b. Quebec City, Quebec, November 13, 1881
d. New Orleans, Louisiana, December 7, 1938

AS GOOD AS HIS WORD

Perhaps most telling, Cattarinich was known to be a man of his word, a man for whom a handshake was as binding as any contract and for whom the word humility could be truly and accurately applied. He gave many favours without seeking credit and never sought the limelight even though his acumen and business success warranted it.

Jacques Plante
Goalie 1952-53 to 1962-63

Jacques Plante wore a mask in practice until a serious injury during a game compelled him to don the protection permanently.

A complex and multi-faceted man, Jacques Plante kept things exquisitely simple when playing goal for the Canadiens: he kept the puck out of the net, and the team kept on winning and winning. In fact, in his eleven seasons with the team, the Habs won the Stanley Cup six times and lost in the finals on two other occasions. If Plante wasn't simply the best goaltender of all time, he most certainly was the most important and influential.

Plante played his junior hockey in Montreal with the Royals where the Canadiens could keep a close eye on him. He made his NHL debut during the 1952-53 season, playing three regular-season games and four more times in the playoffs. His playoff appearances included the first two games of the Cup finals against Boston, but after winning the first game 4-1 the Habs lost the next one 4-2, and coach Dick Irvin went with the experienced Gerry McNeil the rest of the way. Montreal won the Cup in

five games, and the 24-year-old Plante had his name on the Cup for the first of many times.

The next year saw a more gradual progression for Plante. He appeared in 17 games during the season, recording an amazing five shutouts among his seven wins. In the playoffs he bore the brunt of the work and was sensational even though the Habs lost a seven-game finals to Detroit. By this time, it was clear Plante was ready to start a full-time career in the NHL, and he didn't disappoint. Over the next nine seasons he played the vast majority of the team's games, establishing himself as the best in the league.

In his first full season, 1954-55, he played every minute of the playoffs but again was defeated by the Red Wings in a

The backbone of five straight championships from 1956-60, Plante is hoisted Cup-like on the shoulders of his teammates.

Jacques Plante
Goalie 1952-53 to 1962-63

seven-game finals. This was his last taste of defeat for many years. Starting in 1955-56, Plante led the Canadiens to five straight Cup victories, earning the Vézina Trophy every year of this amazing streak.

As important as the Cup wins, Plante became famous for two pioneering and historic contributions to the game. On November 1, 1959, in a game against the Rangers, he was hit flush in the face by an Andy Bathgate slapshot. He was helped off the ice and stitched up, but he refused to return to the game without a mask. Coach Toe Blake was not too pleased, but he had no choice. Every game was important, and teams had only one goalie. A puckstopper of Plante's calibre could not easily be replaced.

Plante returned with the facial protection, the team won the game, but all was not history, as they say. The team went on a lengthy undefeated streak as Plante continued to wear the mask (with one exception later in the season). Goalies in the NHL and AHL had been wearing protection in practice, to save themselves for games, and Plante had tinkered with various designs. It was no accident that he had a mask at the ready after the Bathgate shot, and in many ways this shot marked the terrifying introduction of slapshots as dangerous and intimidating tactics used by some players.

That Plante could wear the mask is a tribute to his reputation, for a lesser goalie would have been banished to the minors as cowardly. But Blake had the best in the business, and the mask showed no signs of interfering with the goalie's ability to play his best. Other goalies slowly

Plante was the fifth goalie in NHL history to capture the Hart Trophy as league MVP.

CANADIENS NUMBERS
JACQUES PLANTE ("Jake the Snake")

b. . Shawinigan Falls, Quebec, January 17, 1929   d. Geneva, Switzerland, February 26, 1986
6'   175 lbs.   goalie   catches left

| | REGULAR SEASON | | | | | | PLAYOFFS | | | | | |
	GP	W-L-T	Mins	GA	SO	GAA	GP	W-L	Mins	GA	SO	GAA
1952-53 🏆	3	2-0-1	180	4	0	1.33	4	3-1	240	7	1	1.75
1953-54	17	7-5-5	1,020	27	5	1.59	8	5-3	480	15	2	1.88
1954-55	52	31-13-7	3,040	110	5	2.17	12	6-3	639	30	0	2.82
1955-56 🏆	64	42-12-10	3,840	119	7	1.86	10	8-2	600	18	2	1.80
1956-57 🏆	61	31-18-12	3,660	122	9	2.00	10	8-2	616	17	1	1.66
1957-58 🏆	57	34-14-8	3,386	119	9	2.11	10	8-2	618	20	1	1.94
1958-59 🏆	67	38-16-13	4,000	144	9	2.16	11	8-3	670	26	0	2.33
1959-60 🏆	69	40-17-12	4,140	175	3	2.54	8	8-0	489	11	3	1.35
1960-61	40	23-11-6	2,400	112	2	2.80	6	2-4	412	16	0	2.33
1961-62	70	42-14-14	4,200	166	4	2.37	6	2-4	360	19	0	3.17
1962-63	56	22-14-19	3,320	138	5	2.49	5	1-4	300	14	0	2.80
TOTALS	556	312-134-107	33,186	1,236	58	2.23	90	59-28	5,424	193	10	2.13

followed suit, and within a decade almost all goalies in all pro leagues were wearing some protection.

For Plante's part, that first game was just the beginning. Intent on improving the mask, he made many designs, both for comfort and safety. In a sense, he was a designer as much as a goalie, and by the early 1970s when all NHL goalies wore masks, they were generally wearing one based on a Plante design.

Additionally, Plante was a student of the game and an innovator over and above the mask. He saw the position of goalie as a subject for study and thought long and hard about how to play goal. Perhaps more than any goalie before him, he understood the concept of coming out of the net to challenge the shooter and cutting down the angle, something no one

considered in the days of the barefaced goalie. But Plante knew that if he came out of his crease, the shooter could see less of the net and had less room to shoot. Indeed, a facemask gave him the confidence to play his position better. He also knew that a goalie with disciplined body position could succeed where others couldn't.

In addition to cutting down the angle, Plante saw no need to sit in his crease and watch pucks trickle behind his net or into the corner. He happily wandered from his crease to play the angled shoot-in of opponents or get to the puck before even his own defencemen. He cut off pucks that went around the net before they got from one forward to another, and he used the area

Plante comes well out of his net to play the puck, a habit for which he became famous.

A maskless Plante focuses on the puck to make a glove save while Leafs' forward Dick Duff tries to poke it free.

behind the goal as a protective area to handle the puck without risk.

Plante communicated with his defenders and worked with them as a third defenceman to get the puck out of his own end faster and more efficiently. To that end, he used his arms and voice to greater effect, raising an arm on a delayed icing call to alert his teammates and talking to them about moving the puck. In essence, the

HART AND VÉZINA A RARE DOUBLE

Jacques Plante made history in 1961-62 when he won both the Hart Trophy and Vézina Trophy in the same year. While the Hart had been won by a goalie only four times previously since its inception in 1924, none of the winners had also won the Vézina. Plante was the first. Previous Hart winners included Herb Gardiner (Montreal, 1926-27), Roy Worters (New York Americans, 1928-29), Chuck Rayner (New York Rangers, 1949-50), and Al Rollins (Chicago, 1953-54). Plante led the Canadiens to first place in the regular season, playing every minute (4,200) of every game (70) while losing only 14 games all year. His 2.37 goals-against average and 166 goals allowed was tops by a wide margin. It was Plante's sixth Vézina Trophy in seven years and marked the last time this rare double occurred until Buffalo's Dominik Hasek turned the trick in 1996-97, some 35 years later. Montreal's Jose Theodore then did it again in 2001-02.

mask freed the goalie to do so many things that previously were either dangerous or foolhardy.

Like all good things, the Canadiens' run of five Cups in row came to an end, early in the 1961 playoffs with a loss to Chicago. The next year, though, Plante was sensational, leading the league in wins and playing every minute of every game, regular season and playoffs. He won his sixth Vézina Trophy and also the Hart Trophy as the league's most valuable player, the last goalie to win until Dominik Hasek in 1997 with Buffalo.

In truth, his contributions to the understanding of the goalie position were so great they overshadowed his purely puckstopping achievements, but in a career so rich it is neither surprising nor a bad thing. Every goalie today owes his safety to Plante, and every goalie who has a goalie coach and who studies his position like it's something special owes Plante a debt of gratitude. He understood that being a goalie did not mean some Neanderthal practice of standing in front of the twine and sacrificing body to keep the puck out. He took a more intelligent and advanced approach, and his seven career Vézina Trophies attest to his unparalleled success in this regard.

Plante used his stellar stick handling skills to move the puck quickly to his teammates.

Plante gets some help from teammate Jean-Guy Talbot as he pokechecks the puck away from his goal.

Sam Pollock
Builder

Sam Pollock, the NHL's most successful general manager, stands in front of the logo for which he served with extraordinary brilliance.

By the time he retired from hockey on September 30, 1978, there was nothing Sam Pollock had not accomplished as a general manager and team builder in the game. In 14 seasons as GM of the Canadiens, he had won nine Stanley Cups. He had orchestrated a seemingly endless string of brilliant trades, built a developmental system second to none with many prospects in the system ready to play at any time, and established a scouting staff that could find a great hockey player under any rock where great hockey players might live and play.

But like many great talents, Pollock railed against people who called him lucky or who suggested he was "blessed" with something that gave the team so many great players and Cup wins. Pollock always maintained one thing and one thing only got the Canadiens their success—hard work. Indeed, he was known to work 18 or 20 hours a day regularly, and he once said that even in the summer when he took a meagre vacation hockey was always on his mind. He may have had luck and been blessed with plenty of fortune, but Pollock worked hard to make his breaks and give himself a chance to win.

Short and pudgy, Pollock never had childhood illusions about playing in the NHL. At age 17, he was manager of a local baseball team in Montreal that, quite amazingly, had three future Habs greats on it—goalie Bill Durnan, defenceman Ken Reardon, and forward Elmer Lach. Within a few years, Pollock oversaw the Midget Canadiens, the level below the Jr. Canadiens which was the junior team of the NHL's Canadiens. He had worked under Wilf Cude and later Frank Currie, and when Currie left he recommended to the NHL Canadiens to hire Pollock as his replacement.

Pollock earned his reputation early. Even on the sandlots as a teen and with the Midget Canadiens a short time later, he was a stickler for detail and travelled all around the city scouting for the best players available. If there was anything God-given about his talents that separated him from every other aspiring coach, scout, manager, or player it was that he had exceptional abilities for identifying talents in players.

SAM POLLOCK

b. Verdun, Quebec, December 15, 1925
d. Toronto, Ontario, August 15, 2007

A GREAT MIND PERPETUALLY AT WORK

Perhaps an even greater sense of Pollock's abilities can be seen in the drafts of 1973 and 1974. Denis Potvin was sure to go first overall in 1973 to the Islanders, but after that Pollock felt there was little difference between the next several players. However, Montreal held the number two selection and Pollock knew that Atlanta, drafting fifth, desperately wanted Tom Lysiak. Pollock traded his second overall choice for Atlanta's first in 1973 and '74! St. Louis, desperate for a goalie, wanted to select John Davidson, so the Blues did just as the Flames had done. Pollock traded his new first selection, fifth overall, to St. Louis for its first in 1973 (eighth overall) and 1974. Pollock selected Bob Gainey with that choice in 1973. The next year, he had two additional first-round draft choices with which he selected Doug Risebrough and Rick Chartraw, two players who were with the Habs through their four Stanley Cups in the last half of the 1970s. In fact, the Cup-winning team of 1976-77 is a vivid representation of Pollock's abilities to acquire draft choices and then use those to select the best player available at the time.

Sam Pollock
Builder

After becoming manager of the Jr. Canadiens in 1945, Pollock started on the road to great success in hockey. He became coach of the team two years later, and in 1949-50 he led the team to a Memorial Cup win. This victory earned him a promotion, and he became the NHL Canadiens' director of player personnel serving under GM Frank Selke. This was a long and fruitful apprenticeship, but the work eventually led to his being named Selke's successor 14 years later.

While Selke was working hard at the NHL level to ensure the Habs kept winning, Pollock was performing heroics in the less-glamourous leagues below the NHL. In addition to coaching the Jr. Canadiens, he was stocking the team and its minor-league affiliates with future stars, ensuring that when age or injury threatened to disrupt Selke's NHL team there was always someone ready to step in for one game, a season, or a lengthy career. Selke and his players were so famous and successful at the NHL level that few knew the name Pollock. But fans of the NHL marveled how the Canadiens always seemed to replenish their roster or re-stock their lineup with a player as good as the departing one.

Pollock won a second Memorial Cup with the Hull-Ottawa Jr. Canadiens in 1957-58, and he guided the Hull-Ottawa Canadiens of the EPHL to back-to-back championships in 1960-61 and 1961-62. A year later, he was general manager of the Omaha Knights that won the CPHL championship, and by this time, like a great player, his time had come.

Selke stepped down as Montreal's general manager in 1964, and Pollock took over. It was a smart but contentious hiring. The only other candidate for the job was Reardon, that one-time ballplayer with Pollock who went on to have a hall of fame career with the team as a player. After Reardon retired, he worked with the Canadiens and was vice president for a decade. He fully expected to be hired as Selke's replacement.

However, Senator Hartland Molson and cousin David, who owned the team, decided to hire Pollock who had acquitted himself well a year earlier when the team asked him to trade Jacques Plante. Pollock sent Plante, Phil Goyette, and Don Marshall to the Rangers for Gump Worsley, Dave Balon, Leon Rochefort, and Len Ronson. The move paved the way for Worsley and Charlie Hodge to share goaltending duties for two Cup wins in 1965 and 1966, and the Gumper stuck around for the last two championships in the later part of the decade as well. Reardon, offended by the slight of not being hired despite his loyalty and playing career, left the team.

One of Pollock's first trades as GM came right after the 1964 Amateur Draft of unsigned 16-year-olds. He sent Paul Reid and Guy Allen to Boston in exchange for Ken Dryden and Alex Campbell, one of his shrewdest moves.

There were two aspects to Pollock's greatness. First, he understood the big picture. He knew that NHL success depended on a strong underpinning and this meant stocking the farm and junior teams with great players. The only way this could be accomplished was through a superior scouting staff.

In addition, he also knew that a young player could not simply join the NHL team as a prospect and hope to contribute as he would five years later after that much more experience. So, as he learned from his mentor, Selke, a prospect must develop, first in junior, then in a lower league, and finally the AHL. Only then could a player be ready to step into the NHL and be an effective player immediately. Pollock was never prepared to do anything out of desperation, and the only way to ensure this was to make sure he was never desperate.

And then there were the trades, specific moments when Pollock made a conscious effort to better his club, for the present or the future, by dealing with other teams. No one in the history of the draft was better than him at this. Of course, one example stands above all others. Pollock wanted the number-one draft choice for 1971 so he could claim Guy Lafleur, hands down the best player available that year. So, he traded Ernie Hicke and Montreal's first draft in 1970 to California for the lesser François Lacombe and California's first overall selection in 1971, reasoning that the Seals would finish dead last and be the team to have first dibs on Lafleur.

The trouble started when Los Angeles proved to be an even worse team than the Seals to start the 1970-71 season. Pollock then traded Ralph Backstrom to the Kings for two players he had no interest in (Ray Fortin and Gord Labossière), and the excellent Backstrom helped prop up the Kings, ensuring the Seals finished dead last. And so, Guy Lafleur wound up in Montreal, not California, and the Canadiens won the Stanley Cup in 1971, 1973, 1976, 1977, 1978, and 1979.

When Pollock retired in 1978, the team was in such good shape that it still won the next Stanley Cup. But in the years that followed, the Canadiens lagged because no one could come in and replace Sam Pollock. Like a player, he had spent years learning his craft in the lower levels, but when he made it to the NHL, there was no one better. He understood what winning was about, and he was passionate about what it took to win. But above all, he won because, as he always said, he worked hard.

Pollock worked for years under the tutelage of GM Frank Selke, and when Selke was ready to retire, Pollock was ready to move in, making his mark immediately.

Henri Richard

Henri Richard won the Stanley Cup eleven times in a 20-year career as a player, a frequency of success unmatched since the Cup was introduced in 1893.

It is impossible not to compare the younger Henri to his older brother, Maurice, but it also seems impossible for people to consider that Henri's career was equal to, if not superior to, his brother's. Henri did not have the charisma of Maurice, and he wasn't as comfortable speaking English. He was never suspended and no riot ensued from anything

CANADIENS NUMBERS
HENRI RICHARD ("Pocket Rocket")

b. Montreal, Quebec, February 29, 1936
5'7"   160 lbs.   centre   shoots right

	REGULAR SEASON					PLAYOFFS				
	GP	G	A	Pts	Pim	GP	G	A	Pts	Pim
1955-56	64	19	21	40	46	10	4	4	8	21
1956-57	63	18	36	54	71	10	2	6	8	10
1957-58	67	28	52	80	56	10	1	7	8	11
1958-59	63	21	30	51	33	11	3	8	11	13
1959-60	70	30	43	73	66	8	3	9	12	9
1960-61	70	24	44	68	91	6	2	4	6	22
1961-62	54	21	29	50	48	—	—	—	—	—
1962-63	67	23	50	73	57	5	1	1	2	2
1963-64	66	14	39	53	73	7	1	1	2	9
1964-65	53	23	29	52	43	13	7	4	11	24
1965-66	62	22	39	61	47	8	1	4	5	2
1966-67	65	21	34	55	28	10	4	6	10	2
1967-68	54	9	19	28	16	13	4	4	8	4
1968-69	64	15	37	52	45	14	2	4	6	8
1969-70	62	16	36	52	61	—	—	—	—	—
1970-71	75	12	37	49	46	20	5	7	12	20
1971-72	75	12	32	44	48	6	0	3	3	4
1972-73	71	8	35	43	21	17	6	4	10	14
1973-74	75	19	36	55	28	6	2	2	4	2
1974-75	16	3	10	13	4	6	1	2	3	4
TOTALS	1,256	358	688	1,046	928	180	49	80	129	181

he did, yet his accomplishments on ice, while far less dramatic, were greater than Maurice's or, in fact, almost anyone else who played the game. He was nicknamed the "Pocket Rocket" because he was younger and smaller in stature than Maurice, but his achievements were anything but pocket-like.

Consider that Henri won the Stanley Cup as a player eleven times. No player since the Cup was introduced in 1893 has been as successful. Henri was also only the ninth player to reach 1,000 career points. He captained the Canadiens for the last four years of his career and is one

Richard appears with what was almost naturally his—the Stanley Cup.

Henri Richard

of a small number of players to play for two distinct dynasties. And, he scored two Cup-winning goals. No one has scored more.

Although Maurice and Henri were brothers, they were more like uncle and nephew because Maurice was 15 years older. By the time Henri was six years old, his older brother was married and playing in the NHL. By the time Henri started his NHL career, Maurice was winding down his. As a result, Henri was like every other kid—he wanted to play like the great Maurice Richard. But, like every other kid, he soon discovered he couldn't.

Henri was a high-scoring centre in junior with the Canadiens, but when he got to the NHL, Habs coach Toe Blake put him on a line with Dickie Moore and Maurice. Henri soon found out the key to success was to get the puck to his brother. Indeed, a glance at their statistics confirms as much. Maurice always had many more goals than assists, and Henri had many more assists than goals.

When he made the Canadiens at training camp in 1955, Henri could not have known what lay ahead for himself. Opponents picked on him mercilessly for two reasons. First, they goaded him into fighting because he was the younger brother of Maurice and obviously not as good (so the trash talking went). And, by picking on him, opponents got Maurice so mad they threw him off his game. What no one realized was that Henri was a good little scrapper who could stand up for himself, make his own mark on the game, and allow Maurice to focus on his own play.

Henri was small and fiery, a competitor in every sense of the word. He worked hard for every inch of ice, every shot, every pass. He won the Stanley Cup in each of his first five years in the league. While some critics said he won because of his brother, Maurice himself refuted the notion by pointing out something more obvious: Henri had renewed Maurice's passion for the game and extended his own career beyond what it might otherwise have been.

Once Maurice had retired in 1960, Henri was freer to establish his own identity on the team, both on ice and in the dressing room. Although the

Richard moves behind the Chicago net looking for an open man.

Richard owns the Canadiens record for most games played, with 1,256.

140

The "Pocket Rocket" chases a puck in the corner while two fellow future Hall of Famers look on—former teammate and defenceman Doug Harvey, and all-star goalie Glenn Hall.

Henri Richard

Centre 1955-56 to 1974-75

team followed its run of five Cups in a row with a drought of four Cup-less years to start the 1960s, Henri was soon leading another generation to four more championships in the second half of the decade, one in which he and Jean Béliveau and Claude Provost were the leaders and Gump Worsley, Charlie Hodge, and Rogie Vachon the goalies.

Richard's finest moment of the decade came in the final game of the 1966 playoffs. Game six of the Cup finals against Detroit went into overtime, and Richard scored the deciding goal, albeit in controversial fashion. He made a pass to teammate Dave Balon at the Detroit blueline and then headed for the net. Balon got it back to Richard in the slot, but he had been knocked down by Red Wings defenceman Gary Bergman and was sliding towards the goal. The puck bounced off Richard's hand and past goalie Roger Crozier. The Wings insisted the goal should have been nullified because of contact with the glove, but officials ruled that the goal was legit.

The crowning glory of Henri's career came the night of May 18, 1971. This was game seven of the Cup finals, in Chicago. Lord Stanley's trophy was in the Stadium, and one team was going to win it this night. The Hawks jumped into an early 2-0 lead midway through the game, but Jacques Lemaire scored at 14:18 of the second to cut the lead to a goal. Richard then scored late in the second and again early in the third after a great deke past defenceman Keith Magnuson, and the Habs won 3-2 to win the Cup.

Typical of Richard, though, his heroics were overshadowed by the

A TEAM ALL-STAR

Despite his amazing success, Henri Richard rarely basked in the glow of individual honours. He was named to the First All-Star team only once, 1957-58, but the singular honour was because there were several other top players at the position during Richard's career. Jean Béliveau had a lock on the spot for several years, and later Stan Mikita and Phil Esposito were frequent occupiers of the position. Henri was a Second All-Star three times and also played in ten All-Star Games. The only individual trophy he won was the Bill Masterton Trophy in 1973-74. Twice he led the league in assists, first in 1957-58 with 52, playing on a line with Dickie Moore and Claude Provost, and later, in 1962-63 playing alongside Béliveau.

Henri Richard beats Johnny Bower on a breakaway as the Leafs' goalie unsuccessfully tries to pokecheck the puck from him.

rookie netminding of Ken Dryden who won the Conn Smythe Trophy. Yet it was the diminutive Richard who was the real hero on the final night of the season in which he won his tenth career Stanley Cup.

Richard won his final Cup two years later and retired after the 1974-75 season. He missed most of the regular season of that last year with a badly broken ankle, but he returned in the playoffs. Despite his quiet demeanour, Richard was the centre of controversy on a couple of important occasions. Prior to scoring the Cup winner in 1971, for instance, Richard had been critical of coach Al MacNeil because the coach had made Richard a healthy scratch for one game. A couple of years later, he and Serge Savard got into a shouting match in the dressing room. And, during Henri's final season, coach Scotty Bowman didn't dress him on opening night during which there were pre-game ceremonies honouring Maurice.

These arguments and outbursts, though, reflected Henri's incredible tenacity and competitive spirit. Throughout his career he was worried about losing his job on the team, even though he was a star the team couldn't do without. Of course, the team retired his number 16, and Henri made it to the Hockey Hall of Fame, two honours bestowed upon Maurice and only a select few in hockey history. Henri can be proud of a career that is second to none. His character, his conduct and professionalism, and his extraordinary level and frequency of success ensure that he will forever be remembered as one of the greats, famous brother or not.

Near the end of a great career, the white-haired Richard was the captain and leader of the Habs, still winning the Cup with enviable regularity.

Lorne "Gump" Worsley

Goalie 1963-64 to 1969-70

He may have been christened "Lorne" but from a very young age anyone who knew him called him "Gump" or "The Gumper."

In the heat of action, the sprawling Worsley twists his body to keep the puck out of the net.

It is almost impossible to conceive, but after winning the Calder Trophy as the NHL's top rookie in 1952-53 with the New York Rangers, Gump Worsley was back in the minors. He is the only player ever to win the Calder and not play a single game the following year.

That post-Calder 1953-54 season saw Worsley play for the Vancouver Canucks of the WHL. He won a league-best 39 games and was named the WHL's most valuable player. It was clear he was too good not to be in the NHL, so coach Muzz Patrick made sure to bring back Worsley for the following season. The Gumper was back in 1954-55 and was the team's star goalie for the next nine seasons, but the team made the playoffs only four times (through no fault of the goalie). Indeed, his brilliance was what led the Canadiens to acquire him from the Blueshirts in a deal that saw Jacques Plante go to Broadway, a stunning deal which, in essence, suggested that Plante was finished and Worsley the preferred goalie for Montreal.

Lorne "Gump" Worsley
Goalie 1963-64 to 1969-70

No one could have been happier than Worsley, who was coming home, but it was not a smooth transition. He played much of the next two seasons (1963-65) in the minors with the Quebec Aces in the AHL—in part because of injuries—but he wound up being a vital

NO ONE HATED PLANES MORE

Gump Worsley came to hate flying honestly. Back in 1949 when he was playing with the New York Rovers, the plane he was on ran into serious difficulties when one of the wings caught fire and they had to make an emergency landing. Ever after, he hated flying, but in the days of the Original Six and the minor pro leagues, trains were the usual method of travel, so he was safe for much of his career. Later, when he was with the Canadiens, another plane hit a large air pocket and the pilot had to turn off the engines for several seconds. The plane dropped swiftly and Worsley was in agony even though the plane continued its course safely. On November 26, 1968, he arrived in Chicago after another horrible incident in the air, took a train back to Montreal, and retired. Two weeks later, he was back playing, but early the next year he left the Canadiens for good, sick of plane travel which, in the post-expansion years after 1967, was standard. He later played for Minnesota, but his fear of flying never abated. Ironically, one of his sons became a pilot in the Canadian Air Force.

ingredient in the team's dynasty of the late-1960s which saw the team win four Stanley Cups in five years. The first came in 1965 when Worsley played eight of the team's 13 playoff games, splitting the duties with veteran Charlie Hodge.

The next year, 1965-66, Worsley was clearly the number-one goalie, playing 51 regular-season games and every minute of the playoffs. He and Hodge shared the Vézina Trophy for their combined record of fewest goals allowed. The next year, the Gumper suffered two injuries that kept him out of the lineup for much of the regular season and all but two games of the playoffs. During that time, Hodge and youngster Rogie Vachon claimed the lion's share of the work, but after the team lost to Toronto in the finals, Worsley was back playing an even greater role the year after.

In fact, the 1968 playoffs might well have been the highlight of Worsley's career. He played only 40 regular season games but led the league with a 1.98 goals-against average, sharing the Vézina Trophy with Vachon,

Incredibly, Worlsey wore a mask for only the final six games of a career that lasted two decades.

148

Not a big man, Worsley had to stretch to make many a glove grab that a taller goalie would have made look more routine.

CANADIENS NUMBERS
LORNE "Gump" WORSLEY

b. Montreal, Quebec, May 14, 1929   d. Montreal, Quebec, January 26, 2007
5'7"   180 lbs.   goalie   catches left

| | REGULAR SEASON | | | | | | PLAYOFFS | | | | | |
	GP	W-L-T	Mins	GA	SO	GAA	GP	W-L	Mins	GA	SO	GAA
1963-64	8	3-2-2	444	22	1	2.97	—	—	—	—	—	—
1964-65 🏆	19	10-7-1	1,020	50	1	2.94	8	5-3	501	14	2	1.68
1965-66 🏆	51	29-14-6	2,899	114	2	2.36	10	8-2	602	20	1	1.99
1966-67	18	9-6-2	888	47	1	3.18	2	0-1	80	2	0	1.50
1967-68 🏆	40	19-9-8	2,213	73	6	1.98	12	11-0	672	21	1	1.88
1968-69 🏆	30	19-5-4	1,703	64	5	2.25	7	5-1	370	14	0	2.27
1969-70	6	3-1-2	360	14	0	2.33	—	—	—	—	—	—
TOTALS	172	92-44-25	9,527	384	16	2.42	39	29-7	2,225	71	4	1.91

Lorne "Gump" Worsley

but in the playoffs the Gumper was sensational. He played in 12 of the Habs' 13 games and was a perfect 11-0, bringing the team its third Cup in four years.

The next year, he played a lesser but still significant role, sharing the duties with Vachon and newcomer Tony Esposito. The team won the Cup again, but early the next year Worsley's nerves from plane travel were shot and he retired. He came out of retirement late in the season to play for Minnesota and stuck around until 1974 with the North Stars. Amazingly, he played 861 NHL regular season games and 70 more in the playoffs, but it was only the last six games of his career, at age 44, that he wore a mask. Indeed, he was the last maskless goalie in the NHL.

Worlsey's career suffered after expansion in 1967. More teams in the league meant a switch from train to plane travel, a method that terrified the otherwise fearless goalie.

Worsley beats Chicago's Phil Esposito to the puck and hustles back to his cage before "Espo" can create a good scoring chance.

A classic Worsley save saw the goalie bobble a hard shot before smacking the puck mid-air to the corner, his calm and hand-eye coordination put to good use.

Frank Mahovlich

Left Wing 1970-71 to 1973-74

The "Big M" may have played only four years with the Habs, but in that time, he won the Stanley Cup twice.

Teamed with Jean Béliveau and Yvan Cournoyer, Mahovlich had some of his finest years with the Canadiens, averaging more than a point a game.

It may have been Sam Pollock's best straight-up trade during his illustrious career as Canadiens GM. On January 13, 1971, he acquired Frank Mahovlich from Detroit for Mickey Redmond, Guy Charron, and Bill Collins. Although Redmond went on to have two 50-goal seasons with the Red Wings, his career was cut very short by a serious back injury. Charron had little effect on the Wings and wound up moving on to lowly Kansas City and then Washington. Collins became an even more itinerant player. Mahovlich played only three and a half seasons with the Canadiens, but he was vital in the team winning the Stanley Cup in 1971 and 1973.

After his arrival in Montreal, Mahovlich was put on a line with Jean Béliveau and Yvan Cournoyer. Coach Al MacNeil knew more than a little of the Big M. MacNeil had played for the Marlies in Toronto at the same time Mahovlich played for St. Mike's, likely the greatest junior rivalry in hockey at the time. Mahovlich came to Montreal in excellent spirits. He had had a good three and a half years in Detroit and was coming to a Canadiens team that included his younger brother, Peter, also dubbed Little M (although, ironically, he was quite a bit taller and heavier).

Mahovlich's impact was felt immediately. He gelled beautifully with the

CANADIENS NUMBERS
FRANK MAHOVLICH ("The Big M")

b. Timmins, Ontario, January 10, 1938
6'   205 lbs.   left wing   shoots left

	REGULAR SEASON					PLAYOFFS				
	GP	G	A	Pts	Pim	GP	G	A	Pts	Pim
1970-71 🏆	38	17	24	41	11	20	14	13	27	18
1971-72	76	43	53	96	36	6	3	2	5	2
1972-73 🏆	78	38	55	93	51	17	9	14	23	6
1973-74	71	31	49	80	47	6	1	2	3	0
TOTALS	263	129	181	310	145	49	27	31	58	26

Mahovlich is checked by a member of his old team, Norm Ullman of the Leafs, in a game at the Forum.

Frank Mahovlich

Left Wing 1970-71 to 1973-74

After playing the majority of his career with the Leafs and Red Wings, Mahovlich made his presence felt immediately with the Canadiens.

two great linemates Béliveau and Cournoyer, and in the 1971 playoffs he almost surely would have been named Conn Smythe Trophy winner except for the exceptional play of rookie goalie Ken Dryden. In the quarter-finals, for instance, the team's remarkable upset of Boston in seven games, Mahovlich scored the first and third goals in the team's 3-1 come-from-behind win in game three. In the deciding game seven, he had two goals and an assist in the 4-2 elimination win to set up a semi-finals date with Minnesota. The Habs won that series in six games,

advancing to the finals to play Chicago.

After the Habs fell behind 2-0 in games and 2-0 after the first period of game three, Mahovlich tied the game late in the second period and scored the insurance marker later in the third of a crucial 4-2 win. In game six, he scored once and added an assist on his brother's goal in the third period to cap a rally and give the Habs a 4-3 win to tie the series at three games each. In all, Mahovlich led the playoffs with 14 goals and 27 points, and the Habs skated off with a 3-2 win in game seven to win the Stanley Cup.

The next season, the Big M picked up where he left off. He had 43 goals and 96 points during the regular season playing on a line with Cournoyer and Guy Lafleur (Béliveau had retired in the summer), the top-scoring line on the team and one of the highest scoring threesomes in the league (Mahovlich finished sixth in overall scoring and Cournoyer eighth). The team was eliminated in the first round of the playoffs, losing to the Rangers in six games, but the year after they were back in the finals.

Again Mahovlich had a great regular season, scoring 38 times and adding a career-high 55 assists for 93 points, and toward the end of the season he scored his 500th career goal, only the fifth player in league history to do so. In the playoffs, he had 23 points in 17 games, and the Habs won their second Cup in three years. After one more excellent season, Mahovlich left the team and signed with the Toronto Toros of the World Hockey Association.

His departure came as no surprise to general manager Sam Pollock. Mahovlich had wanted a long-term contract, but he was 36 years old and that seemed too much for Pollock. As well, the GM was as frustrated as his colleague in Toronto had been years earlier. Punch Imlach always believed Mahovlich was capable of doing so much more than what he did.

The frustration with Mahovlich lay in his style of play. He was a big and powerful left winger, yet he didn't use his size with any physical edge. He was a brilliant skater who seemed to float effortlessly above the ice, but fans and critics thought that "floating" was more lack of effort than balletic grace. He made everything look so easy, people often wondered what he could have done had he put full effort into his game, yet Mahovlich maintained this was how he looked when he did go all out. Misunderstood to the end, it is impossible nonetheless to argue with his extraordinary success.

Between Toronto and Montreal, he won six Stanley Cups, and including his Detroit years he scored 533 total goals and 1,103 points in 1,181 games. He played in 15 consecutive All-Star Games and made the First or Second All-Star team nine times, but after winning the Calder Trophy with the Leafs in 1957-58, he never won another individual trophy. His stay in Montreal might have been comparatively brief, but his contributions were substantial nonetheless and his statistical record with Peter make the Mahovlich brothers one of the finest brother acts in Canadiens history.

NUMBER 500

Frank Mahovlich scored the 500th goal of his career on March 21, 1973, breaking a 2-2 tie and sending the Canadiens on their way to a 3-2 win over Vancouver in a late-season game at the Forum. He became the fifth player to reach the milestone (after Maurice Richard, Gordie Howe, Bobby Hull, and Jean Béliveau), and he did it in his 1,105th game. It was not much of a shot from close range, but it fooled goalie Dunc Wilson and that's all that mattered. The milestone was honoured by the Canadiens near the start of the next season, on November 28, 1973. The team eked out a 5-3 win over Los Angeles that night, a win given a helping hand by brother Peter's two goals and assist. The pre-game ceremonies included a tribute to Frank as his wife, Marie, and three children (Nancy, Ted, and Michael) joined him on the red carpet at centre ice. It was a year and a half later that the next member of the 500-goal club joined when Phil Esposito of Boston achieved the milestone. Mahovlich finished with 533 NHL goals to his credit after this 1973-74 season, although he played four more years in the WHA.

Yvan Cournoyer
Right Wing 1963-64 to 1978-79

If the Montreal Canadiens ever wanted to show a young player how to develop into an NHL star, they need only show a video of the career of Yvan Cournoyer. He was small—too small, critics said—and stocky, but those thick legs of his gave him more speed than just about any player in the NHL. His blazing speed earned him the nickname "Roadrunner." He had a great shot, one of the best in the league, and for this he can thank his dad. Cournoyer, Sr., worked in a machine shop, and Yvan asked him to make a puck made of steel so Yvan could practice his shot. The puck weighed more than three

pounds, and Yvan would practice in the family basement every day. When he got onto ice and played hockey, the real puck felt like a feather for Cournoyer.

Cournoyer liked skating, and he also liked scoring goals. Early in his career, this was both a blessing and a curse. It was a blessing because, of course, natural goal scorers are often difficult to come by. It was a curse because in the early 1960s, when Cournoyer was trying to make it to the NHL, Canadiens coach Toe Blake made no secret of the fact he liked players who backchecked and played solid defence. Cournoyer, by his own admission, was weak in these areas of the game.

Cournoyer began his career slowly, a scorer who played most of the time on the power play. He later became a consistent 30-goal scorer for the Canadiens.

This is one of goalie Ken Dryden's favourite photos. Dryden calmly watches Cournoyer rush up ice, no fear that his teammate could be checked off the puck.

Yvan Cournoyer
Right Wing 1963-64 to 1978-79

The truth was, as Scotty Bowman discovered when he took over for Blake, that as long as Cournoyer was scoring goals, the other team didn't have the puck, thus rendering the backchecking obligations obsolete. Nevertheless, Blake brought Cournoyer along slowly in the early days, and there were both frustrations and rewards for the player.

Despite his clear talents, Cournoyer stayed in junior hockey for three full seasons, 1961-64. In the last of those years he was given an amateur tryout by the team, meaning that he could play five games for the Habs before being returned to the Jr. Canadiens of the OHA. Cournoyer scored in his first game and went back after having scored four times in five games. The next year, he was on the NHL team for good.

THE FIVE-GOAL NIGHT

On February 15, 1975, Yvan Cournoyer joined an elite group of players when he scored five goals in one game in a 12-3 win over Chicago. Mike Veisor was the goalie as Tony Esposito had the night off, but Cournoyer said later he felt particularly good before the game. The previous night, he played tennis, and then the morning of the game he went cross-country skiing. By the time he got to the Forum, he felt energized and ready to go. Although he didn't score in the first period, he got one goal in the middle of the second to give the Habs a solid 4-0 lead. He got his second goal near the end of the period and made it a hat trick in the first minute of the third. He got the fourth midway through the third and the fifth with a few minutes to play. He was the first Canadiens player to score five in a game since Bobby Rousseau in 1964, and before that Bernie Geoffrion scored five in 1955 and Maurice Richard in 1944. Cournoyer's biggest thrill that night, however, came late in the game when coach Scotty Bowman put him out to help kill off a 5-on-3 power play for the Black Hawks, a situation Cournoyer rarely found himself in!

Captain Cournoyer takes a turn around the ice with the Stanley Cup, one of ten he won in just 14 full seasons with the team.

Even still, Blake played him sporadically, using him primarily on the power play because defensive play wasn't as important when playing with the extra man. Cournoyer responded in two ways. First, he scored regularly with the little ice time he got. And second, he didn't complain. Instead, he learned. In 1966-67, for instance, his third full season, he had 25 goals on the year, 19 of which came on the power play. This led the

NHL (Bobby Hull had 18). In 1965-66, he had scored 18 goals, and 16 of them came with the man advantage.

By the time Blake retired in 1968, Cournoyer was ready for full-time duty, and the right winger blossomed into one of the top goal scorers of his era. He was called the

A right winger who shot left-handed, "the Roadrunner" barrels in on his backhand while leaving three opponents in his wake.

Yvan Cournoyer
Right Wing 1963-64 to 1978-79

new Maurice Richard, in part because of the scoring, in part because, like the Rocket, he was a right winger who was a left-handed shot. This meant he always had an advantageous angle when coming in on the goalie.

The comparison was also apt because Cournoyer was a changed man once he got the puck inside the blueline. While he was a good player all over the ice, he was a sensational player in the opposing end, and his eyes were like saucers when he could see a chance to go to the net with the puck. As important, though, all that steel-puck practice had stood him in good stead. Cournoyer had one of the hardest shots in the league, and combined with his blistering speed he simply could not be held in check for a full 60 minutes.

Cournoyer was blessed in another way. His centreman for the first seven years of his career was none other than Jean Béliveau. "Le Gros Bill" was a lefty as well and found it easiest to pass to the right side, and Cournoyer teamed well with him. Claude Ruel, who succeeded Blake as coach, used Cournoyer more, as did Al MacNeil, the next coach.

Of course, these years saw the team perform with tremendous success, and Cournoyer's development was only one story on a team that won four Stanley Cups in the 1960s. While Cournoyer played a lesser role in the first two wins (1965 and 1966), he was a key contributor to wins over St. Louis in 1968 and 1969. The latter ended a season in which he scored 43 times and finished sixth in the scoring race.

It was the 1970s, however, which defined Cournoyer's greatness and which form the balance of his legacy. He had five seasons of 30 goals and 70 points or more, and

he won six more Stanley Cups. He was never more impressive than the 1973 playoffs. First, his 15 goals broke the old NHL record of 14 held by Frank Mahovlich. Second, he proved uncheckable against Chicago in the six-game finals, as Hawks' coach Billy Reay grew evermore frustrated by his players' inability to rein in the Roadrunner. As a result, Cournoyer became the first winger to be named Conn Smythe Trophy winner (a trophy established in 1965).

One of his greatest honours came in 1975 after Henri Richard retired.

CANADIENS NUMBERS
YVAN COURNOYER ("The Roadrunner")

b. Drummondville, Quebec, November 22, 1943
5'7"   178 lbs.   right wing   shoots left

	REGULAR SEASON					PLAYOFFS				
	GP	G	A	Pts	Pim	GP	G	A	Pts	Pim
1963-64	5	4	0	4	0	—	—	—	—	—
1964-65	55	7	10	17	10	12	3	1	4	0
1965-66	65	18	11	29	8	10	2	3	5	2
1966-67	69	25	15	40	14	10	2	3	5	6
1967-68	64	28	32	60	23	13	6	8	14	4
1968-69	76	43	44	87	31	14	4	7	11	5
1969-70	72	27	36	63	23	—	—	—	—	—
1970-71	65	37	36	73	21	20	10	12	22	6
1971-72	73	47	36	83	15	6	2	1	3	2
1972-73	67	40	39	79	18	17	15	10	25	2
1973-74	67	40	33	73	18	6	5	2	7	2
1974-75	76	29	45	74	32	11	5	6	11	4
1975-76	71	32	36	68	20	13	3	6	9	4
1976-77	60	25	28	53	8	—	—	—	—	—
1977-78	68	24	29	53	12	15	7	4	11	10
1978-79	15	2	5	7	2	—	—	—	—	—
TOTALS	968	428	435	863	255	147	64	63	127	47

Cournoyer had nine straight seasons of at least 60 points (1967-76) and captained the Canadiens for the last four years of his career.

November 12, 2005, saw the final honour of Cournoyer's career when the team raised his number 12 to the rafters of the Bell Centre.

The players got together at training camp that fall and voted Cournoyer the new team captain, a moment he cherished from that day forward.

The great dynasty of the late-1970s ended for Cournoyer prematurely. Early in the 1978-79 season, he underwent back surgery which, ultimately, finished his career. He had been playing in excruciating pain for weeks, but it wasn't until he was no longer able to actually walk that he told doctors of his pain. The surgery was successful, but he was told returning to the ice could endanger his post-career health. Cournoyer wisely retired.

In all, he finished with ten Stanley Cup victories, more than any other player in the game's history with one exception—longtime teammate Henri Richard. Because he stopped playing at age 36 when he conceivably had a few good years left, he didn't reach the 1,000-game mark or 500-goal mark, plateaus he surely would have made with better health. Nevertheless, his achievements are among the greatest in the game's history, and his gentlemanly conduct on ice ensures a legacy that will never be tarnished and forever be remembered. His number 12 was retired by the club on November 12, 2005, the final honour for Cournoyer. The Roadrunner was, quite simply, one of the best.

Ken Dryden

Goalie 1970-71 to 1978-79

The classic "Thinker" pose during stoppages in play saw Dryden rest his chin on his glove supported by the butt end of his stick, the tip of which was planted in the ice for balance.

Today, the NHL Entry Draft is a huge deal. It is a two-day fair that travels to a different NHL city every year, drawing thousands of fans and hundreds of hopeful hockey players. Being drafted is the most common way for a young player to get to the NHL. In the infancy of the draft, called the Amateur Draft, in the early 1960s, the selection of players took place in a room at the NHL's offices in Montreal. Only players not already on a team's negotiation list were available, and since most of the best players had been signed to a C-form contract on their 16th birthdays, the pickings were, to say the least, slim.

At the 1964 Amateur Draft, Boston used the 14th overall selection to choose goalie Ken Dryden, a Junior B goalie living in Toronto. In what seemed like a meaningless deal, the Bruins traded Dryden later that day along with Alex Campbell to Montreal for Guy Allen and Paul Reid. Three of these players never made the NHL. The fourth made it to the Hockey Hall of Fame.

As a kid, Dryden dreamed of the NHL, but he was not alone. His brother, Dave, older by six years, also wanted to play in the big league, but these two were a different pair of brothers. Whereas most brothers want to be skaters, or one wants to be a skater and the other a goalie, both Dryden brothers wanted to be goalies. This was difficult because one couldn't shoot on the other for practice. They both had to find places to play. Dave led by example, though, and he made the NHL even before Ken was drafted.

Ken, meanwhile, also had academic aspirations, and in 1965 he left Ontario to attend Cornell University. He stayed there for four years, earning a B.A. in history, but he also played on the university's hockey team. Dryden was nothing short of spectacular, and by 1969 he was ready for a career in the NHL. Or was he? The Canadiens offered him a substantial contract, but Canada's National Team made him a better offer. Dryden signed a three-year deal with the National Team with the condition that he could enter law school at McGill University in Montreal. Deal. He made his debut for Canada at the 1969 World

SUMMIT SERIES EMOTIONS

Montreal's Ken Dryden and Chicago's Tony Esposito played four games each in the eight-game 1972 Summit Series. Dryden started and ended the series, and these games represented the alpha and omega of emotions, the very lowest and highest points a player can experience. Game one in Montreal on September 2, 1972, featured Canada's NHL players, whom everyone at the Forum knew very well, against a group of Soviets about whom virtually nothing was known. When Phil Esposito scored 30 seconds after the opening faceoff, the huge crowd felt what Team Canada's players felt—this was going to be a walk in the park. Two and a half hours later, the Canadians were wheezing, embarrassed, as the final horn went to complete a 7-3 loss. They left the ice without shaking hands. Dryden perhaps had never allowed seven goals in 60 minutes of hockey in any game at any level. Some 26 days later, Canada and the Soviets had each won three games and tied one. Game eight, at Luzhniki Arena in Moscow on September 28, 1972, remains the most important hockey game ever played. Paul Henderson was the last-minute hero, and after he scored the entire team poured off the bench in celebration. Dryden skated the full length of the ice to join in the hugs. He later said the feeling after game one was the worst of his life, and, of course, the elation after winning game eight of the Summit Series was, simply, unmatchable.

Ken Dryden
Goalie 1970-71 to 1978-79

Championship, earning a shutout in his first game, a 1-0 win over USA. He played all of 1969-70 with the National Team, and then the Canadiens stepped in with a new offer. They allowed him to stay in law school and play only home games with their AHL team, the Nova Scotia Voyageurs. Deal.

Again, Dryden was superb. He was called up by Montreal for the final six games of the 1970-71 season, and he won all six. In the playoffs, he appeared in every game for the Habs, but his greatest achievements came in the first round against the previous year's champions from Boston. The team featured Bobby Orr and Phil Esposito, but Dryden was almost unbeatable and the Bruins lost in seven games, one of the playoffs' greatest upsets of the modern era. Dryden continued his heroics against Minnesota and Chicago, taking the Canadiens to the

Cup with only six NHL games to his credit. He became the first player to win the Conn Smythe Trophy before winning the Calder Trophy, which he did the following year.

The Bruins were so frustrated by Dryden's style that Esposito called him an octopus. Indeed, Dryden stood 6'4" and moved his arms and legs with maniacal precision, snaring pucks destined for the corner or kicking out sure goals while on his side. He became famous for resting his chin on the butt-end of his stick during stoppages, the pose a veritable hockey version of Rodin's "Thinker." Most important, Dryden was 24 years old and destined for greatness.

The two lives of hockey player and lawyer, though, continually pulled at Dryden. After leading the Canadiens to the Cup, Dryden went to the U.S. and worked that summer for Nader's Raiders, a group run by Ralph Nader and intended to defeat false advertising and eradicate sales of inferior retail products. That fall, he returned to the Montreal net and picked

Dryden played only eight years in the NHL, winning the Stanley Cup six times and posting an amazing 80-32 record in the playoffs.

CANADIENS NUMBERS KEN DRYDEN

b. Hamilton, Ontario, August 8, 1947
6'4"   205 lbs.   goalie   catches left

		REGULAR SEASON					PLAYOFFS					
	GP	W-L-T	Mins	GA	SO	GAA	GP	W-L	Mins	GA	SO	GAA
1970-71 🏆	6	6-0-0	327	9	0	1.65	20	12-8	1,221	61	0	3.00
1971-72	64	39-8-15	3,800	142	8	2.24	6	2-4	360	17	0	2.83
1972-73 🏆	54	33-7-13	3,165	119	6	2.26	17	12-5	1,039	50	1	2.89
1973-74	—	—	—	—	—	—	—	—	—	—	—	—
1974-75	56	30-9-16	3,320	149	4	2.69	11	6-5	688	29	2	2.53
1975-76 🏆	62	42-10-8	3,580	121	8	2.03	13	12-1	780	25	1	1.92
1976-77 🏆	56	41-6-8	3,275	117	10	2.14	14	12-2	849	22	4	1.55
1977-78 🏆	52	37-7-7	3,071	105	5	2.05	15	12-3	919	29	2	1.89
1978-79 🏆	47	30-10-7	2,814	108	5	2.30	16	12-4	990	41	0	2.48
TOTALS	397	258-57-74	23,352	870	46	2.24	112	80-32	6,846	274	10	2.40

up where he left off. In his first full season, Dryden played a league-high 64 games, winning a league-best 39 times and establishing himself, after just 70 NHL games in total, as the best in the league. He won the Calder Trophy for the great inaugural season.

In the fall of 1972, Dryden was named to Team Canada for the Summit Series, and after that emotional and exhilarating win he returned to Montreal and put in another brilliant performance. He again led the league in wins (33) as well as shutouts (6) and GAA (2.26) for which he won his first of six Vézina Trophies. Yet just as he was becoming the greatest goalie in the game, he ran afoul with the team and left. Dryden had played the first year of a two-year contract and wanted a new deal, but the Habs balked. Dryden left the team for the entire season, deciding to focus on law. He articled in Toronto with the firm of Osler, Hoskins, and Harcourt, but both he and the Canadiens were unhappy and their reconciliation was swift. Dryden had been making $80,000 a season in 1972-73, but in the summer of 1974 he signed a three-year deal worth $600,000 in total.

Although the team lost in the semi-finals that first year, Dryden helped the Canadiens win the next four Stanley Cups thereafter. He never won the Conn Smythe Trophy again after 1971, but he won or shared (with backup Bunny Larocque) the Vézina Trophy five times.

Ever the intellectually restless soul, Dryden retired at the end of this dynastic run, in the spring of 1979. He was only 31 years old and had won six Cups in eight seasons, but he was eager to live a life outside the arena even though hockey was, in one way or another, a significant part of his life for many years after. His off-ice exploits included the writing of a book called *The Game*, a bestseller that describes the lives of players from the Canadiens during their glory years. Dryden's insights combined athletic superiority with descriptive awareness, providing a rich characterization of the game and its essence.

A young Dryden cradles the trophy which is the most difficult in hockey to win, yet which he did even before playing a full rookie-season.

Ken Dryden
Goalie 1970-71 to 1978-79

Dryden was the league's first truly tall goalie, here making a save on one knee with his head still the height of the crossbar.

Dryden's famous red, white, and blue mask became an important part of his in-crease persona.

Dryden later became president of the Toronto Maple Leafs and then moved into politics where he successfully ran for office in the early years of the 21st century. His number 29 was retired by the Canadiens on January 29, 2007, the once awkward goalie number now worn by a new generation of puckstoppers the world over. Dryden may have had interests other than hockey, and his career may have been too short for fans' liking, but what he gave to the game was a gift few players before or since have been able to give—a hero, a belief that the incredible can happen, and a cause to celebrate, well, the game.

Goalie brothers are rare, indeed, but before Ken made it to the NHL his sibling Dave had made it first, albeit without the same fanfare and Stanley Cup success.

166

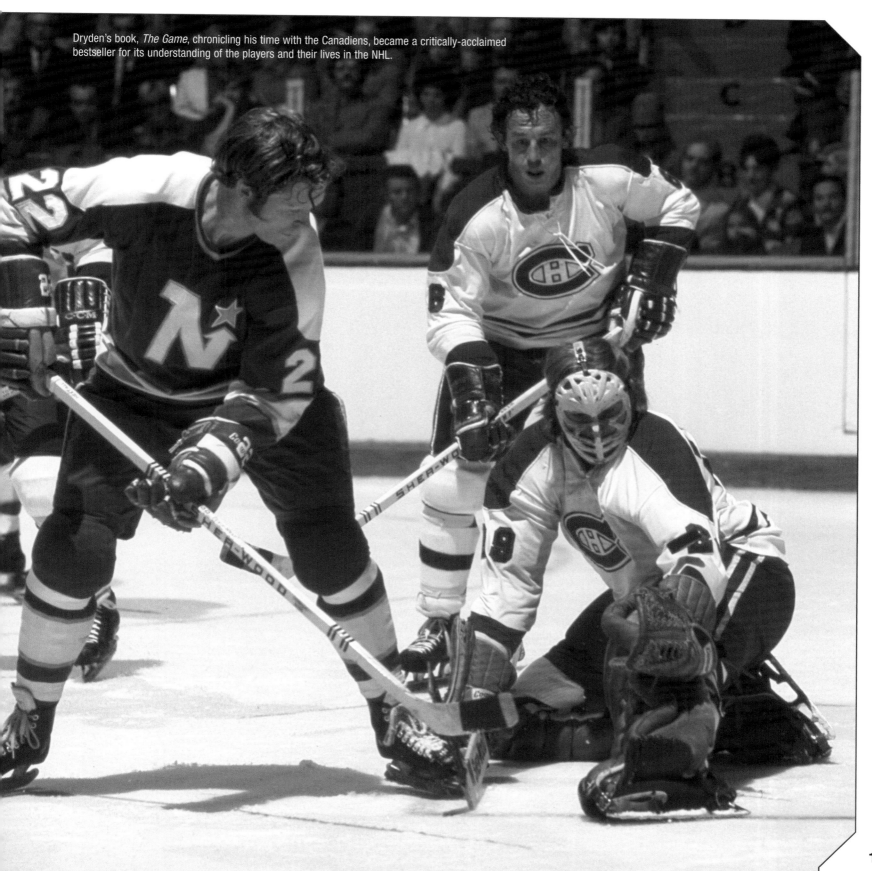

Dryden's book, *The Game*, chronicling his time with the Canadiens, became a critically-acclaimed bestseller for its understanding of the players and their lives in the NHL.

Jacques Lemaire
Centre 1967-68 to1978-79

Not the biggest man in the league, Jacques Lemaire played with an intensity rooted in the great Montreal teams of the 1950s, skilled and fearless in equal measure.

He got the nickname "Coco" while playing junior hockey, but he never knew how the name came about. Perhaps it was apt, however, because Jacques Lemaire never anticipated anything during his hockey career. He went with his instincts, reacted, and trusted himself, and in this way he won eight Stanley Cups and led a varied and happy hockey life that continues to this day.

Lemaire grew up in a hockey household. He had four brothers—Roger, Yvon, Daniel, and Rejean—who all played the game, so he was able to practice and play all the time. Lemaire used to fire a steel puck against his garage door as a way to improve his shot. Incredibly, this was exactly how Yvan Cournoyer developed his great shot as a kid, though nether knew of the other's practice habits. Lemaire's puck came from a friend who had a steel shop, and Cournoyer's came from his father's shop in another town (Lachine).

Either way, Lemaire became well known with the Montreal Jr. Canadiens as a goalscorer and a prospect with a great shot and quick release. After three years in the OHA (1963-66), he was sent to the team's CHL affiliate in Houston and from there it was on to the NHL in 1967. When he joined the Habs he had played most of his career at centre, but the team was deep at that position so coach Toe Blake put him on left wing. However, Henri Richard was injured for several games that season and Lemaire was moved to the middle. He was nothing short of sensational.

By the end of his rookie season, Lemaire, playing on a line with Dick Duff and Bobby Rousseau, had scored 22 goals, a superb number in that era and the signs of

CANADIENS NUMBERS
JACQUES LEMAIRE

b. Lasalle, Quebec, September 7, 1945
5'10"   180 lbs.   centre   shoots left

	REGULAR SEASON					PLAYOFFS				
	GP	G	A	Pts	Pim	GP	G	A	Pts	Pim
1967-68	69	22	20	42	16	13	7	6	13	6
1968-69	75	29	34	63	29	14	4	2	6	6
1969-70	69	32	28	60	16	—	—	—	—	—
1970-71	78	28	28	56	18	20	9	10	19	17
1971-72	77	32	49	81	26	6	2	1	3	2
1972-73	77	44	51	95	16	17	7	13	20	2
1973-74	66	29	38	67	10	6	0	4	4	2
1974-75	80	36	56	92	20	11	5	7	12	4
1975-76	61	20	32	52	20	13	3	3	6	2
1976-77	75	34	41	75	22	14	7	12	19	6
1977-78	76	36	61	97	14	15	6	8	14	10
1978-79	50	24	31	55	10	16	11	12	23	6
TOTALS	853	366	469	835	217	145	61	78	139	63

Lemaire was the consummate leader and team player, a standout and professional in every aspect of the game.

Jacques Lemaire

greater things to come. He lost the Calder Trophy to Derek Sanderson, but Lemaire won something Sanderson didn't that year—the Stanley Cup. And Lemaire wasn't just a part of that team; he was integral to the win. The Habs eliminated Boston in four straight games in the quarter-finals and played Chicago in the semi-finals. With the Habs up 3-1 in games, game five went to overtime tied at 3-3. It was Lemaire who netted the winner at 2:14 of the fourth period to win the series for Montreal. The team went on to play St. Louis in the finals, and in game one Lemaire again scored the OT winner in a 3-2 Montreal win.

That first year saw Lemaire accrue all of 16 penalty minutes, and that was as revealing a stat as his goals. He had it instilled in him by both parents that clean playing was a prerogative to successful playing, both for scoring and for being a role model to kids following the team. He lived by that rule from his first game to his last.

Playing behind Henri Richard and Jean Béliveau at centre was advantageous to Lemaire for several reasons. First, he never got the lion's share of attention, so there was never as much pressure on him to reach various statistical milestones. Second, of course, he got to learn from the best and in time he became the leader to the next generation of players. Also, because of the team's depth, Lemaire was able to develop at a slower pace,

Lemaire won the Stanley Cup eight times in 12 years, missing the playoffs only once in his glorious career.

Lemaire was inducted into the Hockey Hall of Fame in 1984 after retiring in 1979 at age 33, having accomplished virtually all there was to accomplish.

Lemaire's best year was 1972-73 when he had 44 goals and 94 points in the regular season and another 20 playoff points in 17 games.

Jacques Lemaire
Centre 1967-68 to 1978-79

so that by the time Richard and Béliveau were ready to retire, he would be ready to be the leader on ice and off. During his 12 years in the NHL, all with Montreal, Lemaire never failed to score at least 20 goals, and his rookie points total of 42 was also his lowest. He was never below 52 the rest of his career. If he was the model of consistency during the season, he was the epitome of a playoff performer come time for the Stanley Cup competition. In 145 career games, he scored 139 points, a pace of nearly one a game, a pace which few players over such a long time have matched.

More important, Lemaire has the distinction of being one of only half a dozen players to have scored two Cup-winning goals. In his case, the first was as dramatic as can happen. In the 1977 finals, the Habs played Boston for the Stanley Cup. After winning the first three games, Montreal found itself in overtime of game four with the score tied 1-1. Lemaire scored the winner at 4:32 of the extra period to win the Cup for the Canadiens. Amazingly, the goal was also his third-game winning goal of these finals and it made him only the third player after Maurice Richard and Don Raleigh to have scored more than one career overtime goal in a finals series.

In 1979, the Canadiens faced the New York Rangers in the finals. After

Lemaire is one of a select group to have scored two Stanley-Cup winning goals during his career.

Lemaire's style of fighting manifested itself in competitive spirit, not dropping the gloves. He never had more than 29 penalty minutes in any one season, but his gentlemanly conduct was not for lack of aggressive, but smart, play.

four games, Montreal was ahead 3-1, and the team won game five at home with a relatively easy 4-1 win. It was Lemaire's critical goal early in the second period which broke a 1-1 tie and proved to be the Cup winner, giving the Habs their fourth straight Cup and the eighth of Lemaire's remarkable career.

At this point in his life, Lemaire had everything. He was on the best team in the game, at the height of his playing abilities, being very well paid. Yet, at just 33 years of age, he walked away from the NHL and the Canadiens to play in Switzerland. He had grown tired of the game's demands on him and his family and, having accomplished everything on could dream for, he had nothing left to play for.

Lemaire accepted a three-year offer from Sierre, a small club team in Switzerland, to play and coach there, allowing him to enjoy a different culture, learn about coaching at an introductory level, and ease his transition from player to coach. No amount of cajoling or discussion could change his mind, and just like that Coco went from the NHL to Europe, from playing to coaching, from one kind of privileged pleasure to another.

COACH JACQUES

He couldn't have known this in 1979 when he retired from the NHL, but Jacques Lemaire embarked on a career in coaching that has taken him from that day to this. He coached and played in Sierre, Switzerland for two seasons and later coached the Canadiens for a season and a half. After a lengthy break during which time he served as assistant general manager for the Habs, Lemaire returned to coaching in New Jersey, where he spent five seasons. In 1994-95, he became one of a select group to win the Stanley Cup as both player and coach, taking the Devils to the Cup during the lockout-shortened season. Since 2000, he has been the coach of the Minnesota Wild, the team's only coach, in fact, since the new team started playing. In 2007-08, Lemaire coached his 1,000th NHL regular season game, joining another exclusive group to reach that milestone.

Bert Olmstead

Left Wing 1950-51 to 1957-58

In addition to being a star on ice, Olmstead was a popular teammate in the dressing room and an important part of the team's exceptional chemistry.

Although Olmstead began his career in Chicago and continued it in Detroit, he was traded to the Canadiens where he won four Stanley Cups in the 1950s.

CANADIENS NUMBERS
BERT OLMSTEAD

b. Sceptre, Saskatchewan, September 4, 1926
6'1"   180 lbs.   left wing   shoots left

	REGULAR SEASON					PLAYOFFS				
	GP	G	A	Pts	Pim	GP	G	A	Pts	Pim
1950-51	39	16	22	38	50	11	2	4	6	9
1951-52	69	7	28	35	49	11	0	1	1	4
1952-53 🏆	69	17	28	45	83	12	2	2	4	4
1953-54	70	15	37	52	85	11	0	1	1	19
1954-55	70	10	48	58	103	12	0	4	4	21
1955-56 🏆	70	14	56	70	94	10	4	10	14	8
1956-57 🏆	64	15	33	48	74	10	0	9	9	13
1957-58 🏆	57	9	28	37	71	9	0	3	3	0
TOTALS	508	103	280	383	609	86	8	34	42	78

Although he wouldn't be confused with Maurice Richard or Jean Béliveau, Olmstead played with the same character, a combination of ferocity and leadership that defined the meaning of wearing the CH sweater.

INDUCTED 1985

Bert Olmstead demanded a lot of his teammates, but they could never complain because he demanded even more from himself. He was never a team captain, but he was a leader wherever he played and a winner as well. Nobody played with greater determination or overcame a lack of pure talent and skill the way Olmstead did, and by the time he retired he had his name on the Stanley Cup five times. Only a handful of the thousands of NHLers who have played the game can boast as much.

He began his career playing junior hockey in Moose Jaw, Saskatchewan, and wound up in the Chicago system, making his NHL debut during the 1948-49 season. The next year, his first full season, Olmstead had 20 goals and

Upon arriving in Montreal, Olmstead was put on a line with Maurice Richard and Elmer Lach, and the three worked like magic together.

Bert Olmstead

Left Wing 1950-51 to 1957-58

49 points, excellent numbers for a rookie playing for a last-place team. By Christmas of the next year, though, the Hawks traded him to Detroit and the Red Wings flipped him to Montreal for Leo Gravelle, and it was with the Canadiens that he spent the next seven and a half very productive seasons.

Olmstead arrived in Montreal at a fortuitous time. Ever

since the retirement of Toe Blake several years earlier, coach Dick Irvin had been trying to find the perfect left winger for a line with Maurice Richard and Elmer Lach. Olmstead was given a tryout and passed with flying colours, and for several years in the early 1950s he was the second best left winger in the game after Ted Lindsay.

It was this trio that led Montreal to a Stanley Cup win in 1952-53 after eliminating Chicago in seven games in the semi-finals and handling

Olmstead helps out goalie Gerry McNeil as Dick Duff tries unsuccessfully to claim the loose puck.

Boston in five games in the finals. After the 1953-54 season, Lach retired but young Jean Béliveau came on board, and the Olmstead-Richard-Béliveau line became the most dominant threesome in the league. Béliveau always credited Olmstead with the success of the line. Olmstead was a hitter and passer more than a scorer, and in each of the next two seasons he led the league in assists. More important, Olmstead was the leader of the line and demanded dedication and positional play from his two superstar linemates.

Olmstead's value to the team can be understood from the most important fact of all. In eight playoff years with Montreal, the team went to the Cup finals eight times, winning four championships. He was also named as a Second Team All-Star twice while playing with the Canadiens (1952-53 and 1955-56) and he appeared in four All-Star Games as well. Olmstead was inducted into the Hockey Hall of Fame in 1985.

FINALLY, A HALL OF FAMER

Olmstead left Montreal and later Toronto with some bitterness. The Canadiens felt a knee injury had diminished his skills and the team left him unprotected in the Intra-League Draft of 1958. Toronto claimed him immediately. Olmstead had four more productive years with the Leafs, helping them win the Cup in 1962, but the Leafs then released him in much the same way. The Rangers claimed him, but Olmstead preferred retirement to a stint on Broadway. The years passed, and many of Olmstead's teammates from Montreal were quickly inducted into the Hockey Hall of Fame, from Richard to Béliveau, Dickie Moore, Bernie Geoffrion, and Doug Harvey. It wasn't until 1985, as a Veteran Player, that he was inducted, but he refused to let any bitterness spoil the moment. His speech was all about gratitude and perseverance. Yes, he was a Hall of Famer later in life than he had wanted, but he will be a Hall of Famer forever.

Toronto goalie Al Rollins can't stop the shot as Ted Kennedy marks his man, Bert Olmstead, in the slot. Olmstead was elected to the Hockey Hall of Fame in 1985.

Serge Savard

Defence 1966-67 to 1980-81

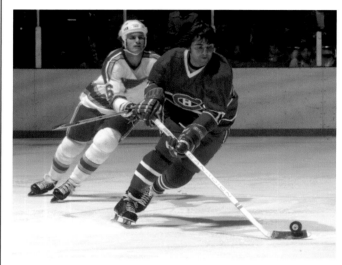

Serge Savard moves the puck out of his own end with a reliability that was his trademark.

Goalie Ken Dryden leaves the puck for Savard to play at the side of the goal. Savard, Larry Robinson, and Guy Lapointe formed the "Big Three" for the Habs in the 1970s.

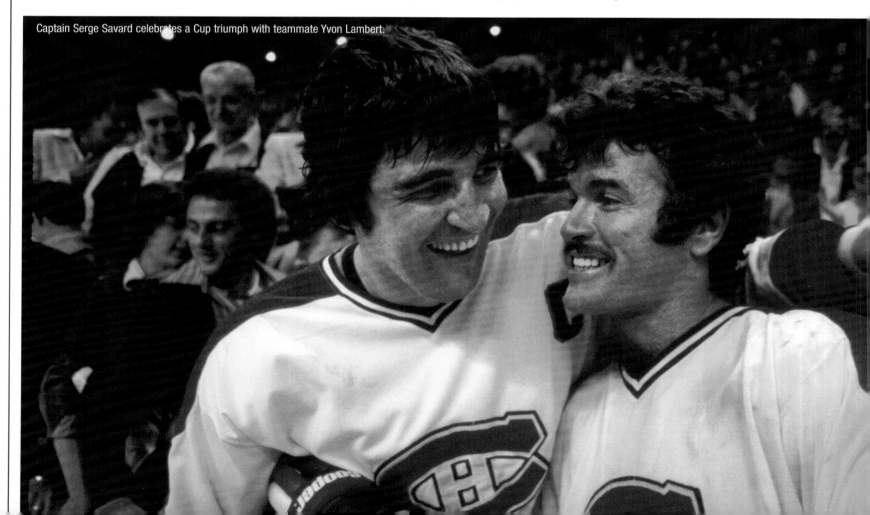

Captain Serge Savard celebrates a Cup triumph with teammate Yvon Lambert.

It was not a straight or well-paved road that took Serge Savard from childhood to the NHL. And, once he got there, he saw his career almost come to a terrible end before it had had a chance to reach its zenith.

As a boy growing up in Montreal, Savard was a forward in Montreal's Metropolitan Junior Hockey League, but his coach, Yves Nadon, a former goalie, decided to move him back to the blueline. It was a move of brilliant serendipity. Savard quickly developed a reputation as a top prospect, so in 1966, eager to continue his education and play serious hockey, he accepted an invitation to go to Winnipeg and play for

Canada's National Team, run by Father David Bauer. But before he had a chance to go, the Canadiens signed him to a pro contract. The rest, as they say, is history.

Cliff Fletcher was in charge of the team's minor hockey development program in Quebec, and when Savard's coach said the player would never amount to anything, Fletcher invoked the Montreal policy of patience. The player was sent to the Houston Apollos, the team's CHL affiliate, and it was there he took his game to another

CANADIENS NUMBERS
SERGE SAVARD ("The Senator")

b. Montreal, Quebec, January 22, 1946
6'3" 210 lbs. defence shoots left

	REGULAR SEASON					PLAYOFFS				
	GP	G	A	Pts	Pim	GP	G	A	Pts	Pim
1966-67	2	0	0	0	0	—	—	—	—	—
1967-68	67	2	13	15	34	6	2	0	2	0
1968-69	74	8	23	31	73	14	4	6	10	24
1969-70	64	12	19	31	38	—	—	—	—	—
1970-71	37	5	10	15	30	—	—	—	—	—
1971-72	23	1	8	9	16	6	0	0	0	10
1972-73	74	7	32	39	58	17	3	8	11	22
1973-74	67	4	14	18	49	6	1	1	2	4
1974-75	80	20	40	60	64	11	1	7	8	2
1975-76	71	8	39	47	38	13	3	6	9	6
1976-77	78	9	33	42	35	14	2	7	9	2
1977-78	77	8	34	42	24	15	1	7	8	8
1978-79	80	7	26	33	30	16	2	7	9	6
1979-80	46	5	8	13	18	2	0	0	0	0
1980-81	77	4	13	17	30	3	0	0	0	0
TOTALS	917	100	312	412	537	123	19	49	68	84

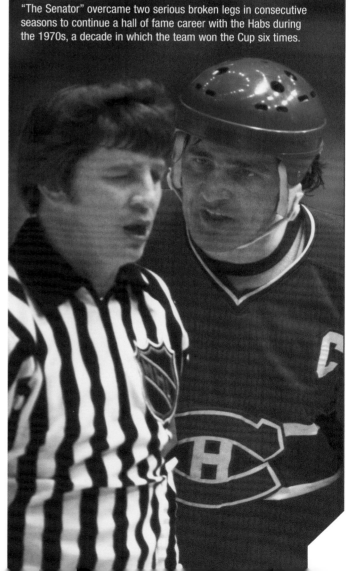

"The Senator" overcame two serious broken legs in consecutive seasons to continue a hall of fame career with the Habs during the 1970s, a decade in which the team won the Cup six times.

Serge Savard

SERGE THE GENERAL MANAGER

Although most fans of the game will remember Serge Savard as a member of the Canadiens during their 1970s dynasty and one of the "big three" on defence (with Larry Robinson and Guy Lapointe), others might not realize that it was under Savard's watch that the Canadiens won their two most surprising Stanley Cups, in 1986 and 1993. Indeed, after retiring from Montreal and being lured to Winnipeg to play for two seasons by Jets GM and former teammate John Ferguson, Savard was hired by the Habs as general manager in April 1983. Since winning the last of four Cups in a row in 1979, the team had lost GM Sam Pollock to retirement, and coach Scotty Bowman moved on to Buffalo. The team had not been playing well and was clearly in need of a shakeup, and Savard was thought to be just the man. He was replacing Irving Grundman, whose tenure was not full of Pollock-like success. Savard started under difficult circumstances and made a significant impact. Under his direction the team drafted goalie Patrick Roy in 1984, and two years later "Saint Patrick" took the Habs on a magical playoff run no one could have anticipated. Savard later called this win as gratifying as any he had won as a player. He did it again seven years later, as Roy again turned in a great performance in goal to win the team's 24th all-time Stanley Cup.

level. He won the rookie of the year honours in his only season in the CHL, earning a playoff call-up to the Quebec Aces and a two-game stint with the Canadiens in the NHL.

Any teenager has attributes and faults, and Savard was no exception. On the plus side, he was big and strong, and a fluid skater who maintained his poise. On the downside, he was weak defensively and had a poor shot, but he was able to overcome the former through experience and coaching and the latter through good old-fashioned practice and hard work.

Savard made the team full-time at training camp in 1967. It was clear he was ready for a limited role with the big club, a role that would grow and grow, and he even played the occasional shift at left wing when injuries left Toe Blake's team a little vulnerable on that side. Indeed, Savard's first two years were marked by tremendous development and improvement. In his rookie season, the team won the Stanley Cup, and the next year it not only won again but Savard himself won the Conn Smythe Trophy for his outstanding playoff performance. The award was given to him based

As many former players will confess, winning the Stanley Cup as a coach or GM is more rewarding than as a player. Savard did this twice, first in 1986 and again in 1993.

on two factors. One, he was the best penalty killer in the playoffs, and two, he contributed key offensive points.

In the semi-finals, against Boston, Savard assisted on all three goals in a 3-2 win in game one. In game two, he scored the tying goal in the dying moments of regulation and assisted on the overtime winner. In game six, he tied the game with a dramatic goal in the third period which Montreal won in overtime. In all, he had four goals and ten points in the playoffs.

The next three years were the most challenging years of Savard's life, however, and there were many times it appeared his career was over. The bad times began on March 1, 1970, as he chased after Rod Gilbert of the Rangers who was going in alone on goal. Savard made a diving try to check Gilbert, but he ended up crashing into the goalpost. In those days, the net was moored into the ice and didn't budge on impact. Savard shattered his left leg in five places. His underwent three surgeries to repair the limb which was placed in a cast for three months.

Savard persevered and returned to the game, but after just 37 games the next year he broke the same leg in a collision at centre ice. This was worse. Doctors had to take bone from his hip to help stabilize the leg and allow it to recover. He needed a year and a half to build his leg strength, and when he returned he was a different defenceman. His days of end-to-end rushes and wild play were over, and he devoted himself to strong positional play and more modest offensive contributions.

Harry Sinden named Savard to Team Canada for the 1972 Summit Series, and it seemed Savard was going to return to the game as good as ever. But in game three of the series, in Winnipeg, he cracked a bone in his right ankle. He missed game four, and doctors told him to rest and recuperate for the long NHL season still to be played. Savard refused. He joined the team in Sweden but missed the two exhibition games, missed game five, and played in the final three games, all historic victories. Indeed, Savard played in five games and was the only Canadian not to play in a loss (four wins and a tie). In the final game of the tour, a 3-3 tie

against a Czechoslovakian all-star team in Prague on October 1, 1972, Savard scored the tying goal in the last minute of the game.

He returned to Montreal and played nine more years before time caught up with him. By the time he retired, he had eight Stanley Cup wins to his credit, the most by a defenceman in NHL history. He had also played in four All-Star Games. Amazingly, he was named to an end-of-year all-star team only once, in 1978-79 when he made the second team. That season, he also won the Masterton Trophy, a truly fitting honour to recognize his amazing return from two horrific leg injuries.

Amazingly, Savard was the only player on Team Canada in the 1972 Summit Series never to play in a loss (four wins, one tie).

Jacques Laperrière
Defence 1962-63 to 1973-74

Lanky Jacques Laperrière didn't develop into an NHLer overnight, but once he had earned a place on the team, he didn't relinquish it.

If nothing else, the Montreal Canadiens were consistent and patient. The team knew how to assess talent, but so did the other five teams during the Original Six. What the Habs specifically did, however, was utilize a strategy and stick with it, no matter what.

Take defencemen, for instance. The Canadiens preferred tall, lean, strong blueliners because a combination of size and skill could overcome opponents more consistently than small and skilled defencemen. Furthermore, the organization knew that the NHL was the final step for any player, and that before he was going to be allowed to take this step he would be given every chance to develop and make mistakes outside the world's best league.

But in the summer of 1961, the team was in a quandary. Their great

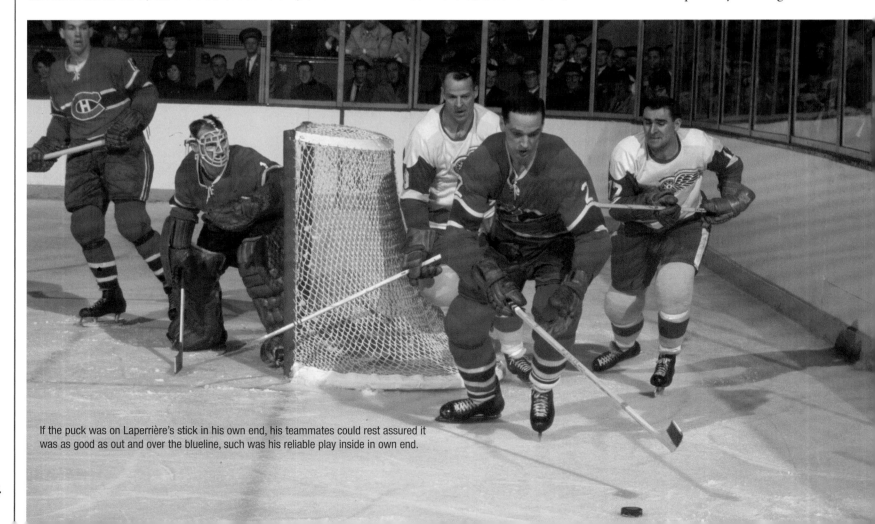

If the puck was on Laperrière's stick in his own end, his teammates could rest assured it was as good as out and over the blueline, such was his reliable play inside in own end.

leader, Doug Harvey, was past his prime and on his way to the New York Rangers, and they had no blue-chip defenceman to replace him. Everyone knew Jacques Laperrière was sure to be great, but although he had finished three years with the junior team he was still only 19 years old at training camp in 1961. So, the team waited.

Two years later, Laperrière had filled out and was a strapping 6'2" and weighed 180 pounds. He was young and talented and ready for the NHL, and when he was given the chance to play full time in 1963-64, he made his bosses look like geniuses once again.

Laperrière had it all. By the end of the year, he was named Calder Trophy winner for his outstanding rookie season, and the Habs, after a couple of

CANADIENS NUMBERS
JACQUES LAPERRIÈRE

b. Rouyn, Quebec, November 22, 1941
6'2"   180 lbs.   defence   shoots left

	REGULAR SEASON					PLAYOFFS				
	GP	G	A	Pts	Pim	GP	G	A	Pts	Pim
1962-63	6	0	2	2	2	5	0	1	1	4
1963-64	65	2	28	30	102	7	1	1	2	8
1964-65	67	5	22	27	92	6	1	1	2	16
1965-66	57	6	25	31	85	—	—	—	—	—
1966-67	61	0	20	20	48	9	0	1	1	9
1967-68	72	4	21	25	84	13	1	3	4	20
1968-69	69	5	26	31	45	14	1	3	4	28
1969-70	73	6	31	37	98	—	—	—	—	—
1970-71	49	0	16	16	20	20	4	9	13	12
1971-72	73	3	25	28	50	4	0	0	0	2
1972-73	57	7	16	23	34	10	1	3	4	2
1973-74	42	2	10	12	14	—	—	—	—	—
TOTALS	691	40	242	282	674	88	9	22	31	101

Laperrière played all 12 years and 691 games with the Canadiens, and his six Stanley Cups is a record that any player can only dream of.

Jacques Laperrière

Defence 1962-63 to 1973-74

off years, were ready to challenge for the Stanley Cup once again. Of course, Laperrière was cut from a different cloth than Harvey. The rookie was a stay-at-home defenceman at the start, with little interest in the opposing end of the ice, but this suited coach Toe Blake just fine. He had an abundance of skilled forwards who could score goals, from Jean Béliveau to Boom Boom Geoffrion, Henri Richard, Bobby Rousseau, and Dick Duff. In time, however, Lapperrière also became an important part of the team's offence as well, not quite as dominant as Harvey, but certainly enough to be called offensively gifted.

A BRAWL INCITES LAPERRIÈRE

When Laperrière was forced into retirement because of a knee injury he was by no means ready to leave the game. So, he turned to coaching, and his first post was as an assistant with Montreal's Junior Canadiens. However, early in his second season he quit the team out of disgust after an ugly brawl at the Forum between the Juniors and the Sorel Black Hawks. This wasn't hockey, he said, and he left. Laperrière took some time off but in 1980 he re-joined the NHL team as an assistant general manager and later assistant coach. He thrived in the role, and for the next 16 years he remained behind the bench working with the defencemen and winning two more Stanley Cups, in 1986 and 1993. He was credited with bringing along many of the team's young and inexperienced blueliners, notably Craig Ludwig, Rick Green, and Chris Chelios.

In Laperrière's second full season, the Habs won the Cup by defeating Chicago 4-0 in game seven at the Forum. The next year, they won again, this time after eliminating Toronto in four straight games in the semi-finals and then handling goalie Roger Crozier and the Red Wings in six games. That second Cup was doubly satisfying because Laperrière was also voted winner of the Norris Trophy. In an era when defensive players often won it, his was the greater honour for being considered the best player on the blueline more for his offence than defence.

Laperrière won the Cup again in 1968, 1969, 1971, and 1973, but he was forced into retirement midway through the next year when he suffered a bad knee injury against Boston on January 19, 1974. Nevertheless, in his 12 years of play, he won six Stanley Cups and came to define the role and play of a defenceman. Laperrière was a master at preventing scoring chances, and although not a gifted rusher of the puck in the way Harvey was, he was brilliant at moving the puck out of his own end. He routinely played against the other team's top stars and was a ballast of the penalty-killing unit. While no one would ever accuse him of being spectacular, he was also the very epitome of the position. And that is most certainly worth a place in the Hockey Hall of Fame.

Laperrière accepts the Calder Trophy as the league's top rookie in 1963-64.

In 1965-66, Laperrière won the Norris Trophy in large measure for his offensive play, this in an era when it was given most often to the best defensive defenceman.

Guy Lafleur
Right Wing 1971-72 to 1984-85

Once he took his helmet off early in his career, the character and personality of "The Flower" seemed to take off.

Few players could come down the right wing and fire a slapshot on the move with the same accuracy and speed as Guy Lafleur.

The story of how Guy Lafleur came to play for the Montreal Canadiens is one of the great moments of general manager Sam Pollock's career. Lafleur was far and away the best prospect for the 1971 Amateur Draft, and the Los Angeles Kings looked certain to claim the first overall draft selection because the team was so weak in 1970-71. This frustrated Pollock because the Canadiens owned the first draft choice of the Oakland Seals, a team he had thought was going to finish last. The cunning Pollock, however, had a solution. He traded veteran Ralph Backstrom, who had been with the Habs his entire 15-year career, to the Kings for no more than minor prospects Ray Fortin and Gord Labossière. The proud Backstrom had nearly a point a game for Los Angeles, helped the team move up the

standings, and ensured Oakland finished last. The Habs used the Seals' first selection to take Lafleur, and "the Flower" became the property of Pollock and the Canadiens.

Of course, Lafleur was the top-ranked prospect for a reason. He was tearing apart the Quebec junior league in a way no player had ever done before. In his five years of QJHL hockey, he became the highest-scoring player in league history, climaxing in 1970-71 when he scored a preposterous 130 goals and 209 points in just 62 games, an average of better than two goals and three points per game.

In Montreal, Jean Béliveau had just retired and the team needed a marquee player to inherit Le Gros Bill's mantle. The team even suggested Lafleur wear number 4, but he demurred, in part out of respect, in part

because he didn't want to enter the league as a rookie with the added pressure of having to perform like one of the greatest players of all time.

Lafleur's first three seasons in the league were very good ones. He scored 29, 28, and 21 goals, but he was by no means scoring at will as he had in junior. He started to question his own abilities when fans grew restless with him. They felt if he were the next Béliveau, he should be scoring 50 goals in his first season. But he needed time, time to learn, time to develop NHL-level confidence, time to mature physically and emotionally. He was also questioned for his toughness. Fans, critics, and opponents wondered if he were a coward because he didn't

like to go into the corners and he never dropped his gloves to fight. At training camp of his fourth season, Lafleur discarded the helmet he had always worn throughout his junior and early NHL career. The result was transforming.

From an aesthetic point of view, fans loved Lafleur's shoulder-length blond hair flying in the air as he streaked down the right wing. The helmetless look also seemed to accentuate just how poetic and brilliantly fast he was on skates, and he received some welcome advice from

Known more for his shot than his stickhandling close to the goal, Lafleur was nonetheless an all-round scorer who could put the puck in the net from just about anywhere on the ice.

Guy Lafleur

Right Wing 1971-72 to 1984-85

RETURN TO THE FORUM

The truth is that when Guy Lafleur retired, he wasn't ready to retire. Yet for four years, that's exactly what his status was. Ironically, his impending induction into the Hockey Hall of Fame caused him to re-consider his career, and just days after the induction ceremonies he was back on ice preparing for a comeback with the New York Rangers. One of the greatest "non-Montreal" moments in Forum history came when he returned to the arena which had been his home for so long and led the Rangers to a stunning 7-5 win over the Canadiens. Lafleur scored two of his 18 goals on the year this night, against Patrick Roy, and every time he stepped on the ice the capacity crowd screamed, "Guy! Guy! Guy!" just as they had for so many years when he wore the tricolore of the Canadiens. He was only the second player after Gordie Howe to play in the NHL after being inducted into the Hockey Hall of Fame. Lafleur's career came full circle in 1989 when he signed with the Nordiques and played with them for the final two years of his career. Some fans who didn't know Lafleur or followed only the NHL saw his signing with the Canadiens' enemy a traitorous act, but in truth Lafleur started his career with the Quebec Aces and Remparts, so he was leaving the game as he entered it, playing at Le Colisée.

Béliveau who told him to relax and keep focused on playing. The goals would come, he assured.

Béliveau was right. In his fourth season, Lafleur went from 21 goals and 56 points the year before and increased those numbers to 53 goals and 119 points in 1974-75. In the playoffs, he led all players with 12 goals, and when it was time to start the next season, he was not a struggling prospect but one of the game's most talented and feared offensive threats. He didn't like fighting? No problem—he did his fighting with goals.

The next four years were historic years for Lafleur and the Canadiens.

CANADIENS NUMBERS
GUY LAFLEUR ("The Flower")

b. Thurso, Quebec, September 20, 1951
6'   185 lbs.   right wing   shoots right

	REGULAR SEASON					PLAYOFFS				
	GP	G	A	Pts	Pim	GP	G	A	Pts	Pim
1971-72	73	29	35	64	48	6	1	4	5	2
1972-73 🏆	69	28	27	55	51	17	3	5	8	9
1973-74	73	21	35	56	29	6	0	1	1	4
1974-75	70	53	66	119	37	11	12	7	19	15
1975-76 🏆	80	56	69	125	36	13	7	10	17	2
1976-77 🏆	80	56	80	136	20	14	9	17	26	6
1977-78 🏆	78	60	72	132	26	15	10	11	21	16
1978-79 🏆	80	52	77	129	28	16	10	13	23	0
1979-80	74	50	75	125	12	3	3	1	4	0
1980-81	51	27	43	70	29	3	0	1	1	2
1981-82	66	27	57	84	24	5	2	1	3	4
1982-83	68	27	49	76	12	3	0	2	2	2
1983-84	80	30	40	70	19	12	0	3	3	5
1984-85	19	2	3	5	10	—	—	—	—	—
TOTALS	961	518	728	1,246	381	124	57	76	133	67

They won the Stanley Cup each year, and Lafleur led the way. In truth, goalie Ken Dryden was an important part of the team, and the "big three" on defence were essential. But the very engine that drove the car was Lafleur. His explosive speed down the right wing, his devastating shot and no-look passes simply terrorized enemy defences and goalies alike.

It is no coincidence that these were his four best years. He scored at least 50 goals and 125 points in each of five straight seasons (1975-80), leading the league for the first three in succession (1975-78). He also won the Lester B. Pearson Award these three years and also was awarded the Hart Trophy for 1976-77 and 1977-78. He led the playoffs in scoring the last three years of this dynastic run (1977-79) and was named winner of the Conn Smythe Trophy for 1976-77 after setting a record with 26 playoff points.

Lafleur wasn't just part of the teams that won those championships, though. More often than not, he was the main reason they won. In the deciding game of the quarter-finals against Vancouver in 1975, Lafleur scored the series winner in overtime. On April 11, 1977, in a playoff game against St. Louis, he tied an NHL record with six points in a 7-2 win. On May 16, 1978, Lafleur scored the overtime winner in game two of the Cup finals against Boston to give the Habs a commanding 2-0 series lead. In game seven of the semi-finals against Boston in 1979, his memorable goal tied the game late in the third period and the Habs won the game and series in overtime.

In May 1978, Lafleur made history of another kind when he snuck off with the Stanley Cup for a weekend. He took it home to Thurso and displayed it on his front lawn, much to the delight of fans and friends. Today, this might not be special, but in Lafleur's day no player was allowed to take the Cup like this.

Lafleur was the first player to score 50 goals and 100 points in six straight seasons. He was the youngest player to reach 400 career goals and he reached 1,000 points in just his 720th NHL game, the fastest ever to do

so. But everything in his life changed in the early hours of March 25, 1981. Driving home after a night of partying, he fell asleep at the wheel. His Cadillac crashed into a post, and he was lucky to be alive when the sun came up. He changed his ways, but the days of 50 goals and 100 points and Cup parties were over.

Lafleur retired early in the 1984-85 season. He had a bad start to the year, and he was seeing less ice time. Too proud to fade before fans' eyes, he left with his skills intact and the memories only great ones. He was the team's all-time leader in assists and total points, and his place in the city's history and hockey history was well assured. The Habs held a special night for him at the Forum and retired his number 10 sweater, and in 1988 he was inducted into the Hockey Hall of Fame. He had won almost everything there was to be won, but ironically he never won the Lady Byng Trophy despite enduring fierce checking without retaliating throughout his entire career. Lafleur was that rarest of player—a remarkable junior talent who came to the NHL and still exceeded all expectations.

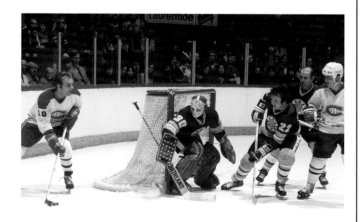

Lafleur led the league in scoring as much because of his passing as his shooting, often finding an open man in an impossible situation or feathering a pass through a maze of players.

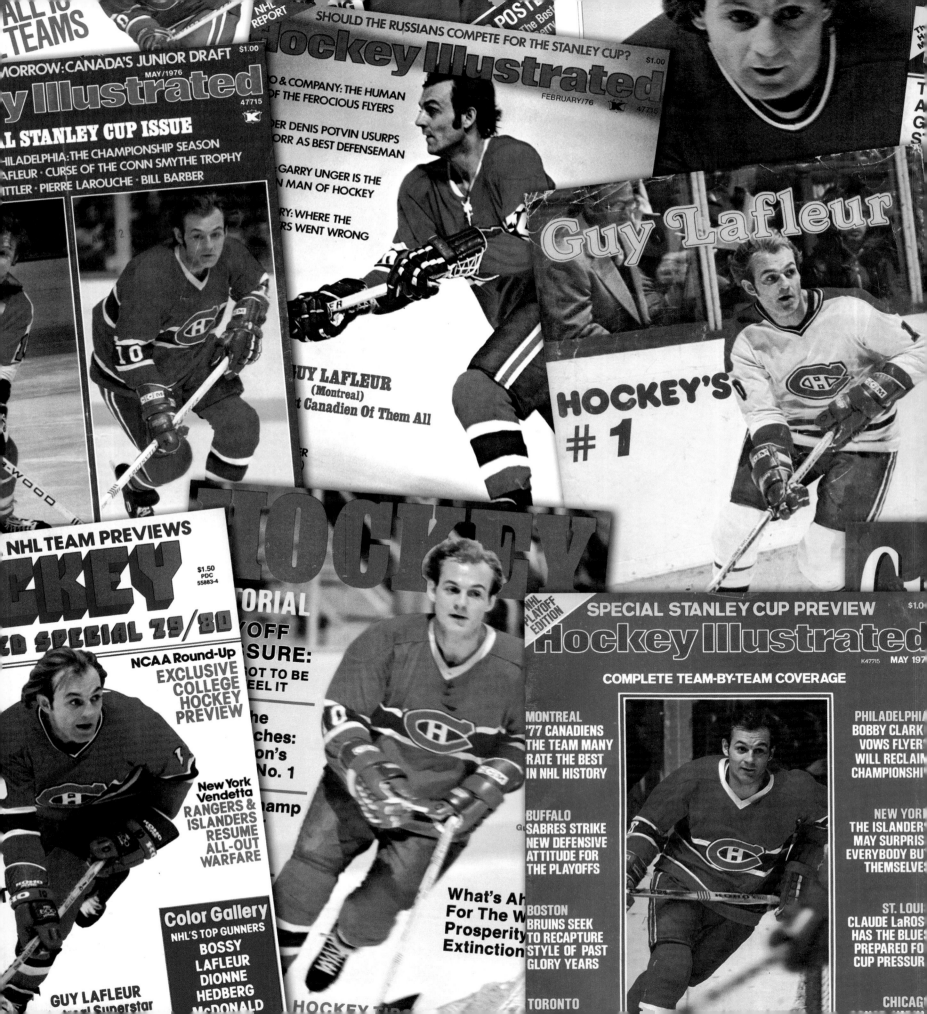

Herbert "Buddy" O'Connor
Centre 1941-42 to 1946-47

The life and career of Buddy O'Connor is so much richer than the statistics on a page suggest. For starters, his nickname came to him honestly. Never before or since has a nicer, kinder man played in the NHL. He never swore, drank with such modesty as to be called, for all intents and purposes, a non-drinker, and played with such gentlemanly conduct despite being a small player that he won the Lady Byng Trophy for the 1947-48 season.

Perhaps most amazing, judging by all accounts of his day, O'Connor was an even better player in senior hockey before he came to the NHL. He played for seven seasons with the Montreal Royals (1934-41), a senior team that made the Allan Cup playoffs five times in that span. Indeed, these were the halcyon days of senior hockey and the nadir of the Canadiens, and the Royals would routinely draw 13,000 fans on a Saturday afternoon while in the evening the Canadiens were lucky to draw 4,000.

O'Connor centred a line called the Razzle Dazzle Line featuring Pete Morin on left wing and Gerry Heffernan on the right side. The Habs were so impressed buy the threesome they signed them all and moved them as a trio to the NHL for the 1941-42 season. But whereas the wingers had brief careers, O'Connor had a Hall of Fame career with the Canadiens and later the New York Rangers. Morin joined the army the next year and never made it back, and Heffernan was back with the Royals after just one season with the Habs.

Despite being a great centre, O'Connor had a tough time gaining the recognition he deserved. After the Razzle Dazzle Line fizzled out, he had to play second fiddle to the Punch Line of Maurice Richard, Elmer Lach, and Toe Blake. The Canadiens won the Stanley Cup in 1944 and

1946, and O'Connor continued to be a superb player as a second-line centre. Heffernan was called back to the Canadiens for the 1943-44 season, and playing with O'Connor he scored an amazing 28 goals while O'Connor had 54 points. That was the last hurrah for two-thirds of the Razzle Dazzle Line.

The true measure of O'Connor's worth could be found in the 1947 playoffs. Near the end of the regular season, O'Connor was hit

O'Connor's outstanding play as centreman on the Razzle Dazzle Line with the Montreal Royals in senior hockey was a big reason the Canadiens gave him a chance.

accidentally by a vicious Bill Juzda stick swing. The Rangers' defenceman had been looking to strike another Canadiens player during a brawl but O'Connor received the brunt of the blow and suffered a broken jaw. Nonetheless, he came back for the Cup finals against Toronto, and although the Leafs won the Cup in six games, O'Connor was in on six of the team's 13 goals.

At season's end, general manager Frank Selke traded O'Connor to the Rangers with Frank Eddolls for Hal Laycoe, Joe Bell, and George Robertson. Selke later called this the worst trade he ever made, and for good reason. The Habs experienced poor seasons for the immediate future, and the Rangers surged, making it to game seven of the 1950 Cup finals. As telling, the three acquisitions in the deal made virtually no impact with the Canadiens.

Just as it took O'Connor several years to make it to the NHL, it took him even longer to make it to the Hockey Hall of Fame. Because he had so many good years in senior hockey and then flew under the radar, so to speak, in the NHL, it was many decades before his true worth was appre-

ciated by the hall's selection committee. Heffernan and Frank Selke, Jr. both petitioned Danny Gallivan, who sat on the committee, to nominate O'Connor as an inductee for the Veteran category (since abolished after its purpose had been served), and in 1988 O'Connor received his due, albeit posthumously.

HART TROPHY WINNER

O'Connor loved Montreal—it was his hometown, after all—and the fans loved him back. When he was traded to the Rangers, he was shocked and dismayed, but he continued to play the only way he knew, with passion and perseverance. In his first year with the Blueshirts, O'Connor recorded 60 points, only one behind Art Ross Trophy winner Elmer Lach, his former teammate in Montreal. O'Connor also won the Hart Trophy as the league's most valuable player and the Lady Byng Trophy as its most gentlemanly, and he was named a Second Team All-Star as well. He was also named Canada's male athlete of the year. In all, he scored 62 goals in four seasons with the Rangers, showing no signs of age or slowing down. The only time O'Connor faced his old team in the playoffs came in 1950 when the Rangers eliminated the Habs in five games, a huge upset given that Montreal finished second in league standings and New York fourth. The Rangers lost the Cup finals to Detroit in overtime of game seven, the first time the Cup had been won in OT of the final game.

CANADIENS NUMBERS
HERBERT "Buddy" O'CONNOR

b. Montreal, Quebec, June 21, 1916 | d. Montreal, Quebec, August 24, 1977
5'8" | 142 lbs. | centre | shoots right

| | REGULAR SEASON | | | | | PLAYOFFS | | | | |
	GP	G	A	Pts	Pim	GP	G	A	Pts	Pim
1941-42	36	9	16	25	4	3	0	1	1	0
1942-43	50	15	43	58	2	5	4	5	9	0
1943-44	44	12	42	54	6	8	1	2	3	2
1944-45	50	21	23	44	2	2	0	0	0	0
1945-46	45	11	11	22	2	9	2	3	5	0
1946-47	46	10	20	30	6	8	3	4	7	0
TOTALS	271	78	155	233	22	35	10	15	25	2

William "Scotty" Bowman
Builder

Almost no one starts out wanting to be a coach, and Scotty Bowman was no different. A forward for the Montreal Junior Canadiens, he had his career come to a shocking end on March 1, 1952, in a Memorial Cup semi-finals game against Trois-Rivières Reds. The Jr.

Canadiens won the first three games and were in control of the fourth, leading 5-1, and in the dying moments, Bowman got a breakaway. Jean-Guy Talbot struck Bowman on the head with his stick, earning a one-year suspension and jeopardizing Bowman's career. Although he played for two more years, he was no longer as effective and retired in

No coach won more Stanley Cup games or championships than Scotty Bowman, his first five victories coming with the Habs in the 1970s.

1954, his dreams of playing in the NHL over.

He had few other interests in life than hockey, but when he finished playing Bowman started to work by day for a paint company in Montreal and coach a Junior B team at night. He took the team to the

There is usually only one reason a coach ever comes onto the ice smiling—to celebrate the Stanley Cup—as Bowman does here with Serge Savard.

championship series and made a great impression on the team's previous coach, another youngster, named Sam Pollock. A year later, Pollock was named general manager of the Ottawa Jr. Canadiens, and he hired Bowman to be his right-hand man. After a year of

WILLIAM "Scotty" BOWMAN

b. Montreal, Quebec, September 18, 1933

INTERNATIONAL RÉSUMÉ

While Bowman was leading the Canadiens to five Stanley Cups between 1973 and 1979, he was also part of three historic international moments in the second half of that decade. On December 31, 1975, he was behind Montreal's bench at the Forum when the team faced the famed Red Army team from Moscow, a game that ended in a 3-3 tie and which to this day many consider one of the finest hockey games ever played. Less than a year later, Bowman was named coach for Team Canada at the inaugural Canada Cup tournament, an event that ended perfectly for Canada when the team defeated Czechoslovakia 2-0 in the best-of-three finals. The deciding game was a 5-4 overtime thriller at the Forum. Then, in 1979, Bowman was again named bench boss for an important international series, the Challenge Cup, a best-of-three series between the NHL all-star team and an all-star team from the Soviet Union, which replaced the NHL All-Star Game midway through the 1978-79 season.

William "Scotty" Bowman
Builder

apprenticing, Bowman became the team's coach. In his first two seasons, he led the team to the Memorial Cup finals. The first year they lost, the second year (now called the Ottawa-Hull Jr. Canadiens) they won the junior championship of Canada.

The Peterborough Petes, the OHA affiliate of the Montreal Canadiens, lured him away by offering him dual duties of coach and GM, and again, like an emerging star player, Bowman rose to the new and greater challenge. He was back in the Memorial Cup finals the following season. From there he became the Canadiens' head scout for Eastern Canada, but three years away from the bench was enough for Bowman.

As luck would have it, the NHL was set to expand from six teams to 12 in 1967, and the St. Louis Blues hired Lynn Patrick as the head coach and Bowman as his assistant. Early in the season, however, Patrick gave way to Bowman who made the team the best of the expansion six. For the first three years after expansion, the Original Six teams comprised one division and the new teams another, thus ensuring that the Stanley Cup finals would be contested between a new and old team. In all three seasons, that new team was the St. Louis Blues.

Bowman knew early on that the key to success was goaltending, and in St. Louis he used two veterans—Glenn Hall and Jacques Plante—who gave the team a chance to win every night. Bowman was tough on the players, but fair. As one player noted, he was a taskmaster. After resigning in the early part of his fourth year with the team, Bowman returned to Montreal. By the end of the year, the Canadiens had fired Al MacNeil and hired Bowman to lead their team. His GM was none other than Sam

Calm, calculating, professorial, Bowman stood behind the bench like a conductor before his orchestra, thinking about his next moves and how they might affect the course of action.

Pollock, and this partnership produced one of the most successful decades in hockey history.

The career of Bowman in Montreal lasted eight years. The team won the Cup five times and lost a total of 110 regular-season games, an average of fewer than 14 per season. The climax of this success came in 1976-77 when the team had a 60-8-12 record, the most wins and fewest losses ever in an NHL season. The team's totals were good enough for 132 total points in the standings, a record that still stands (Detroit later won 62 games in an 82-game season). Bowman's reputation continued to

reach mythical proportions. Players said they hated him 364 days a year. On the 365th, they won the Cup.

Bowman's talents lay not in grooming a group of young players into a winner so much as getting a number of incredibly talented individual players to come together as a team. He was famous for being hard on them when things were going well and easing up during a slump. As in St. Louis, his success started in goal, with Ken Dryden, but Bowman utilized his whole bench with a brilliance opposing coaches could never match. He understood his opponents as well as his own players,

and he was a master of matching lines to maximize his team's fortunes.

In 1979, the Buffalo Sabres signed Bowman as both a general manager and coach and he later he took over behind the bench in Pittsburgh and Detroit, winning the Stanley Cup at both stops along the way. His nine championships is an NHL record, as are his marks for most games (2,141) and wins (1,244). In 30 years as coach, his teams missed the playoffs just once (1985-86, Buffalo).

Canadiens players spill onto the ice to celebrate the successful end to another season—winning the Stanley Cup.

Bob Gainey

Left Wing 1973-74 to 1988-89

Even in junior, Bob Gainey was known as much for his checking as for his scoring ability.

Bob Gainey was a checking forward, to be sure, but he was a cut above the rest. Oldtimers might grouse about the fact that in their day every player in the game was a two-way player, but by the 1960s that was no longer the case. There were scorers and offensive stars, and there were lesser players, checkers, fighters. Gainey was so good at what he did that the league introduced the Frank Selke Trophy in 1978 pretty much as a way to honour Gainey and his unique style of play. Indeed, Gainey won the award its first four years of existence.

Defensive forward is a pejorative term that suggests a player is out of his element and can do little else except nag and hound the opposition. Usually, defensive forwards are born in the NHL. A hotshot prospect arrives in the big league but finds he can't score or create the magic he could in junior, so the coach teaches him to become a penalty killer and defensive specialist, and the player extends the life of his career.

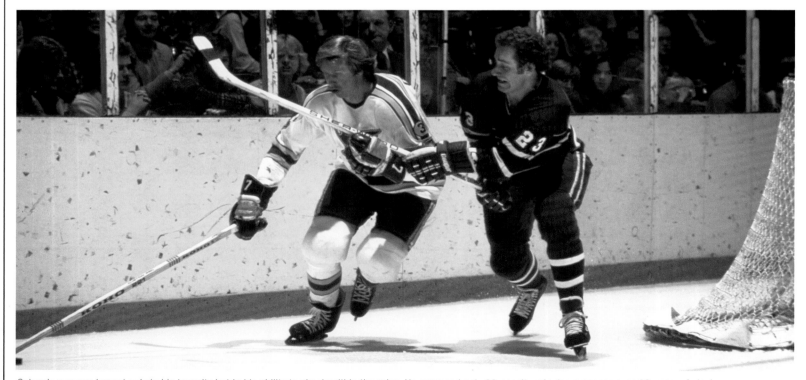

Gainey's success lay not only in his tenacity but in his ability to check within the rules. He averaged only 36 penalty minutes a season over 16 years of playing against the best from the other team.

Not so, Gainey. Even during his two years in junior with his hometown Peterborough Petes, Gainey was known as the best two-way forward in Canada's junior system. His coach, Roger Neilson, and assistant coach, Claude Ruel, started instilling in the teenager the benefits of two-way play. Gainey became the player he did in part because he was an excellent skater naturally and also because he was a quick learner and was highly coachable. Although he was not a prolific scorer, Gainey was nevertheless selected 8th overall by Montreal at the 1973 draft simply because Canadiens' GM Sam Pollock understood the value of a player of Gainey's calibre and type.

Gainey played exactly six games for the Nova Scotia Voyageurs in the AHL in 1973-74 before being summoned to the Forum. He was a fixture with that team for the next 16 years and five Stanley Cups, and as every teammate attested, he was as valuable to the team as scorers like

Guy Lafleur, defencemen like Larry Robinson, and goalie Ken Dryden.

In his rookie season, 1974-75, he scored just three goals, but the year after he had 17. In the fall, he was named to Canada's team for the inaugural Canada Cup, and it was there that the rest of the world learned of his tremendous skills. His club coach was the national coach, and Scotty Bowman put Gainey on a line with Toronto forwards Darryl Sittler and Lanny McDonald, two players with great offensive skills. It was the checker, however, who shone brightest early on, scoring twice and shutting down Anders Hedberg in a 4-0 win for Canada over Sweden at Maple Leaf Gardens. It was Sittler who scored the series-winning goal, but Gainey was praised by virtually

Gainey maintained that his last Cup win, in 1986, was the most rewarding, in large measure because it was the least expected by fans and players alike.

The best rivalry in hockey in the 1970s was between Montreal and Boston, and Gainey was front and centre for most of those classic battles.

Bob Gainey

Left Wing 1973-74 to 1988-89

Gainey won the Selke Trophy each of the first four years it was awarded.

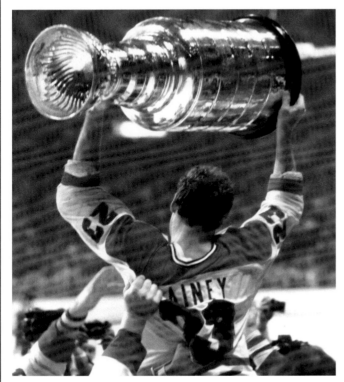

The late 1970s were Gainey's finest days. He won the Conn Smythe Trophy in 1979, and Soviet national coach Viktor Tikhonov called him "technically the best player in the world."

every other team's coach for his dual ability to play in his own end and the opposition's with equal skill and effectiveness.

Gainey was a member of the Montreal dynasty that won the Stanley Cup four times in a row, 1976-79, and he played an integral role in each win. In 1976, for instance, Montreal played Philadelphia in one of the most important finals ever played. The Flyers had used goonery and intimidation to win consecutive Cups in 1974 and 1975 and were on the verge of making it three in a row. This would have dealt the game a devastating blow for teams like Montreal that wanted to play with speed and skill. In the finals, Bowman assigned Gainey to shadow Reg Leach, one of the few skilled players on the Flyers. Gainey recorded only one assist in the finals, but the Habs won the Cup in a lopsided, four-game sweep.

The 1979 finals, however, might have been the best performance of Gainey's career. To wit, game four. Montreal led the series 2-1 in games, but the New York Rangers were winning 3-2 late in the game. The puck came behind the Rangers' net at one point, and Gainey crushed defenceman Dave Maloney against the boards, took the puck while Maloney lay on the ice, moved out front and beat goalie John Davidson with a clean shot. The Habs won the game in overtime, but players from both teams agreed the Cup was won with that hit and subsequent goal from Gainey. At the end of the series, he was named Conn Smythe Trophy winner. Watching this series was Soviet head coach Viktor Tikhonov who went so far as to say that Gainey was, "technically the best hockey player in the world."

That word "technically" was the greatest point of pride for Gainey. He didn't have the hardest shot and he wasn't the biggest man on the ice, but he played the game perfectly. He won key faceoffs, scored big goals, checked his man hard, and, most important, in a game played at top speed, he almost always made the right decision.

Although Gainey was key to those four Stanley Cups, it was his final championship in 1985-86 that remains his favourite memory. By that time most of the players from the 1970s were gone. Gainey, now

captain, was with the team to guide it to another generation of winning. But the team in 1985-86 was hardly a Cup contender until rookie goalie Patrick Roy arrived on the scene and led the team to an improbable championship. Gainey, 32 years old, had scored 20 goals and played his usual great playoffs, but he relished a win that was not expected more than the ones when he and everyone else knew the Habs were the best team in the league.

In 2003, Gainey returned to the team as general manager. In the interim,

he had played in France for a season, coached Dallas and managed the Stars to a Stanley Cup in 2000, and been inducted into the Hockey Hall of Fame. On February 23, 2008, his number 23 was hoisted to the rafters of the Bell Centre in Montreal, never to be used again by another Canadiens player.

CANADIENS NUMBERS
BOB GAINEY

b. Peterborough, Ontario, December 13, 1953
6'2"   200 lbs.   left wing   shoots left

	REGULAR SEASON					PLAYOFFS				
	GP	G	A	Pts	Pim	GP	G	A	Pts	Pim
1973-74	66	3	7	10	34	6	0	0	0	6
1974-75	80	17	20	37	49	11	2	4	6	4
1975-76	78	15	13	28	57	13	1	3	4	20
1976-77	80	14	19	33	41	14	4	1	5	25
1977-78	66	15	16	31	57	15	2	7	9	14
1978-79	79	20	18	38	44	16	6	10	16	10
1979-80	64	14	19	33	32	10	1	1	2	4
1980-81	78	23	24	47	36	3	0	0	0	2
1981-82	79	21	24	45	24	5	0	1	1	8
1982-83	80	12	18	30	43	3	0	0	0	4
1983-84	77	17	22	39	41	15	1	5	6	9
1984-85	79	19	13	32	40	12	1	3	4	13
1985-86	80	20	23	43	20	20	5	5	10	12
1986-87	47	8	8	16	19	17	1	3	4	6
1987-88	78	11	11	22	14	6	0	1	1	6
1988-89	49	10	7	17	34	16	1	4	5	8
TOTALS	1,160	239	262	501	585	182	25	48	73	151

INTERNATIONAL MAN OF CHECKING

In addition to his outstanding NHL career with the Canadiens, Bob Gainey played several important international tournaments, notably the 1976 and 1981 Canada Cup events as well as the 1982 and 1983 World Championships in Finland and West Germany, respectively. But closer to home he played for Montreal in two memorable games against the Soviet Red Army at the Forum in Montreal during the season. The first came on the night of December 31, 1975, a 3-3 tie. The second came exactly four years later, New Year's Eve 1979. On that night the Canadiens won 4-2, and the game-winning goal was scored in dramatic fashion by Gainey. Although it wasn't a bullet drive that beat Soviet great Vladislav Tretiak, it was the play to get the shot off that made the goal special. Gainey beat defenceman Slava Fetisov one-on-one—beat him badly, actually—and that gave Gainey the chance to take the shot which barely crossed the goal line. Nonetheless, Gainey was named Montreal's player of the game, in part for that goal, in part for his superb overall play all game long.

By the 1980s, the Montreal-Boston rivalry had been usurped by Montreal-Quebec, and once again Gainey was front and centre in the league's most bitter rivalry.

Guy Lapointe
Defence 1968-69 to 1981-82

As a teenager, Guy Lapointe wanted to be a police officer more than a hockey player. But his father, a fireman, talked some sense into his son, assuring him he had plenty of time to join the force if a hockey career didn't pan out. As it turned out, Lapointe improved slowly but surely over the years, and by the time he was 25 years old, the cutoff age for joining the Montreal police, he was a Stanley Cup winner and all-star with the Canadiens in the NHL.

Playing junior hockey in the Canadiens' system, Lapointe was nothing more than an average prospect when he joined the team in 1967 as a 19-year-old. In midget hockey he played both defence and forward, but by

Lapointe's offensive skills were many, and he had nine straight seasons with double-digit goals and at least 42 points.

Two of the "Big Three" consult by the players' bench as Lapointe (left) chats with captain Serge Savard.

CANADIENS NUMBERS
GUY LAPOINTE

b. Montreal, Quebec, March 18, 1948
6'   205 lbs.   defence   shoots left

	REGULAR SEASON					PLAYOFFS				
	GP	G	A	Pts	Pim	GP	G	A	Pts	Pim
1968-69	1	0	0	0	2	—	—	—	—	—
1969-70	5	0	0	0	4	—	—	—	—	—
1970-71 🏆	78	15	29	44	107	20	4	5	9	34
1971-72	69	11	38	49	58	6	0	1	1	0
1972-73 🏆	76	19	35	54	117	17	6	7	13	20
1973-74	71	13	40	53	63	6	0	2	2	4
1974-75	80	28	47	75	88	11	6	4	10	4
1975-76 🏆	77	21	47	68	78	13	3	3	6	12
1976-77 🏆	77	25	51	76	53	12	3	9	12	4
1977-78 🏆	49	13	29	42	19	14	1	6	7	16
1978-79 🏆	69	13	42	55	43	10	2	6	8	10
1979-80	45	6	20	26	29	2	0	0	0	0
1980-81	33	1	9	10	79	1	0	0	0	17
1981-82	47	1	19	20	72	—	—	—	—	—
TOTALS	777	166	406	572	812	112	25	43	68	121

Lapointe won the Stanley Cup six times in a nine-year span (1970-79), and he was inducted into the Hockey Hall of Fame in 1993 for his outstanding career.

the time he joined Maisonneuve in provincial Junior A he was concentrating strictly on the former. After two years with the Verdun Maple Leafs, Savard was ready to play major junior hockey with the Jr. Canadiens in the OHL.

He worked hard and proved to be very coachable, and he was given a one-game tryout with the NHL team to get his feet wet. The next year he was sent to the Houston Apollos, Montreal's CHL affiliate, and he acquitted himself well at this next level of play. He also was recalled for five games

with the Canadiens during 1969-70 when he was with the Montreal Voyageurs of the AHL, and again he learned more about the NHL game during his brief stay.

Lapointe's big break came during training camp in 1970 thanks to a series of serendipitous circumstances. First, the Habs were in need of a defenceman to start the season because star Serge Savard was still recovering from a serious injury suffered the previous year when he slid hard

Guy Lapointe
Defence 1968-69 to 1981-82

into the goalpost and broke his leg in five places. Second, Lapointe took the opportunity and played sensationally in the pre-season, proving to be a tremendous physical presence, an offensive threat, and a reliable defenceman who remained calm under pressure. He made the team, and when another steady defenceman, Jacques Laperrière,

suffered an injury early in the season, Lapointe not only got more ice time he became a vital part of the defence. When Savard returned to the lineup midway through the year, coach Al MacNeil had no choice but to keep Lapointe in the lineup, so good had he been.

Indeed, Lapointe stayed the entire 1970-71 season with the team, helped

WISE GUY

Every successful team needs a dressing-room clown, and what a bonus it is when that clown is also one of the team's most skilled players on ice. Guy Lapointe loved practical jokes, and one of his favourite targets was goalie Ken Dryden. In cahoots with his other teammates and the serving staff at lunchtime, Lapointe was at his finest one game day. He knew of Dryden's love for ice cream, so arranged for dessert to be either a fruit cup or ice cream. But, he ensured there was only one ice cream dish. Prior to the meal, Lapointe opened the single-serving dish and replaced the ice cream with sour cream. He topped this with chocolate sauce and replaced the cardboard top. After the main course, everyone got a fruit cup except Lapointe, who received the lone ice cream. He declared himself full from the meal and offered the ice cream to anyone who wanted it. Of course, all teammates remained mum, so Dryden said he'd have it if no one else wanted it. Dryden removed the top, dug into the ice cream, and gagged on the sour cream, much to the delight of one and all. The team won the game that night.

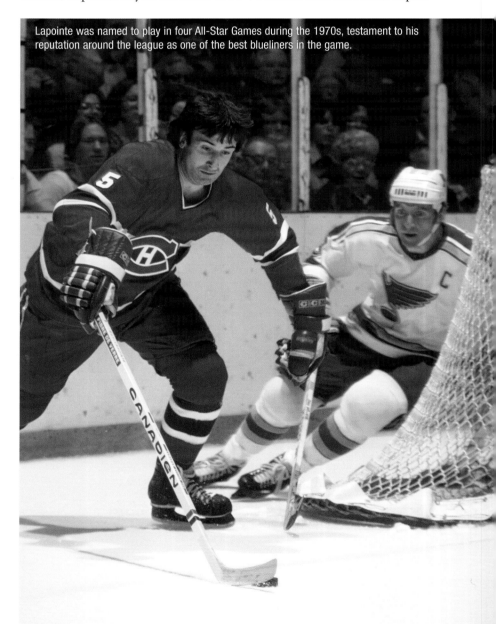

Lapointe was named to play in four All-Star Games during the 1970s, testament to his reputation around the league as one of the best blueliners in the game.

the Habs eliminate the heavily-favoured Boston Bruins in the playoffs, and went on to win the Cup with the Canadiens in his first full season. From then on, there was no looking back for Lapointe. He scored 15 goals as a rookie and proved that, although a little rough around the edges, he was a bona fide NHLer.

He continued to improve in the coming seasons, and the team relied evermore heavily on his complete abilities. He killed penalties, anchored the power play, and moved the puck out of his own end with consistent efficiency. Although he never won the Norris Trophy during his lengthy career, it is only because he played in the era of Bobby Orr, Denis Potvin, and Brad Park. The 1970s was a period defined by its rushing defencemen, and Lapointe's contributions were often overlooked at awards time as a result.

Despite having only two years of full-time NHL play under his belt, Lapointe was named to the historic 1972 Team Canada for the Summit Series against the Soviet Union. He played in seven of the eight games and was a major part of the team's success inside its own blueline. The Canadiens won the Cup again in 1973, and after two years of domination by the fighting Flyers in Philadelphia, Montreal won four Stanley Cups in a row (1976-79). Lapointe was on all six championships in the 1970s, and between 1974 and 1977 he produced three seasons of at least 21 goals. Other members of the team's "big three" on the blueline—Larry Robinson and Savard—might have received more publicity and praise, but Lapointe was just as important to the team's success.

During any long season, a team will have its ups and downs, and Lapointe became a leader in the dressing room not for his inspiring speeches but for his love of practical jokes. Players admitted it was never safe to go onto the ice for practice until Lapointe was on the ice, and it was equally unwise to let him go to the dressing room first off the ice. Whether he was taping shoes together or cutting holes in hats—including his own to camouflage his guilt—Lapointe kept the team loose and made everyone feel like brothers.

Although he was skilled at both ends of the ice, Lapointe was also adept in the dressing room, the team clown who kept things light with his practical jokes.

Toward the end of his stay in Montreal he suffered two scary injuries. In 1977-78, he suffered a serious injury when a deflected puck hit him flush in the eye, and in 1979-80, he suffered a separated shoulder that cost him many weeks of action. He was traded to St. Louis at the deadline in 1982 and retired two years later after a final stint with Boston. In all, Lapointe won six Stanley Cups, was named a First All-Star once (1972-73) and a Second All-Star three straight times (1974-77). He also played in four All-Star Games (1973, 1975, 1976, 1977).

It wasn't until his mid teens that Lapointe focused entirely on being a defenceman. He had played much of his youth as a forward, and this double experience helped him become an offensive threat when he made the Habs full-time in 1970.

Steve Shutt

Steve Shutt was the first player in Canadiens history to score 60 goals in a season, reaching the mark in 1976-77.

It's a strange phenomenon in hockey, but high-scoring left wingers have always been the rarest breed. Top scorers are most often centremen, and right wingers are fairly common as points leaders, but left wingers are less heralded and less successful at being the top players in the game. Be that as it may, Steve Shutt was one of the top wingers from the left side during his career, peaking in 1976-77 when he produced a league record 60 goals by a left winger.

Shutt was a scout's dream. The way he played in junior was pretty much exactly the way he developed and played in the NHL. He wasn't big and fast and flashy, and he definitely wasn't a physical presence who parked himself in front of the net like Dino Ciccarelli or Dave Andreychuk would

later. Instead, Shutt played on the periphery until the exact moment when he knew it was time to get a little dirty and go to the net. For him, timing was everything.

Although he made the team at his first training camp in 1972, Shutt was a raw 20-year-old not ready to play regularly on a club that expected to win the Stanley Cup every year. In his first season, he scored just eight goals in 50 games and spent a fair bit of time in the press box as a healthy scratch. But every game the Canadiens played he learned a little more, either on ice, from the bench, or up high in street clothes. Indeed, the Habs won the Cup in

Shutt didn't develop into a star overnight; instead, he learned and improved steadily over several years before becoming the best left winger in the game.

Shutt played on a line with Guy Lafleur (left) and Pete Mahovlich, a great combination concocted by coach Scotty Bowman.

Steve Shutt

Left Wing 1972-72 to 1984-85

Shutt was deadliest when he found himself in tight with the puck on his stick, making him one of the most potent offensive players in the league.

his rookie season of 1972-73, but Shutt dressed only once in the playoffs and wasn't playing the night the team beat Chicago 6-4 in game six of the finals.

Nevertheless, the next four years saw steady—precise, in fact—improvement from Shutt. He increased his goal production by exactly 15 every year, going from 15 to 30 to 45 to a league record 60 in 1976-77. He finished with 105 points that last year to finish third in NHL scoring behind linemate Guy Lafleur and Marcel Dionne of Los Angeles.

Coach Scotty Bowman put Shutt on a line with Pete Mahovlich and Lafleur, and the threesome became the top-scoring line in the league. Bowman's patience with Shutt, and Shutt's gradual inclusion into the lineup, paid huge dividends over the course of his first three seasons when the winger went from being an up-and-comer to a bona fide superstar in the game.

Shutt was the least "skilled" of the three. Lafleur was magical down the right side with his flowing blond hair, tremendous shot and great speed; Mahovlich could deke through the opposition in a phone booth. Shutt?

Well, he was just there, in the right spot at the right time. No one noticed him until the end of the night when the game summary revealed he had two goals and an assist.

What Shutt also had was a deadly shot, both the wrist and the slapshot.

He was accurate with a quick release, and had a great sense of where the puck was going. As a kid, he played on the family backyard rink with his four brothers, and in the summer he practiced his shot by drawing a goal on the school wall and firing shot after shot at the target.

Shutt liked to think of himself as the invisible forward who always found the net without stealing the spotlight from teammates such as Guy Lafleur or Larry Robinson.

A RARE SCORING JUNIOR WHO KEEPS GOING

Steve Shutt played his junior hockey with the Toronto Marlboros, one of the most storied junior franchises in the country. He played his first games with the team in the 1969 playoffs, and his presence was immediately felt in two ways. One, it was clear he had a superior shot and knack for scoring, and two, he wore his hair long with long sideburns during an era of brush cuts and crew cuts. Shutt, a left winger, was a member of one of the greatest lines in junior hockey history, along with Billy Harris on right wing and Dave Gardner at centre. Shutt scored 133 goals in his final two years, and Gardner led the league in assists both years as his set-up man. Gardner also led the league in points in 1970-71 and Harris was tops the next year. Shutt's 63 goals in 1971-72 also led the OHL prompting Montreal GM Sam Pollock to select him 4th overall at the 1972 Amateur Draft. But while there are many junior stars who can put the puck in the net, few did what Shutt managed after Pollock brought him into the Canadiens' fold—continue the scoring exploits in the much bigger, faster, and more skilled NHL.

Steve Shutt

Left Wing 1972-72 to 1984-85

Shutt later played on a line with Lafleur and Jacques Lemaire after Pete Mahovlich was traded to Pittsburgh, and the new trio continued to dominate. Shutt never again had a 60-goal season, though, but he had at least 30 goals for the next six years, giving his reputation an added epithet—consistent.

Ironically, Shutt's time in Montreal ended as it began. During the 1984-85 season, the 32-year-old found his playing time reduced and his name on the list of scratches as often as not, so when he was traded to Los Angeles it was a welcome move. He retired after that season, however.

Although Shutt never won any individual awards, he won five Stanley Cups with the Canadiens, the first as a rookie and then four in a row to close out the 1970s. He averaged better than a point a game with the Habs in the playoffs, testament to his ability to raise his game when it mattered the most. Shutt was a First Team All-Star once (his 60-goal season), and Second Team member twice (1977-78, 1979-80), and he also played in three All-Star Games (1976, 1978, and 1981). He represented the NHL at the 1979 Challenge Cup, the best-of-three NHL-Soviet Union series that replaced that year's All-Star Game. Although he never got the credit his more colourful line-mates received, his contributions to five Cups speak to his abilities every bit as convincingly.

Shutt on the prowl, moving slowly toward the net while following play, ready to let go a quick shot if the puck comes near him.

CANADIENS NUMBERS
STEVE SHUTT

b. Toronto, Ontario, July 1, 1952
5'11"   185 lbs.   left wing   shoots left

	REGULAR SEASON					PLAYOFFS				
	GP	G	A	Pts	Pim	GP	G	A	Pts	Pim
1972-73	50	8	8	16	24	1	0	0	0	0
1973-74	70	15	20	35	17	6	5	3	8	9
1974-75	77	30	35	65	40	9	1	6	7	4
1975-76	80	45	34	79	47	13	7	8	15	2
1976-77	80	60	45	105	28	14	8	10	18	2
1977-78	80	49	37	86	24	15	9	8	17	20
1978-79	72	37	40	77	31	11	4	7	11	6
1979-80	77	47	42	89	34	10	6	3	9	6
1980-81	77	35	38	73	51	3	2	1	3	4
1981-82	57	31	24	55	40	—	—	—	—	—
1982-83	78	35	22	57	26	3	1	0	1	0
1983-84	63	14	23	37	29	11	7	2	9	8
1984-85	10	2	0	2	9	—	—	—	—	—
TOTALS	871	408	368	776	400	96	50	48	98	61

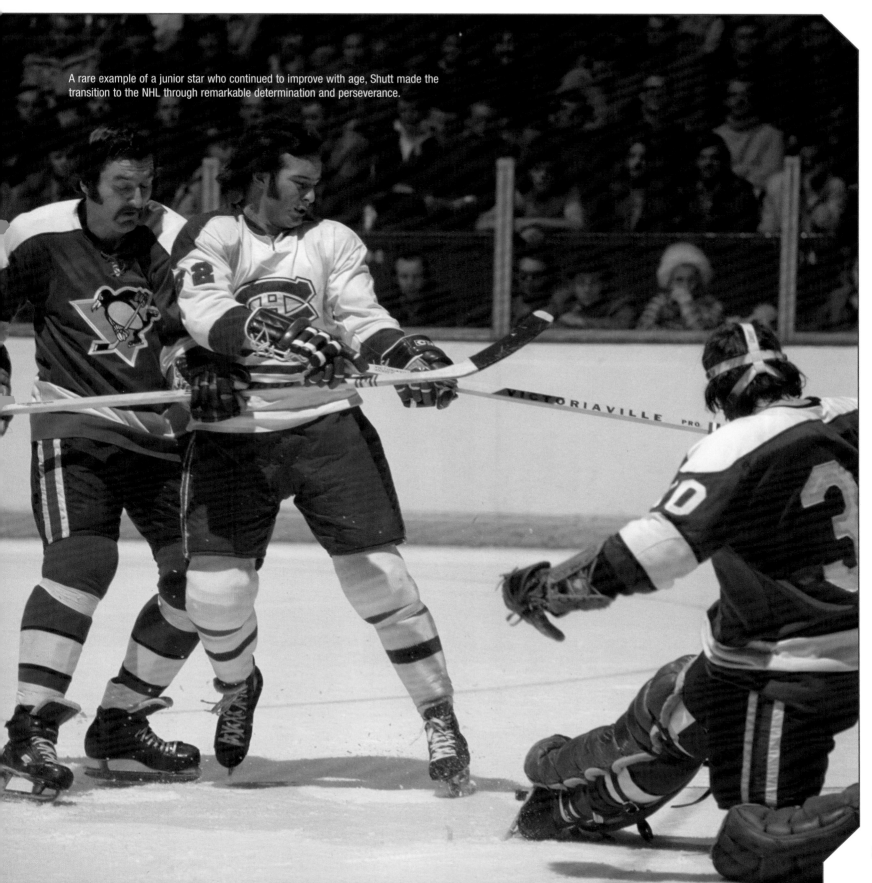

A rare example of a junior star who continued to improve with age, Shutt made the transition to the NHL through remarkable determination and perseverance.

Larry Robinson
Defence 1972-73 to 1988-89

Although he was born in Winchester, Ontario, Robinson grew up in a more appropriately named town nearby. His home of Marvelville could not have been more apt given the incredible career he was soon to embark on after he was old enough to start skating.

Robinson's rise through the ranks was not meteoric, but it was steady, methodical, and unabating. He started as a centreman, and after playing for the Metcalfe Jets in 1967-68 he went on to Brockville where he won the scoring title for the Braves. In his second year with the team he moved back to defence because the team was short of blueliners, and from then on he had found his calling. He developed and improved, and scouts knew of his name, but there was still much to be done before he could be called an NHL superstar.

Robinson earned the nickname "Big Bird" because of his curly hair and his large, angular physique.

Robinson played in the NHL for 20 years and his teams never missed the playoffs. Never.

INDUCTED 1995

In junior with the Kitchener Rangers, Robinson was known as a big and strong player but still gangly and awkward. He wasn't the best skater, and he didn't use his size intelligently, but despite the many rough qualities of his game it was clear he was better than most players. Nonetheless, leading up to the Amateur Draft in 1971, the only teams that expressed interest in him were Los Angeles and Oakland. Of course, this was more Sam Pollock genius. The Montreal GM knew very well of Robinson and had been told by Claude Ruel he was an excellent player with tremendous potential. This was enough for Pollock, and the Canadiens came out of nowhere to draft him 20th overall.

Pollock assigned Robinson to the Habs' AHL farm team in Nova Scotia, and it was there he improved rapidly over the next year and a half. He learned to be intimidating with his size. He learned to use his slapshot. He came to realize his reach was immensely effective and his strength one-on-one unmatchable. His long strides may have looked awkward, but they got him places faster than his opponents. In his own way, he became a superb rushing defenceman who could anchor the power play and be dominating in his own end. In short, Robinson could do it all.

With a head of steam and the puck on his stick, the defenceman turned into a formidable offensive threat.

Larry Robinson

Defence 1972-73 to 1988-89

Midway through the 1972-73 season, Pollock could no longer afford to keep Robinson in the minors. Big Bird was playing too well. From the moment he joined the Canadiens early in 1973, to the day he retired in 1992, Robinson never played in the minors again. He came to the Canadiens and had an immediate impact, helping the team win the Stanley Cup at the end of his rookie season.

Although Montreal failed to win again in the next two years, it was Robinson's physical presence against Philadelphia, the Cup champions in 1974 and 1975, that helped rid hockey of the Broad Street Bullies and restore class and dignity to the chase for the Cup. The team won again in 1976, and in each of the next three seasons, and these were the years when Robinson was at the height of his powers and the most consistent and dominating defenceman in the game. He was named to the First or Second All-Star team in each of the next five years, won the Norris

If he shielded the puck with his body, Robinson was virtually uncheckable without being fouled.

Trophy in 1977 and 1980, and earned the Conn Smythe Trophy in 1978 after a dominating performance in the playoffs.

Nicknamed "Big Bird" after the Sesame Street character because of his curly hair and gangly stature, Robinson was a consistently effective offensive threat capable of breaking a game open with a big goal or end-to-end rush to create a goal. He didn't often do it alone, but he helped others score and he was rarely on for a goal against. Indeed, Robinson never

CANADIENS NUMBERS
LARRY ROBINSON ("Big Bird")

b. Winchester, Ontario, June 2, 1951
6'2"   197 lbs.   defence   shoots left

	REGULAR SEASON					PLAYOFFS				
	GP	G	A	Pts	Pim	GP	G	A	Pts	Pim
1972-73	36	2	4	6	20	11	1	4	5	9
1973-74	78	6	20	26	66	6	0	1	1	26
1974-75	80	14	47	61	76	11	0	4	4	27
1975-76	80	10	30	40	59	13	3	3	6	10
1976-77	77	19	66	85	45	14	2	10	12	12
1977-78	80	13	52	65	39	15	4	17	21	6
1978-79	67	16	45	61	33	16	6	9	15	8
1979-80	72	14	61	75	39	10	0	4	4	2
1980-81	65	12	38	50	37	3	0	1	1	2
1981-82	71	12	47	59	41	5	0	1	1	8
1982-83	71	14	49	63	33	3	0	0	0	2
1983-84	74	9	34	43	39	15	0	5	5	22
1984-85	76	14	33	47	44	12	3	8	11	8
1985-86	78	19	63	82	39	20	0	13	13	22
1986-87	70	13	37	50	44	17	3	17	20	6
1987-88	53	6	34	40	30	11	1	4	5	4
1988-89	74	4	26	30	22	21	2	8	10	12
TOTALS	1,202	197	686	883	706	203	25	109	134	186

A DEFINING MOMENT

In many respects the 1973-74 and 1974-75 seasons were the low point for the NHL. The Philadelphia Flyers won the Stanley Cup both years by using goonery to accomplish their victories, and in the 1976 playoffs they again made it to the finals where they faced the Canadiens. If they had won again, their mini-dynasty would surely have tolerated a new level of violence into the game, but the skating and scoring Canadiens had something to say about the game's history. Montreal had earned home-ice advantage in the series, and as a result the first two games of the best-of-seven were played at the Forum. The finals changed on one play, one very big and clean check delivered by Larry Robinson. He nailed winger Gary Dornhoefer coming over the Montreal blueline during the third period of game two, and the Flyers' player fell hard into the penalty box door. In fact, the door actually broke on the play and the game was held up as the maintenance crew came onto the ice to repair the damage. The Flyers, perhaps for the first time since they started their fighting style of play, looked intimidated, and Montreal goalie Ken Dryden later said it was at this moment that the series was decided. Robinson himself later said he had never felt more at peace than prior to game four when he knew—he simply was fully aware—that his Canadiens would win the Stanley Cup on this night. All thanks to his big hit to ensure the series was headed in the right direction.

Larry Robinson

Defence 1972-73 to 1988-89

scored 20 goals in a season, but he had at least 45 assists in a season eight times. He was the leader on the power play, his great low shots often finding their way to the net.

Despite all his Stanley Cup success in the 1970s with the great Montreal teams, Robinson's proudest championship came during the 1985-86 season. The team would not have won but for the spectacular goaltending of Patrick Roy, but by this time the only two holdovers from the glory years were Robinson and captain Bob Gainey. The elder statesmen reveled in their roles as mentors and leaders, and their play was still at the highest level. It was an unexpected Cup and a rewarding one, to be sure.

Because of his size and style of play, Robinson had his fair share of injuries. A back problem and separated shoulder

Robinson cradles the two great playoffs honours—the Stanley Cup and the Conn Smythe Trophy—which he earned in 1978 as the best player of the post-season.

and other woes kept him out of the lineup periodically over the years, but his worst injury, in the summer of 1987, happened far away from the rink. After his great performance in 1984 at the Canada Cup and his resurgence in the spring of 1986, Robinson was named to Team Canada's 1987 Canada Cup roster. But he broke his leg while playing polo, his summer passion, and missed that tournament as well as the first two months of the NHL season. Another debilitating injury had occurred several years earlier when he was cracked over the head by Wilf Paiement of Quebec. Robinson played it safe and thereafter adopted a helmet, extending the life of his career and enabling him to play with the same confidence as before the high-sticking incident.

In 1989, Robinson was at a crossroads. He had not been pleased with his playing time the previous year with the Canadiens, but he was very much feeling physically fit and energetic. Montreal wanted to go with younger players, and so by mutual agreement the Robinson Era ended. He signed with Los Angeles and enjoyed three more years playing alongside Wayne Gretzky. By the time he retired in 1992 at age 40, he had forced every ounce of energy and skill from his body.

Perhaps two statistics stand out. While numbers don't often tell the story of a player's success or failure, these definitely point to Robinson's greatness because he has almost no equal. During his 20 years in the NHL, Robinson was never a minus player in the plus-minus statistic. He peaked in 1976-77 when he was +120, and his career +/- was an unbelievable +730. Furthermore, in his 20 years in the NHL, he appeared in the playoffs 20 times, a record for successive playoffs and a career record equalled only by Gordie Howe.

And so, it was no surprise when, on November 19, 2007, Robinson's number 19 was raised to the rafters of the Bell Centre, the 13th retired number by the Canadiens. It honoured a remarkable career and a remarkable player, a tough but gentlemanly defenceman, a proud and competitive man, a champion and an idol to the next generation of players in Montreal.

Robinson's number 19 was raised to the Bell Centre rafters on November 19, 2007, to honour 17 tremendous years with the Canadiens.

Denis Savard
Centre 1990-91 to 1992-93

The story of the "three Denis" is so improbable it sounds more like the stuff of myth than fact. Denis Savard, Denis Cyr, and Denis Tremblay played together as a line for the Montreal Juniors in the QMJHL. They all grew up within a few blocks of each other in Verdun, a suburb of Montreal, playing hockey together right up until the 1980 NHL Entry Draft. They were all born on the same day— February 4, 1961. And, they were all NHL prospects.

Denis Savard returned home hoping to win a Cup and was determined to do so even if it meant playing more responsibly in his own end.

Denis Tremblay never made the NHL. Denis Cyr played part-time in the NHL for several years. Denis Savard became a Hall of Famer for his 17 years and 1,338 points. Tremblay was never drafted while Cyr was chosen by Calgary. Savard was a top prospect, and since the Montreal Canadiens owned the first overall selection in the 1980 draft, he hoped the match was perfect. After much debate, however, the Canadiens selected Doug Wickenheiser, a player who was considered as skilled offensively but who was a few inches taller, several pounds heavier, and a good deal stronger. Dave Babych was chosen second overall by Winnipeg, and it was up to Chicago to choose Savard with the third choice. The Montreal boy was on his way to the Windy City, and what a time he had.

Over the next decade, Savard averaged more than 100 points a season, but after 1,013 regular-season points with the Blackhawks he was traded to Montreal for defenceman Chris Chelios and a 2nd-round draft choice in 1991 (Mike Pomichter). The trade was spurred by Savard's frequent head-butting with demanding coach Mike Keenan, but it also ended years of frustration for Savard. During his ten years with the team, the Hawks never made it to the Stanley Cup finals despite going as far as the Conference finals five times (1982, 1983, 1985, 1989, 1990).

Savard missed the final series against Los Angeles in 1993 after suffering a broken foot in the first game, but he was front and centre when the Habs won the Cup, his only career championship.

The frenzy that greeted Savard on his arrival to Montreal was, if not unprecedented, then surely intimidating all the same. Rarely had a French-Canadian player of Savard's stature—who had never played for the Canadiens—been acquired by the team in a trade. Fans and media might have expected him to score every night, but the player arrived with only one goal in mind—the Stanley Cup.

For Savard, this meant happily sacrificing a few spectacular rushes in favour of a more defensive and team-first attitude. To that end, coach Pat Burns moved him from centre to the right wing, and Savard happily made the change to fit in. He became less a scorer or set-up man and more a complete two-way player, and although he no longer appeared to be a superstar he made a significant contribution during his three years with the Canadiens.

Savard scored 28 goals in each of his first two seasons with the Habs and dipped to 16 in 1992-93. The team, however, led by goalie Patrick Roy, charged through the playoffs, winning a record ten overtime games and defeating Los Angeles in five games in the finals to win the Stanley Cup. On the night of the final game of the year, June 9, 1993, Savard was not dressed. He had suffered a broken foot in the first game of the series, but he refused to disappear. He stood behind the players'

bench the rest of the series giving his support to his teammates. At the end of Montreal's 4-1 home victory he charged to the ice to be with coach Jacques Demers and the players in celebration. That Montreal won the Cup in 1993, the 100th anniversary of the first winner of hockey's great trophy, Montreal AAA, was doubly satisfying for Savard.

Savard finished his career in Tampa Bay and back in Chicago, but by the time he retired in 1997, he was the "one Denis," his Cup dreams realized in his home city.

THE CUP TRADITION

As mayhem prevailed in the moments after the Canadiens won the 1993 Cup, captain Guy Carbonneau kept his cool. These were the days before the white-gloved staff of the Hockey Hall of Fame escorted the Cup to a table at centre ice. New NHL commissioner Gary Bettman simply brought the Cup out to give it to Carbonneau, and right behind him was coach Demers. But the captain refused to touch the trophy until Denis Savard made his way over in suit and dress shoes, and as soon as Carbonneau hoisted the Cup, he shifted it to Savard who kissed it and then shook it several times above his head in disbelief. Maurice Richard and Jean Béliveau watched from their seats, the celebration all too familiar for them. Moments later, several players hoisted Savard on their shoulders. The broken foot would not dim his dream of winning hockey's greatest trophy just once.

CANADIENS NUMBERS
DENIS SAVARD

b. Pointe Gatineau, Quebec, February 4, 1961
5'10" | 175 lbs. | centre | shoots right

	REGULAR SEASON					PLAYOFFS				
	GP	G	A	Pts	Pim	GP	G	A	Pts	Pim
1990-91	70	28	31	59	52	13	2	11	13	35
1991-92	77	28	42	70	73	11	3	9	12	8
1992-93	63	16	34	50	90	14	0	5	5	4
TOTALS	210	72	107	179	215	38	5	25	30	47

Rod Langway

Langway was one of the fine young prospects in the Montreal organization before making the team full-time in 1978. He won the Cup that rookie season, his first of four years with the team.

Drafted 36th overall by Montreal in 1977, Hall of Fame defenceman Rod Langway managed to play half a season with the team two years later and get his name on the Stanley Cup. Although his excellent career stretched 15 years, this championship in his rookie season turned out to be the only time he got his name on the Cup.

Langway was part of a trio the Canadiens rescued from the WHA in 1977-78. Mark Napier and Langway were pulled from the Birmingham Bulls, and Cam Connor from the Houston Aeros, and within a year they

were all important elements in bringing Montreal its fourth straight Stanley Cup.

Although born in Taiwan while his father was in the U.S. Army, Langway was brought up in Randolph, Massachusetts, near Boston. He became a superb defensive defenceman and later, with Washington, won the Norris Trophy in consecutive seasons as the league's best blueliner. In the immediate post-Bobby Orr era, when scoring and rushing defencemen were considered the best and most exciting of the blueliners, the promotion of Langway to title of "best" was nothing short of astounding. After all, his Norris honours came during the prime of Paul Coffey's career.

First and foremost, Langway was a large and reliable presence in his own end. He was never a very good skater, but he was physical and rarely made mistakes with or without the puck. Despite his weak skating, he always managed to stay between his man and the net, and during his four years with Montreal the team allowed the fewest goals three of those seasons. He didn't have a great shot, and he wasn't a pinpoint passer, but he could keep the puck out of his net with the best of them, and that was all that mattered to the Montreal coaching staff.

Perhaps most impressively, Langway managed to play an intimidating physical game without incurring frequent trips to the penalty box. And, although his style of play lent itself to injuries, he missed only a few games because of a wonky body during his years in Montreal.

After his rookie season, which he split between the Habs and the AHL's Nova Scotia Voyageurs, Langway reported to camp in 1979 in superb condition, impressing coaches with his summer-long devotion to fitness. From then on he was a mainstay with the team, but he knew hard work and consistency meant no nights off. Unfortunately, he asked to be traded to an American team because of high Canadian taxes, but Langway flourished for another decade in Washington.

CANADIENS NUMBERS
ROD LANGWAY

b. . Maag, Formosa (Taiwan), May 3, 1957
6'3" 218 lbs. defence shoots left

	REGULAR SEASON					PLAYOFFS				
	GP	G	A	Pts	Pim	GP	G	A	Pts	Pim
1978-79	45	3	4	7	30	8	0	0	0	16
1979-80	77	7	29	36	81	10	3	3	6	2
1980-81	80	11	34	45	120	3	0	0	0	6
1981-82	66	5	34	39	116	5	0	3	3	18
TOTALS	268	26	101	127	347	26	3	6	9	42

PROUD AMERICAN

In addition to his outstanding NHL career with Montreal and Washington, Langway was a regular representative of Team USA in international tournaments. He played in three Canada Cup events—1981, 1984, 1987—for his country, but these were lean years for American talent and the team never had much success. His only appearance in the World Championships came in 1982 in Finland, but the team finished 8th (last) and was relegated to B Pool for 1983. Nevertheless, that team included other young stars such as Phil Housley and Gordie Roberts, and it wasn't long after that that the U.S. became much more competitive at the highest levels.

Dick Duff

Left Wing *1964-65 to 1969-70*

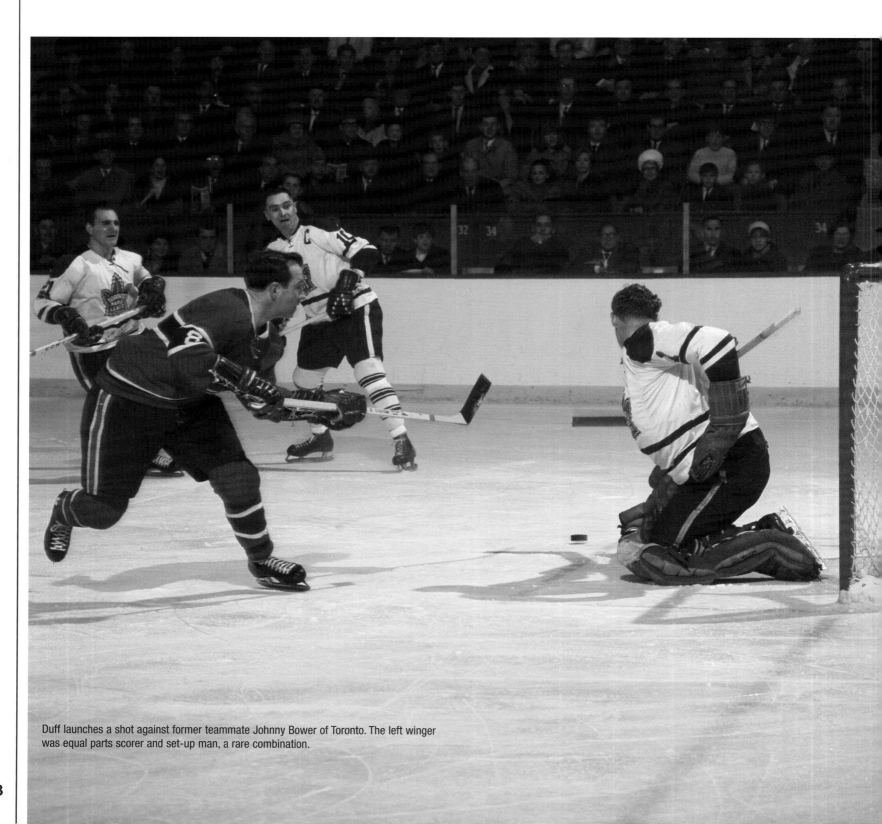

Duff launches a shot against former teammate Johnny Bower of Toronto. The left winger was equal parts scorer and set-up man, a rare combination.

Rare are the players who can make a great pass and score a great goal with equal ability. Usually, a player who scores 50 goals in a season has fewer assists, and often a superb playmaker will be well behind in the goal scoring list. Not so with Dick Duff. Jean Béliveau once said Duff was uncanny around the goal, while Yvan Cournoyer loved playing alongside Duff because of his playmaking skills. This much is certain. In the 1960s, the Montreal Canadiens won four Stanley Cups. The Toronto Maple Leafs won four Stanley Cups. Dick Duff won six Stanley Cups.

A product of St. Mike's in Toronto, Duff went on to play for the Leafs at the start of his career, winning the Stanley Cup twice with his adopted city. Indeed, he scored the Cup-winning goal the night of April 22, 1962, to give the Leafs their first championship in eleven years, and he helped the team win again the next year.

Coach Punch Imlach, however, believed his team was losing its edge during the 1963-64 season. Although it had won the last two Stanley Cups, he decided to shake things up by making a blockbuster trade with the New York Rangers. Going to Broadway were Duff, Bob Nevin, Arnie Brown, Rod Seiling, and Bill Collins, and coming to Toronto were Andy Bathgate and Don McKenney.

Duff wasn't particularly happy with the Blueshirts, and they traded him to Montreal for next to nothing midway through the 1964-65 season. He and little known Dave McComb were on their way to the Forum and the Habs surrendered only Bill Hicke and the loan of Jean-Guy Morrissette. Back in Canada, in a hockey town, Duff thrived with the Canadiens, and just a few months later he

Duff won the Stanley Cup twice with Toronto in the early part of the 1960s, and he won four more titles with the Canadiens in the last half of the decade.

Dick Duff

Left Wing 1964-65 to 1969-70

A RARE HALL OF FAMER

When Dick Duff's name was called in 2006 as one of the new class of inductees into the Hockey Hall of Fame, many critics too young to have seen him play called the selection into question. Duff had, after all, retired just eight games into the 1971-72 season and had not been inducted in 35 previous years, so why 2006? Harold Ballard nominated him in 1987, and this was passed over by the Selection Committee. Sometimes, plain and simple, it takes a while to appreciate a player's performance. Duff was considered by many coaches and general managers of the day to be the best small player in the game, an Yvan Cournoyer of a generation earlier. He also played on left wing at a time the position was dominated by Bobby Hull and Frank Mahovlich, but surely the third best left winger could not be dismissed from Hall of Fame consideration? And, Duff saved his best for last. He was a rare player who excelled during the regular season yet managed to raise his game to another level when the Stanley Cup was on the line. He became only the sixth member of the Hockey Hall of Fame to play for both Montreal and Toronto during his career (along with George Hainsworth, Dickie Moore, Jacques Plante, Bert Olmstead, and Mahovlich). It was a belated but deserved honour, indeed.

Duff played for Montreal for five full seasons, winning the Cup four times and going to the finals the other season.

CANADIENS NUMBERS
DICK DUFF

b. Kirkland Lake, Ontario, February 18, 1936
5'9"   166 lbs.   left wing   shoots left

	REGULAR SEASON					PLAYOFFS				
	GP	G	A	Pts	Pim	GP	G	A	Pts	Pim
1964-65 🏆	40	9	7	16	16	13	3	6	9	17
1965-66 🏆	63	21	24	45	78	10	2	5	7	2
1966-67	51	12	11	23	23	10	2	3	5	4
1967-68 🏆	66	25	21	46	21	13	3	4	7	4
1968-69 🏆	68	19	21	40	24	14	6	8	14	11
1969-70	17	1	1	2	4	—	—	—	—	—
TOTALS	305	87	85	172	166	60	16	26	42	38

was on a Cup team again, celebrating with the likes of Béliveau, Cournoyer, Henri Richard, and Gump Worsley. The Habs eliminated the Leafs in the semi-finals before squeezing by Chicago in game seven for the win. Duff led the way with a goal and two assists in that deciding game.

Over the next four seasons, Duff averaged nearly 20 goals a year and almost as many assists. He perhaps lost a step or two during this part of his career, but his experience and competitiveness more than made up for any loss of speed. Indeed, the finest playoffs he had were his last, in 1969, when he finished second in team scoring behind only captain Béliveau.

The next season was difficult for Duff. He experienced personal difficulties off ice and as a result his performance on ice was adversely affected. He missed two practices and was eventually traded to Los Angeles for Dennis Hextall who was sent to the farm in Nova Scotia and never played for the Canadiens.

Duff arrived and left Montreal under odd circumstances, but his tenure with the Habs had one common factor—the Stanley Cup. His heart was the biggest part of his body, and his skill was virtually limitless. He never won an individual trophy and was never named to a year-end All-Star team, but he was hands down a player any coach in the league would have wanted on his team. Winning was his greatest strength.

Dick Duff (bottom left) was part of all four Montreal Cup wins in the late 1960s. A solid contributor at both ends of the ice, Duff was often overshadowed by his superstar teammates.

Patrick Roy

Goalie 1984-85 to 1995-96

Patrick Roy started his career in 1985-86 and played his way to the number-one position in short order.

Roy stones Calgary's Joel Otto at the Saddledome in Calgary.

For the second time in his career, 1993, Roy almost single-handedly took his team to Cup victory and was named Conn Smythe Trophy winner for his performance.

As a kid, Patrick Roy would watch *Hockey Night in Canada* and wear pillows as goal pads, pretending to be a goalie with the Montreal Canadiens. His real hero, though, was Daniel Bouchard, the goalie for the Atlanta Flames. Roy met Bouchard one time, and the NHLer gave the boy a goal stick which Roy slept with at night, dreaming the dream.

Roy's single-minded determination to play in the NHL began in earnest when he declined to go to Grade 11 in high school and instead attended the training camp of the Granby Bisons of the Quebec junior league. Roy made the team, but he was playing on the worst team in the QMJHL. Nothing could have served his purposes better, however. He had a huge goals-against average and faced close to 50 shots a game, and this extensive game action gave Roy more experience than he could have accrued in any other way. In his rookie season in Granby he had a GAA of 6.26 and in his draft year he was at 4.44. Sparkling numbers these were not.

Still, the Canadiens knew he was something special and claimed him 51st overall at the 1984 Entry Draft. They immediately told him to return to the Bisons for the 1984-85 season, and he did so unflinchingly. Roy played the entire season in Granby with two notable exceptions.

On February 23, 1985, he was called up to the NHL Canadiens. The team had summoned him merely to dress as the backup goalie for one night so he could see NHL

Roy quickly established a reputation as a butterfly goalie, able to go down and spring up remarkably quickly while covering most of the net simply through body position.

Patrick Roy

Goalie 1984-85 to 1995-96

Roy is the only player to win the Conn Smythe Trophy three times, twice with Montreal, in 1986 and 1993.

action up close and get the smallest taste of what it would be like to play in the NHL. As luck would have it, the starting goalie, Doug Soetaert, didn't play very well. After two periods against the Winnipeg Jets, the score was 4-4 and he had allowed a couple of soft goals. Coach Jacques Lemaire figured he'd give the 19-year-old kid a period's worth of NHL action, and Roy responded. He didn't allow a goal and the Habs rallied to score twice. Just like that Roy had his first NHL victory.

Later that season, he played a single game with the Canadiens' AHL affiliate in Sherbrooke, again with Lady Luck on his side. The starting goalie had equipment troubles midway through the first period, so Roy came in. Coach Pierre Creamer was so impressed with his play that Roy finished the game. When the AHL playoffs began, it was Roy who started the first game and every game thereafter. He won ten of 13 games played and had a league-best GAA of 2.89, carrying Sherbrooke to Calder Cup victory.

"Saint Patrick" won ten straight overtime games in the 1993 playoffs, an NHL record that might never be broken.

Only once in Roy's ten years with the Canadiens did the team miss the playoffs, 1994-95, the lockout-shortened season when he played 43 of 48 games.

Patrick Roy

Goalie 1984-85 to 1995-96

In one season Roy had shot past Granby, past the AHL, and was now on his way to the NHL. He never saw the minors again, and he never looked back. At his first training camp with the Canadiens, Roy was ranked third behind Soetaert and Steve Penney, but by opening night Penney was injured and Roy got the call to start. He won the game, and Penney played poorly when he returned to health. Coach Jean Perron stayed with Roy.

He played 47 of the team's 80 games that year, and as a rookie Roy's biggest trouble was consistency and positioning. The former could be worked out over time, and the latter was helped by goalie coach François Allaire. The two

men decided to create a new style of butterfly goaltending. Allaire emphasized that most goals are scored to the lower part of the net, so if a goalie covers that area instinctively, he'll be more successful. It worked for Roy, and by the start of the 1986 playoffs, at age 20, he was playing like a veteran star.

The Canadiens, backed by Roy's impressive goaltending, marched through the first two rounds of the playoffs to set up a conference finals meeting with the Rangers. After winning the first two games, the Habs came under attack in game three, but Roy was almost unbeatable and the Habs won 4-3 in overtime despite giving up 47 shots. Roy later said this was the best game he ever played. The Rangers won game four, but Montreal clinched the series two nights later. In the finals, against

CANADIENS NUMBERS
PATRICK ROY ("Saint Patrick")

b. Quebec City, Quebec, October 5, 1965
6'   192 lbs.   goalie   catches left

	REGULAR SEASON						PLAYOFFS					
	GP	W-L-T	Mins	GA	SO	GAA	GP	W-L	Mins	GA	SO	GAA
1984-85	1	1-0-0	20	0	0	0.00	—	—	—	—	—	—
1985-86	47	23-18-3	2,651	148	1	3.35	20	15-5	1,218	39	1	1.92
1986-87	46	22-16-6	2,686	131	1	2.93	6	4-2	330	22	0	4.00
1987-88	45	23-12-9	2,586	125	3	2.90	8	3-4	430	24	0	3.35
1988-89	48	33-5-6	2,744	113	4	2.47	19	13-6	1,206	42	2	2.09
1989-90	54	31-16-5	3,173	134	3	2.53	11	5-6	641	26	1	2.43
1990-91	48	25-15-6	2,835	128	1	2.71	13	7-5	785	40	0	3.06
1991-92	67	36-22-8	3,935	155	5	2.36	11	4-7	686	30	1	2.62
1992-93	62	31-25-5	3,595	192	2	3.20	20	16-4	1,293	46	0	2.13
1993-94	68	35-17-11	3,867	161	7	2.50	6	3-3	375	16	0	2.56
1994-95	43	17-20-6	2,566	127	1	2.97	—	—	—	—	—	—
1995-96	22	12-9-1	1,260	62	1	2.95	—	—	—	—	—	—
TOTALS	551	289-175-66	31,918	1,476	29	2.77	114	70-42	6,964	285	5	2.46

Calgary, Roy allowed just 13 goals in a five-game series win by Montreal. Of course, Roy was named winner of the Conn Smythe trophy.

After the miraculous victory he was called Saint Patrick, and perhaps no goalie had made a greater impact in his first playoffs since Ken Dryden in 1971. It was clear Roy was the cornerstone of a new generation of Cup-winning teams in Montreal. Unfortunately, despite his heroics, the team around him never grew and developed to produce a dynasty.

Roy's performance in the 1993 playoffs might have eclipsed his rookie season. The Habs were again far down the list of contending teams for the Cup, but he alone seemed to will the team to one win after another. Signs of impending greatness began in the first round of the 1993 playoffs

when the Canadiens faced provincial rivals Quebec in a best-of-seven series. Emotional, tough, dramatic, the series went to six games, Montreal emerging victorious. Four of the games were decided by one goal, and three went into overtime. The Habs won three of the four close games, and two of the overtime games, as Roy proved right away he would simply not allow that game-winning goal.

In the next round, Montreal faced Buffalo, and the Roy legend grew exponentially in this series. All four games were won by a 4-3 score. Three of the games went into a fourth period. And Montreal won them all in a remarkable four-game sweep. By now, Roy's ability to play shutout

Roy's positioning was the best in the league. He never had to flop and dive around the crease; he was always in position, blocking the puck before it hit the back of the net.

ALL-TIME NUMBERS

By the time Patrick Roy retired in 2003, he owned two of the most prestigious goalie records of all time. He became the first goalie to play 1,000 games (achieved in his final season), ending with 1,029 to his credit. He also finished with 551 regular-season wins, the only goalie with more than 500 career victories. Other Roy records include most 30-win seasons (13), and most career minutes played (60,235). And those are just the regular-season records. Roy appeared in 247 playoff games, a number that is light years ahead of the number-two goalie, Martin Brodeur (169). Roy also leads the all-time stats parade with 23 playoff shutouts, 151 career wins, and 15,209 career minutes played. He is also the only player (goalie or skater) to win the Conn Smythe three times (1986, 1993, and 2001).

Patrick Roy

Goalie 1984-85 to 1995-96

hockey in extra time was a certainty, and the Canadiens went to the semi-finals against the Islanders full of confidence. Two of the five games went beyond 60 minutes, and Montreal won both on their way to a five-game series win. The team was on its way to the finals for the first time since 1989, and Roy was the man largely responsible for this trip.

Their opponents were the Los Angeles Kings, led by Wayne Gretzky who had been the hero in game seven against Toronto in the other half of the playoffs. Gretzky was taking the Kings to uncharted waters, the team's first chance for a Cup since entering the league in 1967. Game

one seemed to suggest a great destiny for number 99 as the Kings beat Montreal 4-1 at the Forum. Then Patrick Roy closed the door. Each of the next three games went into overtime, and each time Roy refused to permit the winning goal. The Canadiens won each game and took a 3-1 series lead, winning the Stanley Cup at home, in game five, by a 4-1 score. In all, the Canadiens won a league record ten overtime games during the 1993 playoffs en route to a second Cup backed by Roy who was, again, named Conn Smythe Trophy winner.

The end of Roy's time in Montreal came suddenly and unexpectedly. On the night of December 2, 1995, in a home game against Detroit, Roy had an awful game. It was clear early on this was just not his night, but coach Mario Tremblay refused to pull him until Roy had allowed nine

Roy stops Calgary veteran Lanny McDonald in the 1986 Stanley Cup Finals won by the Habs.

goals. As he finally left the ice, Roy told team president Ronald Corey, who was watching the game from his usual seat behind the team bench, that he would never play for the Canadiens again. A few days later, Roy was traded to Colorado and promptly led the Avalanche to a Cup in the spring of 1996.

That game looms large in Roy's Montreal history, yet it was just one night that obscures an otherwise remarkable career with the Canadiens. Roy almost single-handedly won two Cups for a team that had little business being in the Cup finals those years, and his style of goaltending revolutionized the position. While he left under unpleasant circumstances, his 12 years with the team are testament to a career that started in a blaze of glory and continued unabated for more than 500 games with the Habs.

Patrick Roy retired as the league's all-time leader with 551 wins and 1,029 games played.

Montreal swept Buffalo in the second round of the 1993 playoffs. Every game was a 4-3 score, and three of those games went to overtime.

ACKNOWLEDGEMENTS

The author would like to thank the many people who have contributed to the production and creation of this anniversary edition. First and foremost, to the Montreal Canadiens organization, and their centennial team that contributed to this project, namely Ray Lalonde, Jon Trzcienski, Manny Almela, Alexandre Harvey, Shauna Denis, and Marie-Eve Sylvestre. Also to translator Philippe Germain for capturing the essence of the English text succinctly. To those at the Hockey Hall of Fame for their efforts, starting with president Jeff Denomme, as well as Phil Pritchard, Ron Ellis, Peter Jagla, Craig Campbell, Izak Westgate, Miragh Addis, Darren Boyko, and Steve Poirier. To those at Fenn Publishing for taking the concept and rough material and turning it into a book of substance, notably Jordan Fenn for tremendous enthusiasm in face of this daunting task and designer Laura Brunton whose skill and patience were vital to the book's completion. To Szymon Szemberg for advice and opinion; Paul Patskou for giving the text the once-over; and, to agent Dean Cooke for help at the business end. Without the contributions of everyone, the book would never have come to fruition.

PHOTO CREDITS

8725

This book is an official numbered publication celebrating the Montreal Canadiens 100th anniversary.
To learn more about the unique serial number found on this page, please visit: www.honouredcanadiens.com

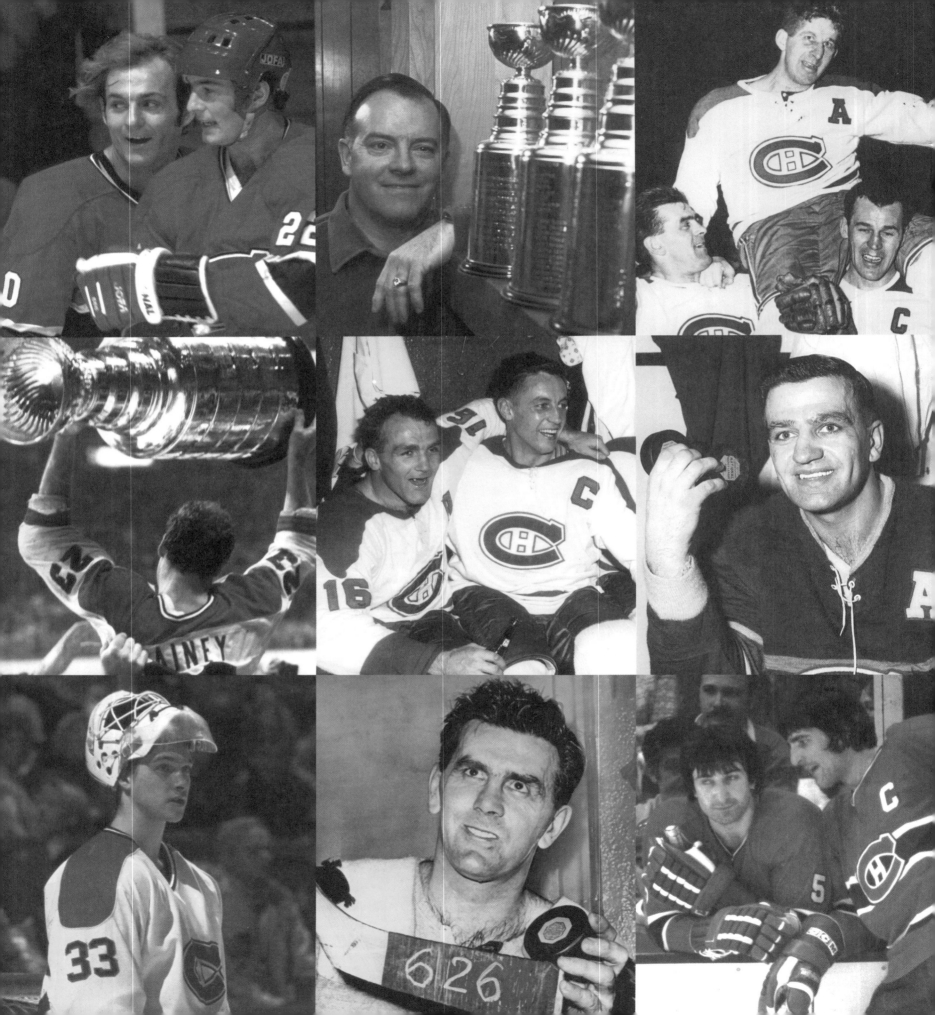